WE ARE WORTH FIGHTING FOR

We Are Worth Fighting For

A History of the Howard University Student Protest of 1989

Joshua M. Myers

NEW YORK UNIVERSITY PRESS

New York

NEW YORK UNIVERSITY PRESS
New York
www.nyupress.org

References to Internet websites (URLs) were accurate at the time of writing. Neither the author nor New York University Press is responsible for URLs that may have expired or changed since the manuscript was prepared.

Library of Congress Cataloging-in-Publication Data
Names: Myers, Joshua (Joshua M.), author.
Title: We are worth fighting for : a history of the Howard University student protest of 1989 / Joshua M. Myers.
Description: New York : New York University Press, [2019] | Includes bliographical references and index.
Identifiers: LCCN 2019002171 | ISBN 9781479811755 (cloth : alk. paper) | ISBN 9781479816767 (paperback : alk. paper)
Subjects: LCSH: Howard University—Students—History—20th century. | African American student movements—Washington (D.C.)—History—20th century. | African American college students—Political activity—Washington (D.C.)—History—20th century. | African American universities and colleges—Washington (D.C.)—History—20th century. | Black Nia F.O.R.C.E.
Classification: LCC LC2851.H84 M88 2019 | DDC 378.1/982996073—dc23
LC record available at https://lccn.loc.gov/2019002171

New York University Press books are printed on acid-free paper, and their binding materials are chosen for strength and durability. We strive to use environmentally responsible suppliers and materials to the greatest extent possible in publishing our books.

Manufactured in the United States of America

10 9 8 7 6 5 4 3 2

Also available as an ebook

To the spirits of those who were responsible for imagining that their moment and time had come, to those who continued the work of the sixties into the eighties and nineties

But politically, I'm clear and always have been. We are worth fighting for, flaws and contradictions galore, we are worth fighting for . . . over and over again.

—April Silver

CONTENTS

Introduction

The Black Arts Movement poet Sonia Sanchez often tells the story of her first few months teaching in the newly created Black Studies Department at San Francisco State University. The year was 1969, and the students had just recently completed a five-month strike in which they had demanded a College of Ethnic Studies. It was a moment when the world witnessed the explosive result of introducing more and more nonwhites into Western systems of' higher education. None of these universities had expected that these students would hold onto their cultural identities instead of simply embracing the canon of Western knowledge or the assumed supremacy of the American project. Sanchez was in the thick of this battle as she was brought in to continue the development of one of these alternative intellectual experiments in this dynamic moment.

One night, Sanchez answered her door to find an FBI agent standing at the threshold of her apartment. This was no raid—although it could have easily been the case. No. The agent had come to ask Professor Sanchez if it was indeed true that she was teaching the work of W. E. B. Du Bois at San Francisco State. Turning to her landlord, the agent then inquired if he knew that he had a subversive as a tenant.[1] Tellingly, the repression visited on Du Bois, Paul Robeson, and on Marcus Garvey had reappeared amid the struggle for Black Studies.[2] What did these figures represent that made the mere teaching of their ideas such a dangerous proposition?

This kind of criminal interrogation may seem unique to the times of the 1960s, but the movement that Sanchez represented continued and continues. Having come to know the work of Du Bois through her brief apprenticeship with the Schomburg Center librarian Jean Blackwell Hutson, Sanchez would not abandon him in her teaching, even as he became persona non grata, in many respects as a result of his own refusal to abandon his radical politics and embrace Cold War liberalism. Sanchez's embrace of radical Black thinkers was an act of preservation, and she would pass that energy on to the future generations struggling along the lines of Du Bois and Hutson—to those struggling to make Black spaces incubators of radical traditions working toward the liberation of African peoples.[3]

One such generation would emerge almost twenty years after the knock on Sanchez's door. In the nervous moments before perhaps the most important event in this late 1980s iteration of Black student radicalism, it was none other than Sonia Sanchez who would provide inspiration and motivation to its young spokeswoman, April R. Silver, who recalls fondly that

> Sonia Sanchez, who guided me so carefully during this time (over the phone), made it all clear to me one night when we, as a group, had decided to go through with the plan to shut down the school. In effect, she said, in the most maternal way, "April, when people ask you why you are fighting against your own school, when they try to tell you that you are wrong to protest against President Cheek, when they ask you why are you going through with shutting down the school (a plan that was unknown to most at the time), you have to tell them it's because you love Howard University, because you love Black people. You have to tell them that you are fighting because what you believe in is worth fighting for. It's up to you all to make sure that Howard fulfills its mission to you. We fought too hard to let our Black institutions end up in the hands of people who oppose us."[4]

These were all the words she needed. The moment was drawing nigh. And by ensuring connections to those who had participated in similar struggles a generation or two earlier, the Howard student radicals were extending a tradition. The protest would not succeed otherwise.

We Are Worth Fighting For is a history of the Howard University student protest of 1989 as told from the perspectives and worldview of its participants. It frames the actions of the students involved in this movement as a part of a long genealogy of Black renegades who resisted the notion that peoples of African ancestry should remain wedded to the ideals of American universalism. Rather than pursuing détente with an inherently oppressive political regime, this genealogy of Black radicals pursued self-defined norms and self-determined actions for securing a just society for their group and for humanity. And thus the Black Radical tradition found itself at center of the controversy at Howard University during the key moment in the appearance of what some of have called the "hip hop generation."

At the center of this story is the student organization Black Nia F.O.R.C.E (Freedom Organization for Racial and Cultural Enlightenment), which was the catalyst for the coalition of organizations that developed and went through with the plans for the takeover of the university. While the overriding ideals of this organization and this movement were geared toward self-determination and Black solidarity, the precipitating event was Howard president James Cheek's decision to support the appointment of Republican National Committee Chairman Lee Atwater to the university's board of trustees. Yet this was but one—albeit the most objectionable—of the many issues that caused these students to demand changes from the university.

The events of 1989 demonstrated that Black youth were not passive receptacles of the neoliberal values of the Reagan era. Against the trend prominent among many educated Americans that saw them take their place among the "Yuppies" and reject the "sixties values" of their parents, a significant number of Black youth, inspired by those of their communities that felt the "underside" of Reaganism, chose to resist its imposition.[5] While the roles Black youth played in the anti-apartheid struggle, as well as in the political campaigns that rejected the conservative values of the 1980s, have been acknowledged, the Howard protest of 1989 represented an extension of the still-vibrant questions of self-determination and institutional autonomy that have always been associated with Black political activity. It was a nationalist movement that was conversant with and connected to the spirit of the Black Radical tradition.

While this nationalist resurgence of the early-mid 1990s has been commented upon, the protest of 1989 became an outlet for its expression in a space—Howard University—that continued to be known as the "Mecca" of global Blackness.[6] That the conditions at Howard produced a clash that pitted a sizable student population inspired by nationalist ideals against an administration committed to neoliberal ones assuredly has implications for how we understand the dualities at play in Black institutional life in the 1980s and now. *We Are Worth Fighting For* pays close attention to the ways that nationalist politics influenced student action at Howard in 1989 and what this means for comprehending the wider Black community's response to what some have dubbed the "high eighties."[7]

The evolution of this protest cannot be understood without an appreciation of the long trajectory of Black radicalism, nor can it ignore the specific political context of 1980s America. In many ways, these two might be understood as being bound together. For had Black radicalism not existed, some of the measures put in place to secure "order" in American society might not have produced the brand of politics that was responsible for the center-right politics that came to define the period.[8] While there has been much interest in what some have sardonically called the "heroic era" (the Civil Rights/Black Power movement) in American historical studies as well as in studies of the New Right, less attention has been given to the continuity of the Black freedom movement in the "post–civil rights" era.[9] If there has been a significant amount of conceptual work on the long Civil Rights/Black Power movement, less work has been done on how the ethos of that era actually extends into the decades that lead up to the present.[10] In fact, the entire American twentieth century might be read as the struggle to contain Black radicalism as it intersected with a range of other movements. For these reasons, *We Are Worth Fighting For* pays just as much attention to the forces at work *off* campus as to those in play on the Yard.

This is a history that fills both temporal and conceptual gaps. It adds to the historical record, but it also contributes to how we go about comprehending the nature of historical movement—that is, the historicity of these actors and, by extension, the historicity of Black radicalism. The takeover of Howard University by its students in 1989 helps us better appreciate that student protest activity both continued into this period and also took bold steps to ensure that nominally Black institutions reflected what the students considered to be the political interests of the largest segments of the Black world—those normally rejected in both mainstream and Black elite spaces—thus continuing a tradition of Black radicalism that centered "the least of these."

But given the above, this work does not merely seek to make a historical intervention. More than a matter of presenting historical data, this work responds to the Africana Studies imperative to ensure that connections between past, present, and future movements to realize a new world are known and maintained. The pursuit of historical memory is not an act of scholarly inquiry as much as it an act of *re-membering* our collective body.[11] The intent is for readers to see both historical antecedents, contemporary adherents, and future activists as intimately connected by a vibrant, though multilayered, tradition of Black struggle.[12] The narrative is based upon the voices of the students, not because they—as Silver warns us—were without contradictions or flaws, but because they *were*. At the core of understanding their resistance is the question of what motivated these students to act, particularly given the political and social forces that reigned, but also what it meant to *be* who they were. This book, finally, interrogates what lessons from this protest can be extended to those generations to come, with the central premise that connections between radical traditions are always present and must continue to be accented and highlighted. As such, the narration of this story derives its meaning from maintaining linkages between movements of yesterday and today. History—if it is to be meaningful—must breathe.

* * *

The power of memory inheres in its ability to frame the future. Our memories create the pathways that we follow, that our descendants follow. In the face of modern assaults on our humanity, African intellectual traditions have over the last two hundred years generated philosophies of history that were guided by the particular memories—and modalities—of people of African ancestry.

With regard to understanding the recent past, this intellectual practice becomes ever more urgent. The advent of the professional and public narrative of the Civil Rights era has generated "official" memories of the events of the 1950s–1960s "Negro revolution."[13] We see its impact every February: "whites only" signs, dogs and hoses, marches, "We Shall Overcome," and finally the Civil Rights Act of 1964. These images are juxtaposed to stock images of "Black anger"—Malcolm X, Watts, and gun-toting Panthers—and then we are often told that such anger was misplaced or misapplied.[14] Consensus historiography has touted the triumphal Civil Rights era as the long-awaited fulfillment of American promise, simplifying the multiplicity of voices and agendas that characterize it, rendering longer narratives of Black resistance as inessential to fully explaining the terms through which Civil Rights workers engaged the problem of American democracy.[15] Even the two most recent trends in American history, the "long Civil Rights movement" and "Black Power studies," are simply improvisations upon this master narrative, ultimately expanding the consensus to different fields, which now includes the Black student movement.[16]

This supposedly self evident framing of the movement assumes a teleology of Black thought faithful to and acceding to the U.S. founding documents and a recognition of the inevitability of inclusion within the logics of the American nation-state, ideas relying chiefly upon the ambitions of a middle-class component of the Black community. Its modern manifestations are the victorious appellation of the United States as "post-racial." However, both transnational and African-centered frameworks for understanding the Black American experience would caution us against accepting such easy kinds of assumptions.[17]

In coming to terms with the history of this student protest at Howard University, we would do well to place these students in more nuanced political and cultural constructs than those that have animated the dominant trends in American history thus far. Recent work on Howard University's activist history simply follows the received triumphalist narrative of the Civil Rights/Black Power era. In these formulations, Black folk rescue the idea of American exceptionalism from the clutches of reaction by overcoming segregation and/or instituting the still-unfinished projects for diversity.[18] In rethinking this framing, we reduce the probability that the history of student movements becomes construed as attempts to provide Black paint to an often overdetermined, hackneyed conception of the "American dream." Such a move also redefines for the coming generations what "activism" is beyond the imagery and iconography that have been force-fed us by officially sanctioned portrayals of the Civil Rights era. Instead of being led to reproduce the mere *imagery* of a movement, an alternative narrative would allow Black people to imagine how they might contribute to a living, breathing, actual movement for something larger and more grand, one that is connected to a tradition of "conquering the world by thought and brain and plan."[19] For when it was all said and done, the 1989 protest rested on assumptions that were against and beyond the motivations of those who have accepted the notion that American ideals were the only ones worth fighting for.

* * *

We Are Worth Fighting For is divided into three parts. Part I considers the cultural, social, and political contexts of the student actions of 1989. In contextualizing the movement in this way, we can further glean how the protest was both unique and representative of certain tendencies among Black students across time and space, while maintaining an awareness of the ways it engaged and resisted the dominant political structures at work. Chapter 1 gives a brief overview of student protest at Howard University. The best-known protest on campus occurred in March 1968 and has been somewhat of a model for subsequent actions. This chapter considers how the dominant framings of Black political struggle have affected our understanding of the meaning of student activism at Howard. Chapter 2 charts the evolution of American national politics and tells the story of how its rightward turn converged with James Cheek's tenure as Howard president and the emergence of Lee Atwater as a political operative at the close of the 1980s. While electoral politics produced Atwater, this chapter shows how his emergence was part of a broader reckoning with questions of race that marked the American century. Chapter 3 examines Black youth movements during the 1980s, giving further context to the political scene of the era. The anti-apartheid movement, the insurgent presidential campaigns of Jesse Jackson, and the cultural movement around hip hop provided much needed space for young people to cut their teeth.

Part II is a narrative of the actions leading up to and through the 1989 takeover. Chapter 4 explores the founding of Black Nia F.O.R.C.E (BNF) and its early activities on campus. Founded in January 1988, BNF espoused a nationalist philosophy that combined elements of study, protest, and cultural programs on campus. After hearing of Atwater's appointment, its leaders were responsible for convening the meetings that led to plans to shut down the university. Chapter 5 covers the actions of the students at Howard's Charter Day Convocation of 1989. It discusses the development of the demands and the disruption of these activities, which preceded the more militant actions to come. The convocation protest was important, for just as in previous protests, it gave the administration the opportunity to prevent those more militant actions. Just as much, it demonstrated and galvanized support for those who were still on the sidelines as well as solidarity among those who were outside of the university. Chapter 6 details the events of the Mordecai W. Johnson Administration Building takeover, which occurred days after Charter Day. Along with a narrative of the events, it explores the meaning of direct action within this context, the students' philosophy of struggle, and the nature of outside support that saved the protest from disastrous results.

Part III closes this story with an assessment of the impact of the protest. Chapter 7 explores both how the students came to understand the meaning of their actions after the protest had been called off, leading to the resignation of President Cheek, and the ways that this shifted campus politics and culture. Chapter 8, the final chapter, reveals the ways that the Howard protest influenced on-campus struggles at other historically Black colleges and universities. It also details the work of BNF at Howard and beyond in later years, showing how BNF members attempted to force permanent changes premised on the spirit of the demands voiced during the 1989 protest, as well as their broader national growth and influence.

The kind of university that BNF and the students who participated in the 1989 protest imagined was one that rested on the reality that Black lives have always mattered. But what to do once that declaration had been made has not been resolved. Their central question remains: What is a Black university?

The Howard student protest of 1989 laid bare the implications of this question in a critical moment in American political history. As the scourge of late capitalism continues to envelop the social environment and as neoliberal alternatives continue to represent the "common sense" of contemporary life, we might think with these student radicals about what kind of future is possible for our people. It is becoming more and more necessary to anchor our futures with such memories. In the face of a higher education industry that continues to fail us, it is quite refreshing to remember in our times of despair that we are heirs to a long tradition of forerunners who said: "No." And then imagined otherwise.

PART I

Contexts

1

A Space for Black Ideas

At present, Howard is primarily Western civilization oriented. It is unrealistic to educate Black students as if they
were exclusively products of Western civilization and in fact
totally integrated into that civilization. Our blackness is the
principal reality of our lives—and what we want is a Howard
University oriented to that reality.[1]
—UJAMAA, Howard student organization

Historians have generally framed Black political thought as the tension between competing notions of liberation: self-determination and
assimilation.[2] These are not neat categories, nor are their stable ones,
yet this friction informs the sorts of political and social agendas at work
within Black institutional spaces and could also be thought to determine
questions of identity and an institution's raison d'être. Historically Black
colleges and universities (HBCUs) are unique sites of this ambivalence.
It becomes quite easy to misread the nature and scope of student activism at Howard absent this sort of contextualization. For leaders and
students alike, the ongoing question seems to revolve around whether
Black peoples should engage, embrace, and embody the ideals of the
American national project, or if they would do well to reflect upon and
craft national identities of their own, which might better meet their
collective political needs. As such, it is necessary to see the Black university both in institutional terms as well as communal terms, as both a
bureaucratic space beholden to larger societal interests and a subversive
"undercommons" devoted only to the self-identified group progress of
African peoples.[3]

Although there has been some "interest convergence"[4] between those
representing these concerns, allowing for some unity in purpose, it is
often the assimilationist creed that overdetermines the way we think
about university matters and, by extension, the context for student

activism. And for good reason. It was indeed within the administrative realms—the space that often represented this Black elite dream of assimilation—that students found themselves most directly embroiled in various confrontations. But there is no reason to divorce these concerns from larger political and social contexts or to assume that students at Howard were unaware of the institution's imbrication with agendas set by dominant power structures beyond the campus' borders. Their struggle was not merely on campus; it was also in the world.

It is in that sense that it becomes logical to place Howard student activism—as well as the struggles of the Black faculty—within a political context that allows us to see multiple valences of Black radicalism at work. In some ways, struggles within the campus community were mirrors of the deep political differences that reigned beyond those boundaries. A communally oriented self-determination was most often the inspiration for Howard student activity (and when it suited their needs, the administration would assume that cloak as well). Student activism represented the quest for intellectual and cultural freedom in a national context that required a sort of Black self-annihilation in order to achieve certain liberal ideas of progress.[5] Struggle at Howard was not new in 1989. It was connected to a larger tradition, one that saw fit to resist the external imposition on peoples of African ancestry and one that saw the cultivation of Black spaces that would protect and center their cultural identity.

Foundations

As Howard University existed—and continues to exist—in a social and political cauldron that makes Black radicalism a necessity for survival, an approach to understanding what has happened within its walls must also give credence to the impact of Black intellectual traditions informed by and developed through what Cedric Robinson describes as "an accretion, over generations, of collective intelligence gathered from struggle."[6]

Following Robinson, we might endeavor to trace the ways in which Howard students and scholars engaged and employed the historical memory of the Black Radical tradition in order to create movements for revolutionary change in the twentieth century. Robinson's work on Black social and political movements suggests that without this sort of orientation it is doubtful that we would be able to connect traditions of Black resistance over time, ultimately following conventional historiographical tendencies that consider it less than plausible that insurrections like the Haitian revolution had anything to do with the social movements of the Black Power era, except for serving as "inspiration."[7] While questions of whether movements have inspired one another are appropriate, Robinson shows that the foundation of the Black Radical tradition functioned as not merely inspiration but also as a specific cultural foundation for developing and acting upon revolutionary theory. The very nature of the Black Radical tradition was what guided action.[8] Just as Robinson utilizes this process to locate the orientation of the theoretical works of eminent scholars like W. E. B. Du Bois, it would not take a leap of imagination to see how his contemporaries and colleagues might have embodied similar ideas at other Black universities.

Founded during that moment where "Black folk" attempted to "reconstruct democracy in America," Howard's origins were shrouded in the belief that education for the formerly enslaved was a necessary precursor to citizenship.[9] The white Congregationalist ministers, along with Freedmen's Bureau head Oliver Otis Howard, imagined a university that stood for the universalist creed of "Equal Rights and Knowledge for All."[10] And yet these presumptions also guaranteed an authoritarianism that produced racial tensions. As Black scholars began to teach at Howard— beginning with the lawyer and poet George Vashon—it should seem obvious that they imported ways of understanding and reading the world that were unique to Black thought. We must not assume that Western training—only the terms of their employment—was more powerful than the honing of identity and cultural memory in convened Black spaces. Beyond the obvious racist and dictatorial machinations of bureaucratic or "institutional" Howard during the university's early years, a historical approach that recognizes the above factors might uncover that the influence of Black scholars upon student subversives might be one of the deciding variables in the struggles between Black faculty and the white administrative structure, since it certainly explains the later struggles.[11]

An additional consideration, as Zachery Williams argues in his *In Search of the Talented Tenth*, is the extent to which Howard's intellectual community was influenced in its shared milieu within the interstices of the racial uplift tradition and the New Negro movement, of which Washington, DC, was a critical location.[12] As Du Bois and others struggled against the various strands of Black political thought housed within the archetypal politics of "racial uplift," it would be a mistake not to interrogate whether these battles affected the consciousness of Howard students, particularly those who emerged from the very communities responsible for enacting the events Robinson narrates in his "historical archaeology of Black resistance."[13]

While it is true that much of what would constitute radical thought at Howard led to robust considerations of class, it was significant that such declarations were often made from *Black* spaces, a point raised in Jonathan Scott Holloway's work on three of the Howard thinkers.[14] Further, as Sterling Stuckey relates, a consideration of class dynamics within nationalist thought was practiced in its earliest iterations dating back to the plantation. As such, there need not be a binary epistemology of race and class where none actually existed; Africans were able to recognize the economic foundations of racism because their very relations to the state were its product.[15] When one considers the development of Howard student activism from its origins, but particularly in its "Black Power" manifestation in the 1960s, the importance of nationalist consciousness cannot be discounted. Neither can we dismiss its effect on Howard institutionally with the advent of the Mordecai Wyatt Johnson administration in 1926. As the institution's first permanent Black president, Johnson imputed more nationalist tendencies onto the bureaucracy, although it would be disingenuous to suggest that it was of the same form and intensity that we would find in the undercommons.[16] Placing these concerns within a more expansive tradition would allow us to apply Stuckey's methodological technique to a range of actors in Howard's student activist history.

Very few thinkers would refute the contention that elements of Howard's culture—from the development of musical education and theology to the extracurricular activities of fraternities and sororities and the marching band—could not be understood without a consideration of its African roots, particularly the ways in which what Stuckey calls the "the shout" was improvised in some of these contexts.[17] If, for Stuckey, these ritual practices had everything to do with the constitution of nationalist identity, then it would follow that, in their persistence and transformation in various forms, we might also trace the form and function of nationalist theory as it existed and influenced the trajectory of student unrest at various periods in Howard history. Understanding student activists as carriers of a historical tradition of Black struggle would reveal the extent to which the disputes with administration reflected the latter's alienation from the foundations of Black intellectual and political cultures and the complicated, often deleterious, fallout from such arrangements.

A Tradition of Struggle

With our expanded view of Black traditions of resistance, the history of student activism at Howard rightly begins with the appearance of Black students—those for whom education under any guise was for many considered a "conceptual impossibility."[18] For a university founded by a group of liberal white "architects of Black education," the mere presence of Black students created the conditions for deeper entanglements.[19]

Records exist of student protest activity stretching back to at least March 1913, when Howard students participated in the suffrage movement. Students were also active in struggles against racial capitalism, articulating their ideas in the *Howard University Journal* and in organizational vehicles like the Intercollegiate Socialist Society, the Social Science Club, and a student chapter of the National Association for the Advancement of Colored People (NAACP). Each of these organizations housed important conversations and reflected ideas that ran the gamut of the political identities that represent Black thinking in those years. In the era before the emergence of the New Negro movement, Howard students had developed critical spaces to discuss radical thought and the question of race in the absence of a university curriculum that directly addressed such issues. As a student, E. Franklin Frazier's "undercommons" experience listening to the Howard philosopher Alain Locke discuss race relations at NAACP forums or inviting W. E. B. Du Bois to lecture on similar topics were instrumental and could be seen as indicative of the direction that intellectuals had begun to take—toward a Black university.[20]

This undoubtedly prepared the ground for perhaps the best-known student protest movement prior to the "heroic" 1960s: the May 1925 student strike. Concerned largely with the imposition of mandatory ROTC requirements, the transplantation of what Raymond Wolters calls "the

New Negro on campus" seemed to be about much more—not least the resistance to the continued paternalistic control of Negro education. In many ways, students fought for shared governance, a concern that would emanate within many future struggles in higher education. Students understood ROTC requirements as irrelevant to the kind of education that they understood would be necessary to advance their interests. Moreover, they resented that they did not have the authority to choose for themselves.[21]

For many, it was this strike, along with pressures from the faculty and alumni, that led to the downfall of the last white president, James Stanley Durkee, and the ultimate resolution to find a president of African ancestry. The presidency of Mordecai Wyatt Johnson can be said to be rooted in New Negro sensibilities—which, as Alain Locke argues, was merely a new political (and in the case of Harlem, geographical) context for more authentic and audacious forms of cultural Blackness.[22] In this manner, Howard students joined other Black college students at Fisk and Hampton in uniquely extending a tradition of Black resistance to spaces like the university.

The cultural vitality of the New Negro movement resulted in radical denunciations of white respectability politics on campus, a tradition one must remember is rooted in much longer trajectories than the more famous articulations in the 1960s. Indeed, as the 1920s closed, Howard students would link these respectability politics to the "race" problem in the United States as well as internationally. Founded in 1924, the student newspaper, *The Hilltop*, increasingly became a central space where these concerns were voiced. As the decade turned, Howard students participated in a number of political activities off campus, fueled in large measure by what historians assign as the rise of Popular Front politics but that was perhaps most solidly linked to a Black radicalism, the spark that ignited the latter, especially in the "Black belt."[23] Howard students were involved in everything from support for federal antilynching legislation and the desegregation of the nation's capital, to questions of economic justice and socialist and communist concerns, to thinking through and organizing resistance to the Italian occupation of Ethiopia. The diversity of the students' activist interests converged with the faculty's, an intellectual environment that, as Holloway shows, began to disaggregate class-based issues from the liberal racialism that engulfed the mainstream civil rights organizations.[24] Although class analysis became popular, if not essential, these questions were often subordinate to the larger environment of white nationalism, making necessary the continuity and maintenance of what Du Bois thirty years earlier called "race organizations."[25]

The transfer of Lyonel Florant, a student expelled from Fisk University for his activist politics, represents a key chapter of the history of Howard University student activism. Along with an active role in on-campus work with the Liberal Club—a social protest organization advised by Ralph Bunche—and as a contributor to *The Hilltop*, Florant helped spearhead the development of a class-based approach to questions of race within the youth division of the National Negro Congress (an organization that also included Howard faculty), eventually hosting a major youth conference on these issues at Howard in May 1936, a year after the major conference at Howard on the New Deal that led to the creation of the Congress.[26] Joining him were students, like James E. Jackson, the eventual Communist Party organizer, who were central to the formation of the offshoot of the National Negro Congress's youth council, the Southern Negro Youth Congress, a significant development that addressed the deeply entrenched tentacles of racial capitalism by imagining programs for economic justice as well as supporting the work of anticolonialist movements abroad.[27] As the radical Trinidadian-born organizer George Padmore had realized in an earlier era, these organizers saw Howard's Pan African population as the critical location to organize on anticolonial and anti-imperial terms.[28]

This energy boomeranged to on-campus concerns, perhaps energizing the Howard University football strike of 1936, which galvanized students across campus to organize a one-day solidarity strike.[29] It was clear that Howard students were participants in larger movements to harness the power of working peoples to strike a blow to the capitalist system. Eschewing the racial liberalism dominant in the NAACP, students were able to capitalize on their access to the Howard "Young Turks" faculty members, whose influence was undoubtedly felt strongly.

Labor's defeat (or compromise) at the hands of the New Deal coalition would have an impact on Black student struggle and the larger theater of Black politics. It would seem that liberalism became the only game in town. The next decade saw a rough transition from more expansive economic and internationalist social justice concerns to a narrower civil rights agenda. Although Howard students and faculty evinced the same level of involvement in these broader initiatives, buoyed through the various Red Scares by President Mordecai Johnson's stalwart defense of academic freedom, their work in the school desegregation cases under the rubric of *Brown v. Board of Education* in some ways represented a greater focus toward the domestic (rather than the international) manifestation of racial capitalism: Jim Crow.[30]

Social justice activism on HBCU campuses dovetailed with the emergence of white resistance to court-mandated desegregation movements across the South in the mid-1950s.[31] One of the offshoots of this activity was the creation of the Nonviolent Action Group (NAG), a nonofficially recognized, though very active, student group on Howard's campus. An affiliate of the Student Nonviolent Coordinating Committee (SNCC), which was founded in 1960, NAG insinuated itself in many on-campus issues, particularly around the persistent de facto policy of in loco parentis, the controversy surrounding the awarding of the contract to construct Burr Gymnasium, and the development of Project Awareness (their only university-funded work), which brought to campus speakers of the stature of James Baldwin, Harry Belafonte, Bayard Rustin (NAG's mentor), and Malcolm X, who debated Rustin on the merits of integration in Cramton Auditorium in 1961.[32] But as then-student and NAG member Stokely Carmichael relates, theirs was not simply a "student movement," in the strict sense of the term, for they participated in the broader human rights issues and militant reform beyond the boundaries of campus, including the struggle to desegregate the restaurants and gas stations around Route 40.[33] Along with Carmichael, who would later become a national leader in SNCC and a life-long Pan African activist (changing his name to Kwame Ture in honor of his influences Kwame Nkrumah and Sekou Toure), students involved with NAG included such figures as Cleveland Sellers, Courtland Cox, Ed Brown, Mike Thelwell, and Mary Lovelace, as well as a handful of white activists like Tom Kahn. Many of these students came to Howard with activist sensibilities, which were then sharpened and refined before being transformed into tools necessary for lifelong engagement with social justice concerns and the broader movement for African liberation.

When Robin Gregory, an Afro-donning SNCC staffer, was elected homecoming queen in 1966, the Howard student body thrust itself full force into the Black consciousness pervasive among Black youth across the nation.[34] It is this period that ushers into existence what historians have begun to call "Black Student Power" and the "Black Campus movement."[35] The work of NAG and previous iterations of Black student activism at Howard University provided the roadmap for students in the second half of the 1960s. The continued activities of Black student unrest reached yet another inflection point, beginning with the conflict with President James Nabrit's administration over the question of student judicial processes in 1966 (as well as the *Brown* litigator's dream of a more racially mixed university), ultimately reaching its apogee with the five-day takeover of the Administration Building in March 1968.[36] This, by far, is the best known of all the student protest activity at Howard, having been chronicled by the popular documentary *Eyes on the Prize*, replete with freedom songs, fiery rhetoric, and the supposed "calmer heads that prevailed." Indeed, these are the images we have of this moment. And for most, the events of 1968 are clear: the student discontent over the direction of the university regarding questions of governance, curricula, Howard's relevance to the community, and, eventually, questions of violence, when students became horrified at the events in Orangeburg, South Carolina, that February. The proposal to make Howard "Black" was named the Orangeburg Ultimatum in memory of the victims of the Orangeburg Massacre. Next came fifteen demands.[37] And then the takeover.[38]

When mentioned by historians, March 1968 at Howard University is routinely seen as possible only within a larger context of student protest across America.[39] Yet this episode's significance is rendered more profound when placed in context of the larger tradition of Black intellectual and political insurgency, the kinds suggested by Robinson and Stuckey. Its principle demand for a Black university was at once larger than the internal quips with administration as well as a rearticulation of sorts of the expansive visions articulated by Kelly Miller decades before.[40] The quest was for a relevant intellectual space in which to solve the problems faced by Black communities around the globe, to construct a world "Africa inspired."[41]

We must resist the perception that Howard students were simply attempting to establish an increased presence in university decision-making bodies. This was a movement against a sort of paternalism, but it was more deeply against what that paternalism obscured—that is, the default position of the university was whiteness, Europe, the West. Its patresfamilias were our supposed "Yankee Stepfathers."[42] The quest for student governance must be placed into a larger context of Black struggle—within and beyond Howard—in which the 1968 protests continued a quest for liberation from the intellectual and psychological fetters inhibiting Black humanity. At the core of the demands listed by students we can extract what we could call the "suprademand": the destruction of a white supremacist lens for knowledge, so that Black students might better know themselves and their communities; or for the creation a Black space. In the words of the sociology professor and student advisor Nathan Hare, one hears the logic of Black radicalism, not only speaking through the community and addressing their concerns but also speaking their languages, dreaming their futures. In the words of Adrienne Manns, of Michael Harris, of Gary Ayers, of Ewart Brown, one hears the idea that community, Blackness, is what makes the universe of knowledge.[43] Their demands were sacred enunciations of Black freedom, they were their fathers and their mothers—their words became their children's.[44] This was but an inflection point of an expansive tradition of struggle that never really stopped—even now. And it is not insignificant that they used song and chant not only to rally their troops but also to fortify their spirits and to remember. As Vincent Harding makes clear in his work on the "Black university," this action constituted an affirmation that "dying copies of whiteness were no longer needed."[45] This is what animated the large and lesser-known convening—November 1968's "Toward a Black University" conference, which sought to extend W. E. B. Du Bois's "field and function" argument to that moment. Its organizers included figures like Acklyn Lynch and held that a Black university should be more than a label for the population of its student body.[46]

The struggle continued into 1969. After the "Toward a Black University" Conference, which sought to conceptualize the "Black university," the following spring saw students orchestrate a decentralized takeover of various university buildings. These were heady times, considering how militant demands at other Black universities had quickly descended into violence that precipitated armed defense among the students. At Howard, the tactics were far more advanced than they were in the previous year, including a high degree of coordination and planning among various student organizations, resulting in the closure of the campus for a week. The 1969 takeovers would have no easy resolution, as federal agents were called upon to evict the students from various buildings and students were formally charged. These protests demonstrated the broader support for change as even the law and medical students were engaged.[47] It also demonstrated, however, the seriousness of students' demands for the fulfillment of the grand idea that Black knowledge could permeate higher education.[48] From arguing that the university should change its name to Sterling Brown University to arguing that it should play an instrumental role in the community life of Washington, DC, a sizable number of students sought a true remaking of what it meant to do knowledge work at Negro colleges.[49]

James Cheek's arrival on campus was both a boon to this idea and an eventual repudiation of it. The structural conditions that led to the football protests of 1927 and 1936 were not resolved and led to more unrest in the 1970s. As Howard students and faculty members increasingly placed pressure on the administration to create a university representative of and responsive to the global Black community's issues and concerns, student protest returned in 1983 when *The Hilltop*'s editor in chief, Janice McKnight, was expelled by Cheek's administration for publishing articles related to a sex discrimination suit.[50] This action showcased a willingness by students—already less than thrilled about the university's rightward leaning posture—to return to the protest tactics of a generation ago. The student-led quest to require Afro-American Studies classes as a condition for *all* students to graduate in 1986 demonstrated the continuity of the demand for affirmations of Black identity and curricular change within the university.

How we remember events matters. The movements represented in the images of the sixties were not merely (if at all) for academic and popular consumption, for those images represent what Vincent Harding calls "the river."[51] They are for orienting how we might continue to be vessels for changing what Malcolm X characterized as "this miserable condition on this planet."[52] Insofar as we frame these earlier protests as the distant past, best remembered in museum exhibits, we ultimately miss the importance of that moment, its ability to reveal the ways that certain components of the Black university continue to exhibit a fealty to the architects of our oppression. With this framing the student revolt on campus in 1989 must be seen as an extension of the larger fights for freedom that have animated Black life. It was a declaration that the work of the sixties, of the thirties, and of the twenties was unfinished. It was a declaration that merely studying Black people does not a Black university make. It was a declaration that "Blackness can," and it must.[53] It was a declaration that "We are the primary sources of information," and from those sources we can construct our institutions in our image.[54] It was a declaration that our blood memory reminds us that our destiny cannot be fulfilled if we go for money at the expense of our greater Spirit—for the latter sustains us in ways that the former never can.[55] As Du Bois stated, the great question of the Negro college was: "How far and in what way can we consciously and scientifically guide our future so as to insure our physical survival, our spiritual freedom and our social growth? Either we do this or we die. There is no alternative."[56] The fraught politics of the American and global twentieth century would provide the context for the necessity of new imaginations.

2

Racist Etiquette

We know what Willie Horton did to the campaign, we
know the environment that it created. It had many people in
America thinking that that's the truth about Black men.
—William Simms[1]

Of the more consequential moments of the American twentieth century,
the most prominent was the shift toward the political and cultural right,
a move that coincided with what has generally, albeit imprecisely, been
labeled the "post–Civil Rights era" (1968–present). This moment and
movement not only had an immense impact on the long-term fortunes
of the traditional Democratic Party coalition and its electoral successes,
which were built in part upon race-specific domestic policies and the
political apparatus of the New Deal, it would also determine the shape
of higher education policy. Beyond the cultural assaults of the Right
(i.e., Ronald Reagan and the Free Speech movement and the so-called
culture wars of the 1990s), this rightward lurch was also responsible
for a range of policies that endangered the funding of public universities, as public monies were reallocated to other "entitlement" programs
(e.g., military expansion).[2] Historically Black colleges and universities
(HBCUs) were among the first targets, particularly in the 1970s. The
choices made by university administrators across the higher education
landscape, then, were largely influenced by their professed need to adapt
to the neoliberal environment that structured the academy in America
and the larger world.[3] By the same token, the kinds of political movements that students developed were cognizant of these sorts of shifts,
and the university-based "quality of life" and curricular critiques were in
some ways understood as part of this larger momentum, which affected
American and global political realities.

Race has never been incidental to American politics. To use the
phraseology of an earlier era, the "Negro problem" was and continues

to be endemic to the kinds of political worlds created by Western modernity, particularly its "exceptional" exemplar, the United States. But what needs to be clarified is exactly how the racialization of Africans determined the possibilities for their survival in America at various points in the evolution of its history. In other words, what forms has this systematic racism taken as American history unfolded? In addition, the questions of how racism influences and affects the ways in which the state is governed and how democracy is constructed along racial lines become crucial considerations for assessing the possibilities of freedom for African peoples that reside in these structures.

The latter quarter of the twentieth century provides a case study for what Ronald W. Walters called a unique form of "white nationalism" that pervaded American society, serving as an effort to curtail even the limited "gains" achieved with the erosion of Jim Crow. The aftermath of the Civil Rights era, then, saw the repositioning of racialized power.[4] But, as in all other eras, resistance to the very order of this kind of society continued. In documenting the nature of this shift, we would then clarify that changes in form did not produce changes in function: 1989 represented the continuance of a long, beautiful struggle to enact a Black freedom. Race shifted the meter of American partisanship and the ideological formations (though not the broader American ideological project) that characterized the last half of the twentieth century, leading to the merging narratives of the Lee Atwater saga and Howard University's own right turn.

Liberal Fissures

For those Africans in America who have defined freedom as ascension into the American body politic, the Democratic Party in the twentieth century was their means. The Democratic Party's "friendship" was largely conditional and came from an intense effort to force Franklin Delano Roosevelt to extend the benefits of the New Deal to Black communities. In exchange, the party was able to secure the votes of disaffected Black Republicans in the urban North, but as a result it created a New Deal coalition—composed also of liberal intellectuals, labor (largely white ethnics), and the South (overtly white racists)—that was destined to fail.[5] Despite sharing some nominal economic interests—although even the New Deal was administered via the same racial logics that had always existed—the coalition would sputter largely because of the ways in which race came to influence the direction of policy during the Civil Rights movement.

Much of the impetus for the Southern retreat from the Democratic Party stems from the 1948 election, which saw the emergence of the "Dixiecrat revolt" of Southern politicians who were dismayed by the civil rights orientation of Harry S. Truman's administration, signified by its creation of the Civil Rights Commission. Led by Strom Thurmond, the Dixiecrats' articulation of an anti-civil rights posture would serve as the beginning of a rallying point around which segregationist forces would converge. Despite the fact that the New Deal political project would likely not have threatened the racial order, the mere pretense of a Truman pivot toward the destruction of Jim Crow—only the extreme manifestation of that order—was enough to generate a political response with deep implications for future of the American duopoly.[6]

It was, however, with John F. Kennedy's New Frontier and Lyndon B. Johnson's Great Society that the Democratic Party's coalition, rooted in the New Deal, began its demise. In the late 1950s, Americans had felt that "something" was wrong, a sense generated by the uninspiring response of Dwight D. Eisenhower's administration to the crises of desegregation in Little Rock, Communist revolution in nearby Cuba, the space race with the launch of Sputnik, and the economy. Coupled with Richard Nixon's "mixed political legacy," this may have played as much a part of the success of the Democrats in 1960 as anything.[7] Although there were the murmurings of defection and some Southern support for Barry Goldwater's late push for the nomination in 1960, the coalition remained largely intact, helping propel Kennedy to victory.[8]

Kennedy's pro-business posture endeared him to the same sorts of corporate leaders that Roosevelt had courted to make the New Deal possible. And in so doing, it also endeared him to a political coalition led by certain Black leaders who did not question the fundamental nature of liberal democracy.[9] Proponents of American liberalism, then, viewed the American project as in need of a few repairs—of these, the elevation of Black citizens to equal players (i.e., as laborers) within the existing capitalist order. The New Frontier essentially argued that the nature of American society could be extended, that exceptionalism could be taken to new heights (e.g., the moon). But what Kennedy could never imagine was the ways that Africans in the United States would force liberalism to confront what is more than a simple tension: its racial legacy. To use Malcolm X's formulation, U.S.-born Africans struggled to force into existence a "version of freedom larger than America's prepared to accept."[10] Of course, this has been historically labeled the "Civil Rights movement." But following Charles Cobb and others, its most significant elements might be most appropriately understood as the Black freedom struggle or the "freedom movement."[11] To many struggling under its aegis, Black liberation presaged the destruction of racial capitalism, which in effect meant the undoing of American liberalism, not the simple smoothing of its rough edges. The structure itself had to end.

It is out of the violence that Black liberation projects met that the national shame became visible enough to secure the concessions—read elsewhere as Kennedy's moral vision or "awakening"—that erupted into legislative changes during the 1960s. While it is important to acknowledge the benefits of such legislative action, doing so from the flawed premise that they flowed simply from moral revelations, rather than a racial crisis at the core of the liberal tradition, creates significant confusions. It not only obscures the racialist meaning we should ascribe to the very notion of American citizenship, it also leads to a propensity to misread the resulting conservative backlash as simply "backward." It was, and remains, more complicated.

While liberation was the larger, more central goal, Black people of varying class sensibilities also sought to force the state to live up to its professed ideals (even as some viewed this as *the* goal; this friction led to important internal cleavages within the movement). It was during Johnson's tenure that these elements of the Black freedom struggle forced America into a deeper consideration of what Black citizenship might mean. By 1964, the struggle had seemingly become synonymous with Democratic Party politics, as more activists sharing this vision saw in Kennedy's legacy and Johnson's administration an opportunity to affect real change. Johnson's presidency, as is well known, saw the legislative victories of the Civil Rights Act (1964), the Voting Rights Act (1965), and the Fair Housing Act (1968), but it also generated a series of antagonisms. Liberalism could provide only piecemeal changes to the American racial order and the ways in which it imagined citizenship.

Such a reading can be applied to the War on Poverty. According to Ira Katznelson, part of Johnson's energetic response toward the idea was due to the connection those in his cabinet saw between poverty among Black youth and the ways that it rendered them "unqualified" for military service.[12] Other origins for this "war" were the Kennedy administration's development of an antidelinquency program and the intellectual elite who saw an occasion to test the "opportunity thesis." This idea argued that both delinquency and poverty resulted from an institutional lack—structurally, poor people had no alternatives.

Remedying this lack would require social programs that prepared African Americans for true citizenship. And "citizenship" meant participation in what came to be known as "community action" and preparation for productive labor within, as opposed to against, the structures of a still-racialized capitalism, as it became clear that such foundations of inequality would not be seriously addressed. For the social science intellectuals who engineered these programs, racial oppression was reduced from an antagonism inherent to the systems that ordered American society to one that could be solved by addressing it as a marginal concern. The failure of the War on Poverty was, in other words, written into the very logic of the policies themselves.[13]

And the fate of the Great Society—at least its ability to fully resolve the question of race—was prefigured. At his commencement speech at Howard University in 1965, Johnson revealed what was no doubt a shared concern among well-meaning liberal ideologues, the idea that the amelioration of generations of racial discrimination had to be dealt with through positive liberalism—corrective measures had to be taken. Johnson followed others who labeled this "affirmative action."[14] These ideas contributed to his wider vision of a Great Society, in which all Americans would ostensibly benefit from American prosperity (which was extracted, in part, from its imperial victims). The *liberty* of traditional American liberalism had to become responsible to the visions of *equality* of the liberals in the Democratic Party.

The opportunity to participate in an unquestioned "mainstream" of American life was the bellwether of the Johnson administration's coalition with the Civil Rights movement. As more of "America's prosperity" was needed to attempt the containment of communism in Southeast Asia, the more strident economic demands of the movement were either never considered or betrayed. Having both guns and butter was a political dream that could not measure up to reality.[15] While the failures of the Great Society have been attributed to many factors (including its identification as a "Black program"),[16] what remains most clear is that it was not wholly synonymous with how many Black people had envisioned a new society. While certain organizations veered toward the idea that the legal, political, and economic policies in place would best secure freedom, Black radicals took "freedom" to mean self-determination, only possible through a revolutionary disavowal of the logic of American liberalism that underpinned the current structure.[17]

The latter half of the 1960s saw this evolution of Black resistance toward more radical ends coincide with both the escalation of the student movement and the antiwar movement. As Johnson correctly identified this new-old radical orientation as discordant with the American liberal tradition, American cities began to burn. Watts, Detroit, Newark, and other rebellions were generated largely in response to what urban Black folk considered the inadequate attention given to the structural conditions of racial capitalism within the Black freedom struggle. Their model was a wider vision of Black freedom, inspired by the Revolutionary Action Movement, the Black Panther Party, and the post-1965 incarnation of the Student Nonviolent Coordinating Committee (SNCC).[18] In partial response to these upheavals—replete with the imagery of Black resistance—the political cudgel of "law and order" was born. These conceptions of Black liberation were visions that Johnson and the Democratic Party vision would not and could not fully engage and were often met with state violence. This violence was undoubtedly the result of the age-old conflation of Black liberation projects with criminality. But despite Johnson's late attempts to assuage the American fear of a Black freedom, the politics of crime became the final nail in the coffin of the Democratic coalition.[19]

The white ethnics who witnessed the long hot summers and the solid white South, which sought to massively resist positive liberalism for Black people (but not for themselves), were dismayed by the Democratic response to the law-and-order issue. (One wonders what their reaction might have been had they been aware that Johnson's Pentagon chiefs were actively drawing up plans to deploy the army in American cities).[20] Ascendant now were the politics of resentment, which, ironically enough, framed the political attitudes of mostly white working-class Americans. Mortified by the brashness of American youth and the audacity of Black resistance, the traditional voting blocs of the Democratic Party fractured and led to the rise of the first influential third-party candidate since Henry Wallace in 1948: the demagogic George Wallace.[21] It was Richard Nixon, however, who took control of the law-and-order narrative, eventually upending Democrat Hubert Humphrey and, with the help of Strom Thurmond, Wallace's insurgent campaign.[22] But Wallace's run charted an electoral strategy, one in which racial appeals could constitute a workable stratagem in national elections. And Nixon's embrace of "conservative" issues proved the viability of the wider conservative movement, especially in the wake of the Democratic Party's disarray—pulled apart by the rift between party traditionalists and the insurgents who were inspired by the Black freedom movement.[23] Nixon and the Republican Party would elevate the "silent majority" as the most important constituency in subsequent elections and the base from which to launch a political project to challenge the best of American left-liberalism. Whatever gains the latter had procured would thereafter be in grave danger.

Conservative Futures

Prefiguring Nixon's success, however, was the movement that produced the language of conservatism he so strategically appropriated. At the core of this movement and the various factions that coalesced under the name of conservatism was the idea that Lyndon B. Johnson's social programs—"the liberal establishment"— had gone too far, that the "new class" it supported and created had to be stopped.[24] While the Republican Party's approach to Black voting blocs was traditionally similar to that of the Democrats, the evolution of its strategy of employing and benefiting from racial appeals had, and will continue to have, implications for conservative politics in America. The story of this evolution follows.

In the United States, what has come to be known as "conservatism" began as a political orientation that was premised upon "liberty" as the key principle of liberal democracy. While it has been argued that this was already the defining ethos of American society, and always had been, the greater emphasis placed on the freedom of the markets in the middle of the twentieth century characterizes the movement in particular ways. This free-market ideological orientation also set the ground for what historians of conservative politics have identified as the other tendencies of the movement: anticommunism and moral traditionalism.[25] Each of these would have reverberations for questions of racial justice. The highly interventionist programs that marked the New Deal and the Great Society were considered violations of the sanctity of the market, while anticommunist forces both accurately and erroneously sought to extirpate the "red" influence from the Black freedom struggle, all the while eschewing the "permissiveness" of the 1960s, which, of course, also had much to do with mainstreaming of Black student movements and popular culture. Although each of these spheres is interconnected, much of the racial meaning of the Republican shift can be assigned to the first issue.[26] Race played an important role in the failure of the Great Society. By the end of the decade, long-standing conservative intellectuals would be joined by liberals who were disenchanted with the idea that the central state might solve the problems of inequality, crime, fair housing, and other racially inflected issues that formed the backdrop of American life.

As the 1950s closed, much of the intellectual edifice of the conservative movement was being developed by thinkers like James Burnham, Frank Meyer, Friedrich Hayek, and Russell Kirk. But in the political realm, conservatives had no discernible leader. Into this fray entered the Arizona senator Barry Goldwater. Perhaps not ironically, Goldwater had supported civil rights earlier in his career and had led a chapter of the National Association for the Advancement of Colored People (NAACP) in his home state, but by 1960 he would place his name on the ghostwritten *Conscience of a Conservative*, which quickly became a bible for the movement.[27] Goldwater then launched himself into presidential politics, running on conservative principles. Although he would lose the nomination to Nixon, his speech at the Republican National Convention galvanized the "conscience" of the most ardent supporters and financiers of the conservative movement. Their backing allowed Goldwater to secure the nomination of the Republican Party for the 1964 presidential election, where he was trounced by Johnson.[28]

While his loss was monumental, Goldwater's badly run campaign created the conditions that would guarantee the rise of the "New Right" in subsequent years by generating important bases in future conservative strongholds and by articulating his support for conservative principles on a national platform. Important also was Goldwater's refusal to support the Civil Rights Act of 1964. To many, the Republican Party's embrace of a candidate who styled himself as an opponent of civil rights signaled a leap to the right wing of the party and a disavowal of its traditional moderate wing, led by Nelson Rockefeller, among others. It further positioned the Democrats as the champion of the Civil Rights movement in the imaginations of many, which had an immediate impact on the fortunes of both parties. Finally, Goldwater's campaign was the training ground for a new crop of organizers, running the gamut of conservative sensibilities. It helped these organizers build an important following for conservative issues, which was in turn courted by the growing conservative news media and the growing conservative student movement. This final legacy of the Goldwater presidential campaign, in many ways, presaged the conservative movement's electoral success in the years to come.[29]

The conservative movement's emphasis on moral traditionalism provided a "home" for those Americans unsettled by the events of the 1960s. The election of 1968, which finally resulted in the successful election of a conservative president (at least "optically"), marked the real entrance of the movement to power. Conservatives, however, quickly soured on Nixon, who did not roll back Johnson's Great Society to their liking (while extending his misadventure in Vietnam). Nixon was less an ideologue and more concerned with winning elections, and he was thus the improper vehicle for extending the conservative movement's principles as understood by its hardliners.[30] Nixon's ambition directly led to the Republican Party's lone black eye of the era, the Watergate scandal in 1974.

After the lame-duck tenure of Gerald Ford, the centrist Jimmy Carter was able to appeal to the newly emergent evangelical constituency to win on the Democratic Party ticket. Carter's presidency, which appointed Black leaders to visible positions, generated somewhat of a thaw in the civil rights arena, while also attempting a moderately successful and short-lived remaking of U.S. foreign policy as the extension of "human rights."[31] Despite Carter's efforts—and some might argue because of them—the needle of American politics was solidly to the right by 1980, pushed there by the sapping of American national confidence.

Against the tendency to view this period as a decline of the Black freedom movement, it is imperative to note that many of the high points of Black twentieth-century political work occurred during this period (e.g., the work of the National Black Political Convention, the Congress of Afrikan People, the African Liberation Support Committee, and the Combahee River Collective), including the election of many important leaders to local and national electoral positions.[32] It is perhaps also significant to note the ways in which the federal government actively worked to undermine many of these radical programs for revolutionary change, which held at bay the potential for America to undergo the "revolution of values" that Martin Luther King argued would be necessary— more necessary than the legislation passed by Johnson.[33]

The passage of these laws, however, was enough for conservative strategists to "mobilize resentment" within "the silent majority." This mobilization took place in the seventies beginning in large measure with the ideas of Kevin Phillips and the work of individuals like Howard Phillips and Richard Viguerie.[34] Premised on short historical memory, little empirical data, and on purely racially motivated appeals, this resentment had much to do with the perception that Black gains meant somehow that "middle America" would have to "lose." Conservatives pounced on this and coupled their arguments for less government intervention with the idea that social programs compromised the efficiency of the markets, arguing that rational actors would eventually lose their "taste for discrimination" on their own.[35] The writing was on the wall for "affirmative action," particularly the strong version that emphasized "equality of outcome." As Jean Hardisty shows, this resentment would also be mobilized within antifeminist and antigay politics, which had a curious convergence with the emergence of Jerry Falwell's Moral Majority in the late 1970s and other mass-based Christian conservative outfits that preceded it.[36]

While extremist organizations such as the John Birch Society and populist nativist movements achieved broad support and sometimes tepid sanction of the party elite, they were less important than organizations that became collectively known as the "Christian Right." While the former eventually had to be publicly disavowed by most elements of mainstream conservative leadership, the Christian Right was embraced as a moral foundation for the movement. Outright racist and nativist fundamentalisms were to be rejected, but Christian fundamentalism could be useful. Able to mobilize for conservative ends with perhaps some of the largest bases available to political strategists, pastors and other religious leaders involved in the conservative movement were able to generate a windfall for the Republican Party. Their main ideological contribution to the movement—and the proverbial price for their support to the party—was the idea of "family values." The Christian Right was able to expand the concerns of the moral traditionalists to concerns of the stability of the "ideal American family" in the face of feminist and LGBT (lesbian, gay, bisexual, transgender) movements, which they argued destabilized notions of the ideal. As Robert Self argues, this created a political environment that eroded support for many of the "positive rights" (e.g., government support for unwed mothers) that were part and parcel of the liberal victories of the long progressive era, as the Republican Party embraced its many extremist manifestations (e.g., the Stop the Equal Rights Amendment movement and the pro-life movement) to achieve electoral victories in the 1970s and 1980s.[37] Although values were its domain, the Christian Right would also come to embrace the politics of austerity, the freedom of the market, and an anticommunism that supported American imperial efforts abroad.[38] In the end, the family's stability was secured by liberty, not equality.

Another important constituency, one able to deliver not simply votes but an ideological justification for conservative policy as well, was the neoconservatives. Famously characterized by Irving Kristol as "liberals, who were mugged by reality," many of the neoconservatives were disaffected Trotskyists, democratic socialists, who were simply no longer enamored with the radical movements that brought them to politics.[39] Concerned with the anti-anticommunism of the student movement and what they considered to be an overreach of the welfare state, these intellectuals began an outright assault on the liberal consensus. The neoconservatives were among the loudest dissenters to forms of positive liberalism, such as affirmative action, offering that it failed to deal sufficiently with racial harm, which was individual as opposed to collective. This of course, opened the door to the imaginary ideas of "reverse racism," which led to the uses of the Fourteenth Amendment to address the "harm" done to members of the dominant group.

In addition, a movement in social science that challenged the tenets of the welfare state was coupled with new kinds of cultural explanations for the prevalence of a supposed Black inferiority, as environmental ex-planations replaced the biological ones of yesteryear. Joining the Christian Right, the nativist "Americanist" movement, and the libertarians who had also benefited from the exodus of disaffected student liberals, the neoconservatives rounded out an important quartet of conservative elements.[40] Perhaps because of the ways that these intellectuals came to the movement, the robust media platforms they secured, neoconservatives have had an outsized influence on defining the conservative and, by extension, the larger Republican agenda—so much so that neoconservatism has become somewhat of a metonym for the New Right. Many of the neoconservative movement's key figures ended up playing influential roles in the administration of the figure who has often been seen as the most celebrated political exemplar of the New Right: Ronald W. Reagan.[41]

Reagan's rise and eventual ascendancy to the presidency was not inevitable. It was the product of a genuine shift in American political consciousness during a period of "malaise"— the designation attributed to the 1979 speech that came to define Jimmy Carter's presidency. The late 1970s saw the economic fortunes of the nation grind to a halt, character-ized by an energy crisis and "stagflation," which furthered eroded any confidence in the Keynesian system that underpinned American liberalism. Coupled with the deepening geopolitical convulsions, which made a thawing of the Cold War seem less plausible, the economic "crisis of confidence" cost Carter the 1980 election.[42] But as Doug Rossinow has argued, the election of Reagan was not simply a repudiation of Carter; it was also an affirmation for a large majority of Americans that "the time had come" for a conservative president.[43] Reagan was able to capture the presidency by appealing to the free-market, anti-tax, white backlash, individualist, masculinist, patriotic, and corporation-friendly sensibilities of the American electorate at the same time—all without appearing as an extremist. His acting background perhaps made this possible, for Reagan was generally likable, despite embracing political positions that in other eras might have been dismissed prima facie. But in the difficult days of the late 1970s, they would come to symbolize a "return of confidence" in America.[44] With the election of Reagan, the conservative movement had finally won the soul of America. The 1980s proved to be a decade that would demonstrate the extent to which conservative principles, such as the unadulterated freedom of the market, could stand for what Rossinow calls "common sense" American ideals.[45]

Much ink has been spilled both labeling Ronald Reagan with charges of racism and absolving him of the same. This either serves to create in Reagan a singular villain or a flawed but well-meaning hero. Both depictions fail. They do not take seriously the more meaningful question of how racism was already within the normative logic of American democracy and in every sphere of human activity, producing a tension that could not simply be resolved by allowing access for the few. The racial contract, as outlined by Charles Mills, fundamentally shapes and orders the modern world—of which America, of course, sees itself as the exceptional leader.[46] Thus we might consider the deeper significance of conservatism as an implicitly (and sometimes, unnecessarily explicit) racist political doctrine.[47] While Reagan's personal racism and his use of language such as "welfare queen" is revolting, ultimately they matter less than the question of whether he would produce policy that would either exacerbate or reduce the impact of racial capitalism on Black communities. Tellingly, however, his willingness to embrace a conservative worldview necessarily meant "conserving" a political order that reduced (even made impossible), rather than expanded, the possibilities for Black citizenship. In other words, race mattered to Reagan's political vision. Whiteness, it seems, had to be "conserved."[48]

Of course these political ideals had to be rendered in more coded language. The approach of a George Wallace had to be repudiated. Reagan had famously opened his campaign in Neshoba County, Mississippi, the infamous site of the 1964 killings of Michael Schwerner, Andrew Goodman, and James Chaney. But when the rubber hit the road, he could not openly accept his endorsement from the Ku Klux Klan.[49] In the place of overt racist appeals, this period saw the emergence of what Amy Ansell calls the "new racism." Arguing that it was no longer appropriate to use brazenly racist language to court the silent majority, Ansell claims that the "New Right" created more sophisticated propaganda, more subtle language that invalidated policies that targeted (or failed to target) what they considered America's racial minorities.[50]

Rather than asking if Reagan was racist, the better question is to ask to what extent he—and/or America itself—benefited politically from what Ronald W. Walters calls "policy racism," as generated through the levers of American governance.[51] The racialized impact of policy would be felt through the imposition of the free-market fundamentalism and the antiregulation ideals of the Right. Race would factor into the ways that the anti-tax movement dovetailed with the perception that much of government spending went toward social programs that benefited Black communities. Policy racism would be felt in the atomization of the individual and the repudiation of the concept of group harm in antidiscrimination jurisprudence. The question of racism and its link to coloniality would also be felt in the "peripheries" of Latin America and Africa as Reagan's foreign policy sought to conserve American power abroad, no matter the struggles of self-determination then raging in the so-called Third World. In these ways, Reagan's orientation toward race was not unlike that of the vast majority of American presidents. As David Theo Goldberg has argued, racism irrevocably marks the emergence and sustenance of the modern state, and America is perhaps a clear manifestation of these vexed origins.[52] This larger question, however, has been somewhat subsumed as historians and political theorists are more willing to question how race was used to secure political power for candidates, rather than simply remarking upon its implicit meaning for political power itself. This generally characterizes prominent analyses of how the GOP was able to hold onto the silent majority as a base in the 1980s, even as Reagan's image as hero waxed and waned.

Perhaps the most significant domestic impact of Reagan's administration was its economic policy. Buoyed by a dubious concept of supply-side economics, the administration engineered what amounted to the evisceration of whatever was left of the liberal reforms of the 1960s. These and other views would collectively come to be known as "Reaganomics." The plan was simple, perhaps so simple that it predictably could not pass scientific muster. Known also as "trickle-down economics," the theory supposed that eliminating or reducing the top marginal tax rates would stimulate economic growth as the funds that would have traditionally filled the federal government's coffers would be diverted toward private investment. The economics behind this, known as the Laffer Curve, were shaky at best (rumored to be explained at a restaurant and mapped out on a napkin) but received a ringing endorsement from the energetic head of the Office of Management and Budget, David Stockman, along with many others within the Reagan administration (though not among many trained economists). It also represented the culmination of the "tax revolt" that had received a boost from lawmakers Jack Kemp and William Roth, whose Kemp-Roth 30 percent tax breaks had become enshrined as the official Republican position.[53]

The results were as predictable as the economics were fallacious. According to Thomas Byrne Edsall and Mary Edsall, the effective tax rate for those in the bottom quintiles of income rose while those in the top quintiles fell, programs like Aid to Families with Dependent Children and the Food Stamp Program were slashed, the reduction of the size of government affected the employment opportunities in those areas where nonwhites traditionally worked, and the shrinking of the regulatory state affected the safety of workers and nonwhite communities located in areas of heavy industry.[54] (The one bureaucracy that was spared and even expanded was the military, prompting some analysts to claim Reaganomics as an example of "military Keynesianism.")[55] What the Edsalls call "a top-down coalition" helped to engineer such drastic changes in the role that the state played in the lives of the working class, which in the end received sanction because of a "conservative egalitarianism" that appropriated the banner of equal opportunity from the civil rights struggle and sought the slashing of such programs because they supposedly harmed white citizens.[56]

The result was that, despite the aspirational reception of middle-class visuals on television's *The Cosby Show*, the Reagan era saw the further tightening of the American racial order.[57] What changed, if anything, was how this "changing same" was understood. Ansell argues that the shift in discourse about race made possible the concealment of the policy racism of the 1980s by rendering them in language that was "color-blind," that used the concept of equality of opportunity, that regarded harm as individually based—as opposed to group-based or historical—and that read targeted policy as "reverse racist."[58]

In addition to the above economic issues, Reagan's administration dragged their feet on questions of civil rights with appointees to the Department of Justice like William Bradford Reynolds and Clarence Pendleton, who were outspoken against affirmative action. Conservative jurisprudence sought (with mixed results) to overturn the idea that historical discrimination was deserving of any form of legal remedy. For these thinkers, only current, individual harm constituted a violation, and those sorts of violations could go both ways. In line with this world-view, the Reagan administration appointed a score of federal judges who have shaped the common law in ways that continue to reverberate over thirty years later.[59]

One of the biggest issues that Black communities had with Reagan's administration, however, was its failure to levy sanctions against apart-heid South Africa. It is necessary to draw linkages between policy racism at home and abroad. It is meaningful, even if not altogether surprising, that Reagan and others in his administration put international com-mercial considerations ahead of the lives of Africans, not just in the United States, but throughout the world. Not only was Reagan's support of apartheid South Africa received with disdain, the 1983 invasion of Grenada roiled Black leftists as well. In addition, many Blacks joined other liberals in questioning the support of the American government toward the Contras in Nicaragua, a major foreign policy concern. For the African world, the Reagan era was another nadir.[60]

Historians and political scientists have long debated whether the con-servative ascendancy beginning with Reagan constituted a true political realignment.[61] But this question seems less important than the fact that it contributed to the development of a seemingly permanent neoliberal order in American political life. In other words, regardless of electoral outcomes, what has certainly been realigned is the very conceptual vo-cabulary of politico-economic discourse. The consolidation of the power of the Right in America lies not only in electoral victories but also, and perhaps more important, in how what counts as politics, as issues, and as problems are constructed and discussed.[62] Even in elections in which it has not been successful, the GOP has created a policy environment that renders traditional liberal values as less viable, putting Democrats in somewhat of a permanent defensive mode and causing many to move toward the center in order to compete. In some senses, both American political parties are neoliberal, hewing toward a kind of politics that ren-ders the market as inviolable and American power abroad as paramount to the achievement of this goal. It has been the power of conservative media, conservative foundations and think tanks, and clever electoral marketing that has made this possible.

According to Thomas Ferguson and Joel Rogers, the corporations that had traditionally aligned with the New Deal coalition shifted loyalties in the mid-1970s as a result of the recession of that period.[63] Indeed, as Jerome Himmelstein argues, business swung from an ideological basis in "corporate liberalism" to "corporate conservatism." The economic and political shifts of the 1970s created conditions in which corporations were less willing to entertain the short-run costs resulting from the compromises between labor and capital of earlier eras.[64] What quickly followed was the development of the Business Roundtable and the flowering of conservative think tanks like the Olin Foundation and the Scaife Foundation, which were quickly joined by newer organizations like the American Enterprise Institute, the Cato Foundation, Manhattan Institute, and the Heritage Foundation. Together, these organizations generated the intellectual justification for conservative policies. These new foundations, of course, were developed alongside a multiplicity of single-issue organizations that worked together to deliver votes to the Republican Party, representing a range of concerns from pro-choice advocacy to gun rights. For Himmelstein, these institutions constituted the "New Right," brought together by both a disdain for the liberal elite and the elevation of "issues" as the entrée into conservative movements.[65]

These institutions were aided by the dominant presence of neoconservative media—for example, publications such as *Public Interest, Commentary*, and *New Criterion*—which joined paleoconservative mainstays like William Buckley's *National Review*. Television and radio would also benefit from the eventual lapsing of the Federal Communications Commission's fairness doctrine, which had been put in place as a mandate to achieve some semblance of balance. This kind of deregulation paved the way for the kind of political education that only Fox News and Rush Limbaugh could provide.[66]

Along with the foundations and the media, a number of political action committees—which went from 89 to 1251 from 1974 to 1980—benefited from the increase in corporate support for conservative politics, so much so that the Republicans were able to outspend the Democratic Party in the much-needed polling that helped to secure electoral victories throughout this era.[67] The Republican National Committee was able to employ a number of campaign specialists, all experts in understanding and shaping public opinion, such as Richard Wirthlin and Roger Ailes. As electoral contests assumed the kinds of marketing bonanzas that resembled commercial advertising, the role of political operatives became that of public relations specialists.[68] It is here, in the rough-and-tumble world of political campaigns in the 1980s, where we meet Lee Atwater.

Can't Say "Nigger"

When George H. W. Bush's presidential campaign decided to "go negative" by appealing to the racial fears of swing voters in order to secure the presidential election of 1988, they were not charting new ground. The fear of the African, the savage Black body, was of course inscribed into the very nature of American life and lore and thus political discourse. In fact, Nixon had used a variation of the same tactic to defeat the waffling, soft-on-crime liberal campaign of Hubert Humphrey, as discussed above. But there was something new about 1988. Where it would not have hurt Bush's chances to use overt, obvious racist language—say, that of a George Wallace—in previous epochs, what Tali Mendelberg calls the new "norm of equality" rendered such a tactic unviable in 1988. Instead, the Bush campaign team mastered the new discursive tactics for employing both race and the media strategies that allowed them to disavow any racist intent, which they would need to do constantly. The impact of these "implicit" uses of race to impugn the electability of their opponent secured a victory for Bush and forever linked Michael Dukakis with William Horton, as well as the association of the Bush campaign with racism, in the annals of American history.[69]

Harvey LeRoy "Lee" Atwater was one of the masterminds behind this strategy. Atwater was one of a crop of young, brash political masterminds willing to go above and beyond ethical codes of conduct to secure wins for their candidate and their party. Atwater's rise to the top of the GOP after his successful management of Bush's campaign in 1988 capped an extended political career defined by deceit, underhandedness, and duplicity, which earned him the negative endorsement of Congresswoman Pat Schroeder as "probably the most evil man in America."[70]

This was no hyperbole. Perhaps irrevocably scarred by a childhood accident that saw his brother killed by scalding oil, Atwater was never able to develop the kind of human empathy that served as a check on actions that might harm others. Yet none of this excuses his laundry list of what might have been considered crimes if they had not been committed in the realm of the privileged: stolen elections, creating false candidates, and ruining the careers of other operatives. Atwater's true talent, however, was for manipulating the media. Where stories could be planted, where sound bites could ruin an opponent, where racial fears might be played upon, there was Lee Atwater, son of the New South: too egalitarian to be a "racist," too American to ignore the power of race.[71] In a well-known 1981 interview, Atwater explains the nonracist racist strategy:

> You start out in 1954 by saying, "Nigger, nigger, nigger." By 1968 you can't say "nigger"—that hurts you. Backfires. So you say stuff like forced busing, states' rights and all that stuff. You're getting so abstract now [that] you're talking about cutting taxes, and all these things you're talking about are totally economic things and a byproduct of them is [that] blacks get hurt worse than whites. And subconsciously maybe that is part of it. I'm not saying that. But I'm saying that if it is getting that abstract and that coded, that we are doing away with the racial problem one way or the other. You follow me—because obviously sitting around saying, "we want to cut this," is much more abstract than even the busing thing, and a hell of a lot more abstract than "nigger, nigger."[72]

Eight years later, he would have the opportunity to test this strategy when the campaign became aware of the name and story of William Horton.

The Republicans had developed a team devoted to researching possible issues that could be used in a negative campaign. After defeating Bob Dole in the primary using a similar strategy, the team turned to Michael Dukakis, where they quickly found grounds to challenge his patriotism, his commitment to militarism, and most crucially, his supposed softness on crime. The accuracy of Dukakis's record on any of these issues was not important. What attracted Atwater and others was whether they could use them to their advantage. Atwater, it could be argued, was less concerned with conservative ideology and more concerned with winning; it was as if politics was a game.

The William Horton story had been publicized in the papers of the *Lawrence (MA) Eagle-Tribune*, the setting of Horton's initial crime. After being convicted of the murder of Joseph Fournier, Horton, along with three accomplices, was sentenced to life in prison without the possibility of parole. After a tumultuous first few years that saw him transferred back and forth between maximum- and minimum-security prisons, Horton was finally allowed to participate in a prison furlough program after having his sentence reduced. None of this was unique or even "liberal"; these were normal procedures for the carceral state during this era that gave some semblance of a value toward rehabilitation, as opposed to incarceration motivated by revenge. Horton escaped during his tenth furlough, moving along the Eastern Seaboard and doing odd jobs. He eventually settled in Upper Marlboro, Maryland, where he committed the crimes for which he is most consistently linked. On April 3, 1987, Horton stabbed and tortured Cliff Barnes and raped his then-fiancée Angela. After briefly escaping the scene, he was caught and convicted and sentenced by a Maryland judge to life in prison. The judge overseeing the case refused to extradite him back to Massachusetts, remanding him to more "tough-on-crime" Maryland, where he was destined to "never breathe a breath of free air again."[73] These events provided the basis for a Pulitzer Prize–winning series of articles on the furlough program written by the journalist Susan Forrest, some of which, it was later revealed, contained factual errors. What started as a series of articles became an entire community's quest to hold Governor Michael Dukakis accountable for the actions of its corrections department. And it is this crusade that made the Bush campaign aware of the story.

Bush was not polling well. For his campaign team, it was time to pull out its "silver bullet." In April 1988, Atwater's team had convened a focus group composed of "Reagan Democrats" in Paramus, New Jersey. After asking them a series of questions related to crime, the prison furlough program, and other issues, the campaign operatives noted how quickly they changed their preference for Dukakis and became likely supporters of Bush. This convinced the team that they had the means to close the polling gap. After convincing Bush that this was the way to go, the name "Willie Horton" began appearing in stump speeches. It was an easy way to not only encourage Dukakis's "wimp" status in the American imagination, but to also paint him as a liberal, a bleeding heart who believed that even savages should get a second chance. Atwater was aflutter; he immediately set to making "Willie Horton a household name."[74]

While at a July 4 dinner with his family in rural Luray, Virginia, Atwater was surprised to overhear other diners discussing the July *Reader's*

Digest article that had catapulted the issue into a national story,[75] which to his mind further proved that they had found their key issue—if only they could associate the crime issue with the racially coded protocols of white fear. These most obvious racist intentions were revealed with clarity later in July during an Atlanta speech in which he stated that Horton might as well be Dukakis's running mate, after relating a story of seeing the latter in the company of Jesse Jackson. This insinuated that Dukakis—and his softness toward people like Horton—was in league with Black folk. Horton became Black without Atwater ever mentioning his Blackness, giving the team plausible deniability that the issue was solely about crime, not race.[76] This obfuscation held—until the television ads.

According to Kathleen Hall Jamieson, television had the power to alter the perceptions of electoral issues in ways that were unique, giving it "Svengalian powers that print and radio" lacked. In her work, *Dirty Politics*, she examines how political campaign strategists were able to use the twin tools of campaign advertisement and news media coverage to shape whatever narrative they wanted but usually "to heighten the power of visceral appeal."[77] In an age in which scooping other news outlets trumped fact checking, in which scandal was more newsworthy than actual records, campaign strategists had a tool that could easily captivate the electorate. Whoever could manipulate the narrative around wedge issues could effectively sway voters. Those unwilling to embrace the deviance of this environment were susceptible to defeat. Ironically, the truth would not be enough.

Two campaign advertisements—one official, the other from a political action committee—would electrify the campaign. The first appeared in the second week of September and featured the image of Horton. The creator of the ad was the National Security Political Action Committee (NSPAC), which, despite its other moniker, "Americans for Bush," disclaimed any official association with the Bush campaign. Officially, NSPAC could not claim the association with the Bush campaign, for the ad was patently racist. Featuring Horton's mug shot, the ad openly played on the racial fears of its captive audience by linking this image of a "brazen murderer" with the so-called liberal policies of Dukakis. It stated that the Democratic nominee was in support of "weekend passes" for criminals like Horton and told the story of his subsequent crimes.

The official campaign ad on the furlough issue, appearing first on October 5, featured a revolving door at a makeshift prison. Strategists proclaimed its nonracial attributes by pointing out that most of the actors in the prison were indeed white, but in a moment of truth during the ad the one black prisoner stares into the camera, right as the narrator states how many "murderers" had escaped.[78] The message was clear. And many of the claims in the ads were lies.[79] But it did not matter. The damage was done.

It also did not that matter that these ads only ran for two weeks each. Once they had appeared, the news media would repetitively show the images of Horton's mug shot as they covered the campaign issue. In their coverage the media solidified the image and the "story" in the mind of the voters, who associated them, replete with their half-truths, with Dukakis. Atwater's strategy of forever linking Dukakis with Horton had been successful, but with the constant news coverage, the name *and* Horton's image became engrained in the public mind. It was not until Jesse Jackson came out against the use of the ads in late October, rightfully calling them racist, that the news media would cover the Horton case as a "racial" one.[80] The immediate disavowal of racist intent became the rehearsed response of the Bush team, which would largely escape any of the retribution that would have normally followed any explicit appeal to race. For Mendelberg, the "outing" of the racist foundation of the strategy came too late to have an impact on the election.[81] Meanwhile, Bush would continue to evoke the issue in his campaign speeches. In the presidential debate in Los Angeles on October 13, Dukakis was forced to address the issue of crime. In his response to Bernard Shaw's question of whether he would sentence his wife's hypothetical rapist-murderer to death, Dukakis committed a blunder, according to analysts, by not appearing genuine in his response that he would stick to his ideals. His soft-on-crime image was confirmed. The gap was closed. Bush won the election.

It was only in the aftermath of the election that Atwater was forced to answer for his negative tactics. At a post-election forum at Harvard, he engaged in a heated exchange with Dukakis campaign manager Susan Estrich, who charged that they knowingly used the issue of crime in ways that emphasized race.[82] Atwater dishonestly disclaimed any foreknowledge of Horton's race until much later in the campaign. Questions were also raised as to the campaign's knowledge of NSPAC's use of Horton's image in the "Weekend Passes" advertisement, its possible involvement in the planting of the July 1988 story on Horton in *Reader's Digest*, the campaign's use of "Willie"—a name he did not use—as opposed to William, and its refusal to use the many white escapees that had committed crimes while on furlough as their cause célèbre.[83]

In many ways the GOP's deployment of the Horton issue reveals little about the ways that criminal policy actually structured Black life during the era, which in reality was validated by somewhat of a bipartisan consensus—Dukakis was more neoliberal than "soft on crime." The Democrats, who would move further to the right after the 1988 election, were no better or worse than the Republicans on this issue, as Bill Clinton would show six years later.[84] The question here was one of electoral strategy, not policy. The resulting fallout revolved around the question of whether it was appropriate to use race as a means through which to assuage or intensify voters' fear of crime. What Jamieson and Mendelberg revealed in their works was that the question of winning elections seemed to supersede any consideration of morality. Ethics, after all, was not Lee Atwater's strong suit, as even his famous deathbed confessions of guilt might be read as political calculation. As much as Atwater wanted to make Horton Dukakis's running mate, Horton became Atwater's own "tar baby."[85]

Grand Ole Bison

To some, it was a surprise that officials associated with Howard University—ostensibly a Black university—would embrace the Republican Party politics of the New Right. After all, the Black electorate had been solidly Democratic since 1964, save a consistent cadre of moderate Black elite establishment icons.[86] But even their identity within the GOP had begun to wane as the Southern and Sunbelt-based silent majority replaced the Eastern Establishment faction of the party. How do we make sense, then, of various leaders—including President James Cheek—who remained Republican even as the party often employed not only racial appeals to win elections but also created austerity policies that seemed to transgress many of the liberal norms that some believed would solve the problems of racial inequality? What were the incentives that university leaders sought by remaining bipartisan, even as it meant courting right-wing politicians during the Reagan era? These are critical questions, as they not only serve as the important background for the precipitating actions that preceded the 1989 student protest, they also help us understand the long struggle to create free Black spaces within the modern world and the role that historically Black colleges were imagined to play.

As the university's historian Rayford Logan reminds us, the long association of Howard with the GOP began at the moment of its birth in 1867, with the Radical Republicans playing a central role in its founding.[87] Since then, Howard has adopted somewhat of an unofficial bipartisan approach to U.S. politics. But this does not mean that there were not important tensions existing between students and the administration, between the faculty and the administration, and among faculty and students. Much of what produced these tensions has been the idea that Howard should in fact be partisan, embracing political positions that serve to benefit populations of African ancestry. This sensibility goes back to at least the late nineteenth century and has been most acute in times of great upheaval within the larger community—for instance, the 1920s New Negro movement and the 1960s era.[88]

James Cheek arrived in the midst of one such moment. As discussed in chapter 1, his predecessor, James M. Nabrit, Jr., was embroiled in a crisis where his vision of the university ran counter to what many of the student and faculty bodies had envisioned. Nabrit's tenure came to an end when the consistent pressure placed upon his administration by student upheavals forced a change. Cheek arrived in 1969, a thirty-six-year-old divinity scholar who had served as president of Shaw University since he was thirty, in tune with the times and poised at least in theory to make Howard a "Black university."[89]

One of the reactions to stagflation and the general loss of confidence that attended the late 1970s was a reorientation in the meaning of higher education. Although in their nature these changes might be based on a foundation that goes back to the 1890s, the move from the liberal arts–influenced view of higher education as a repository of national culture to a market-based view that has understood education as preparation for nationalist dominance in economics and global political power is bound up with the machinations of the Right.[90] With the latter in mind, universities began to operate as institutions more beholden to market forces. The managerial elite that ran corporations encouraged intellectuals to embrace these models as well. It is no coincidence, then, that competition over potential students was and continues to be read in economic terms—students lost to other institutions is read literally as the loss of potential revenue. Students in turn have increasingly come to read higher education as an investment in a careerist future as deindustrialization, globalization, and other factors have made college education more of a commodity, as it is the key to accessing the only jobs that are left in the United States. Despite tensions in the concept of mass higher education, the older functions of the more exclusive universities continue—that of the reproduction of an elite.[91]

At HBCUs, the pressure to adapt to these new conditions in the higher education space was often read as a matter of life and death. The idea that Black colleges should modernize—read as both the embrace of elite models and the diversification of its student body—both preceded and attended the financial crises that had beset them beginning in the "era of Reagan." Integration created both a crisis of identity and discernible changes in the populations of both the professoriate and the student body. Public institutions faced increased pressures as it became clearer that state legislatures, despite being paragons of the New South, were chomping at the bit of austerity.[92] For private institutions, the economic issues were certainly there, but there was also a crisis of vision that dovetailed with the ascendancy of Right-wing politics: What does an HBCU look like in a post-soul, post–Civil Rights era? For many associated with Howard University, it was "Yale, Johns Hopkins, and Stanford."[93] In the 1970s and into the 1980s, as intellectuals based at Howard fought to institute the visions of intellectual freedom launched by the freedom fighters of this and earlier periods, they ran against the brick wall of an administration concerned about both an economic future and the continued support for the national interests of the federal government.[94]

Howard is different in important ways, owing to its status as the only HBCU to receive an annual appropriation from the federal government. At various times in its history, the continuance of such an appropriation, rightfully considered a unique arrangement, has come under question. In fact, on many occasions Mordecai Wyatt Johnson's deft handling of the politics of Black education ensured its stability at times when it was considered marked for death at the height of the New Deal.[95] In many ways the tightrope walk around questions of partisanship has had much to do with ensuring the continuity of these operating funds, which at the time of James Cheek's embrace of Reaganism accounted for over half of the university's budget.[96] Coming out of an era in which recessionary pressures had many HBCUs confronting questions of their survival, Cheek could confidently assert that "it's just as inappropriate to be concerned about Howard's survival as about Yale's."[97] The elite foundations of Howard held sway, ultimately engulfing whatever revolutionary momentum that Cheek's arrival had countenanced. It was then unsurprising that Howard's administration decided that it was better to embrace the neoliberal, rightward shift resonant in America and in the politics of higher education. Cheek's administrative approach became openly partisan.

This was not inevitable. In many ways Cheek's public profile as a Republican began, like many Black moderates in the GOP, as an attempt to force the party to adhere to the demands of the Civil Rights movement. Disgusted by the lack of fiscal parity between Black colleges and majority institutions and the tepid response to the state violence that was converging upon HBCU campuses, Cheek led a delegation of Black college presidents to Richard Nixon's White House in 1970, demanding a federal response. When asked by the president if HBCUs were even necessary, given the successes of integration, Cheek and his fellow presidents, including Maceo Nance of South Carolina State University and John A. Peoples of Jackson State University, responded that the closing of any HBCUs was unthinkable.[98] As a result of this meeting, Cheek was appointed special advisor to the president on Black colleges, where he implored Nixon's administration to increase its support for Black institutions, thereby beginning a lifelong association with Republican Party politics.[99]

A decade later, inspired by Ronald Reagan's pledge to support Black colleges, Cheek would hew even closer to the political strategies of the Republican Party, often as a matter of pragmatism, stating matter-of-factly that "we always got more [funding] from the Republicans than the Democrats."[100] As Reagan's proposed budgets slashed the economic programs designed to curtail poverty, Howard's appropriation *increased*.[101] As Cheek became comfortably ensconced at the White House, appearing at state dinners and strategy sessions, he openly defended Reagan's wider austerity project from assaults from faculty, students, and the larger Black community. He would need to double down on this gambit as the university faced deficits in 1981 and 1982, and he did so by inviting George Bush to deliver the 1981 commencement address, amid student protest, and President Reagan himself to a fundraiser on campus the next year, amid faculty and student protest. While the university's operating budget received a shot in the arm and Cheek received the Presidential Medal of Freedom, students, faculty, alumni, and the larger community became increasingly suspicious of this arrangement, wondering if Cheek's coziness with such an unpopular president was worth it.[102]

Importantly, this was a moment in which many Black elite figures had begun to think about "Black Alternatives"—the title of a conference convened by Howard alumnus Thomas Sowell that attracted eminent Black thinkers, many formerly associated with liberal or radical views. It was also a period in which a new energy around Black conservatism was cultivated with an increased media attention given to figures such as Clarence Thomas and Sowell and the popularity of organs like the *Lincoln Review*.[103] Although Cheek's association with the party and with conservatism is of an older lineage, it is important to note these changes that rendered his actions as unremarkable, even as they were clearly troublesome to significant swaths of the Howard community.

As Republican National Committee Head Lee Atwater announced his Operation Outreach, an initiative to woo minority voters in the wake of the 1988 election, his selection to a position on Howard's board of trustees in early 1989 was similarly unremarkable—or so the board thought.[104] Whether or not it was a genuine attempt to address Black people's interests during the Reagan revolution (it was likely not), this initiative and the Howard strategy that Atwater had in mind was a step too far.[105] Although Howard faculty and staff were willing to somewhat tolerate the pragmatic politics of the Cheek administration up until this point, issues came to a head with the embrace of a political operative willing to trade on the racist logic of Black criminality for political success. They were no longer willing to abide the presumed benign Howard tradition of political friendships. As the Howard political scientist Ronald W. Walters stated, "It was perceived as heavy-handed. We're not naïve about Republican ties . . . but there was a sense of [Cheek's] imposing [Atwater] on our community."[106]

The macropolitics outlined above filtered into the decade of the 1980s, in Black communities beset by the imperial and neoliberal regimes of the era. As in other epochs in the modern world, these sorts of politics were met with resistance. Before we reach the story of the resistance of the Howard students of the late 1980s, it is necessary to think about Black youth resistance generally during the era. Its challenges, its victories, and its energy not only influenced the Howard protestors—they were also part of the same struggle.

3

The Message

> With knowledge of self, there's nothing I can't solve
> At 360 degrees, I revolve
> This is actual fact, it's not an act,
> It's been proven
> Indeed and I proceed to make the crowd keep moving
> —Rakim[1]

When Martin Luther King, Jr., commented, near the end of his life, that he feared that his dream had turned into a nightmare, he likely could not imagine how true that would be of the 1980s.[2] The Reagan era, as it has been univocally labeled by historians, has been remembered as one of prosperity, patriotism, and American strength. The disappearance of de jure racism, the rise of a Black middle class and elected officials of that ilk, and the emergence of a Black intellectual class that commanded the national spotlight became evidence that such prosperity had also reached Black America. The race problem, it appeared, had been solved. It was "morning in America," as Reagan's 1984 campaign slogan reminded us—"the decade of nightmares" had passed. Although critical of many of his policies, the general tenor of historical and public memories of the 1980s is encapsulated by this sort of framing. Americans felt good about themselves, and they had a lovable, good-natured president to thank. Ronald W. Reagan continues to be admired as a paragon of American ideals, able to rescue them from what the filmmaker Lawrence Kasdan imagined as "the big chill," a characterization that signaled the limits of the free-flowing ideas and the raucous days of the youthful sixties.[3]

The memory of Reagan's term in office is recalled with less fervor in some quarters. Race remained the fundamental contradiction at the core of the American national project. Racial capitalism could not be vanquished by civil rights, nor could it be wished away by clever marketing strategies of political campaigns or chants of "USA!" at the Los Angeles Olympic Games. American capitalism's growth during the decade, like the much-celebrated end of the Cold War, came at a price—the racialized other in the urban cities and poor people across the world would again bear the costs of U.S. ascendancy. In some ways, then, it *was* "morning" again in America—the problem was that that was not necessarily a great thing for those who had been previously branded as its "internal enemy."[4] To them, "morning" was akin to awakening to an ongoing nightmare.

Organizations like the National Urban League, in its annual, *The State of Black America*, consistently showed the unequal distribution of income and wealth, the divergence in employment figures, serious fraud in the allocation of public housing resources, and the disproportionate rates of imprisonment and deaths from treatable diseases in the Black community. The optimism spewed by the Reagan campaign in the year 1984, for example, tended to obscure the fact that the previous year's recovery had yet to reverse the historical trends associated with Black working-class suffering—unemployment figures were almost double that of whites, and income figures were almost half. Entrenched poverty, decaying schools, and the emergence of underground economies that brought increased crime rates were the logical results of such economic distress. Neither had more openly racist incidents of police brutality and hate crimes totally ceased.[5] There was a shift that did occur, however, and that was the neoliberal logic suggesting that such maladies were no longer the result of structural issues. The civil rights struggle, such pundits suggested, had eliminated the structural flaw that prevented Black Americans from succeeding. In the 1980s, Black Americans who did not achieve the good life had only their own behaviors to blame. This rhetorical gambit, coupled with the more racist backlash politics, removed any possibility of lengthening the "second reconstruction," resulting instead in the strengthening of Reaganism and its military Keynesianism. But these politics were now supported by the emergence of a cadre of Black conservative thinkers who received an "economy of expression" to project a different brand of Black politics.[6]

The irony is that the share of taxes paid by poor people increased as the programs that these taxes had previously paid for—welfare and entitlement programs that benefited the poor—were repeatedly placed on the chopping block. To add injury to insult, the legal avenues through which some of these issues might be alleviated were becoming more difficult to access as the language used by neoliberal thinkers began to alter how discourse around affirmative action and civil rights protections were imagined. By the end of the decade, the ravages of the AIDS virus, initially ignored by the government (and curiously blamed, in part, on Haitians), and the "crack epidemic" had begun to deepen the inequities at the heart of Reaganism.[7]

These domestic challenges were both deeply connected to the foreign policies generated from the Reagan administration and just as sinister. Reagan has been remembered as the ultimate Cold Warrior, able to strong-arm the Soviets into undoing its "evil empire."[8] But it is necessary to remember that, in many ways, the Cold War was "hot" for Africans across the world. A small sampling of the loss in human lives amid the foreign policy adventures in Central America, Libya, Grenada, Angola, and South Africa, inasmuch as they contributed to American victories, provided opportunities for young Black activists to hone in on the contradictions of empire. Movements such as the nuclear-freeze and anti-apartheid struggles, not to mention the perennial issue of Israel-Palestine relations, placed important constituencies of Black America at direct odds with American Cold War stratagems (which, of course, was nothing new).[9] Amid the administration's visceral responses to terrorism, Howard University students, for instance, were among the loudest and most consistent voices that condemned the Grenada invasion, as well as the Reagan administration's response to terrorism, even sending a contingent of student government leaders to visit Muammar Qaddafi's Libya on special invitation in 1986.[10] But it was in their music that the most salient political expressions would be made.

Do the Knowledge

During this period, the political grammar of Black youth was hip hop. It was there that the meaning of their lives was not only narrated but theorized upon and that the articulation of how they thought about and read the worlds created by Reaganism was launched. Hip hop emerged on Howard University's campus through the consistent flow of students from New York who brought the emergent culture with them, ensuring that the energy forged in those Bronx and Queens summers would not be extinguished by a party DJ that might not have been hip to the latest sounds.[11] If the DJ, the MC, and the cipher were transferable, it was not simply *because* Howard students brought it. It was much larger than that. For what hip hop signified was already there, not simply in DC, but wherever Black people were. It was an expression of life in what Christina Sharpe calls "the wake."[12] It was but an instantiation of what Richard Iton calls "the Black fantastic," made manifest and made to articulate a politics of resistance that could also be found in the cultural authority of Go-Go and other modes of music then resonant in the Black world. Hip hop was a powerful mode, one that was easily transferable because it costumed youth discontent and rage in the Blackness and bluesy traditions of sound and thought of times past.[13] B-boys and B-girls were unique extensions of an older, consistent thread.

While the historiography of the birth of hip hop remains centered in New York, it is nevertheless critical to remind ourselves that its explosion would not have been possible if not for its diasporic roots. The soundscapes that emanated from the turntables, if not the very technologies that produced them, were not rooted in space or place as much as they were rooted in a consciousness of the world. That consciousness of how to create rhythms, how to sort a loop, how to develop a sample, how to move the crowd would prove just as critical as the message embedded in the rhythm. It is clear, however, that, as Tricia Rose argues, one must be able to think about hip hop as both an extension of a tradition and a direct response to a particular moment.[14] These should not be conceived as negations.

But what did in fact prove consequential were the ways in which the cultural product (i.e., that which is/was made) would be converted into a commodity, or a market product (i.e., that which is/was made in order to be sold). This transition occurred amid the "first death" of hip hop in the late 1970s and ushered in a new form of the tradition, a "hip hop record," one that Grandmaster Flash, for one, skeptically dismissed as "absurd." In that sense, one could argue that the first death of hip hop, as characterized by Jeff Chang as the decline of the technical maneuvers of the mid-1970s, was a "death" *also* instantiated by the record itself, the act of placing the music on wax.[15] For others, this may be too rough a binary. The fact remains, however, that the hip hop we "consume" today, which continues to (re)make how we understand Black youth expres-

sion, is a product of, and conceived as, both a movement and an industry.[16] If that is true, what makes the era of "message rap" so compelling
is its attempt to break out of that contradiction while having to express
itself *within* it.

Rather than evaluate message rap's political impact by attempting to
project its practitioners as "political activists," it is more critical to frame
the question as one of the effect that the music and culture have had
upon those who defined themselves as activists or participated in political activities during this period.[17] The explicit force of the words and,
yes, the "message" of rap acts, beginning—as most scholars do—with the
1987 appearance of Public Enemy's debut, *Yo! Bum Rush the Show*,[18] is
an important point of departure for how Black youth came to see themselves vis-à-vis the larger world and its oppressive features.

Owing in part to the aforesaid ravages upon Black communities of
the Reagan era, the evolution of the same political forces that inspired
Jesse Jackson's presidential campaigns and caused the deepening of the
crises in Southern Africa also became the backdrop for an aggressive
form of critique resonant in Black youth music and culture. Emergent in
these critiques of the police, the church, violence, and drugs was a message inherent in rap that made clear that things could no longer be what
they were as well as a sense that identification with all things Black/Af-
rican had to be central to any viable future. While some have criticized
the "attitude" of hip hop, it clearly was one of many forces that allowed
student activists at Howard to create space to challenge the university's
contradictions during the key moments that led to the protest of 1989.
Hip hop became a powerful medium to express not only discontent but
to imagine otherwise and to live it *now*. One of the lasting features of hip
hop consciousness was the way in which it inaugurated a new style, an
improvisation of a way of being in the world.[19]

Public Enemy's announcement of this new mode of hip hop music
based its emceeing on an emergent nationalism—premised on the idea
that Black folks must begin and end any question of liberation on the
central fact of a cultural and social Blacknesss—that decentered liberal
notions of progress and imagined Black unity as a bulwark against the
increasing hostility of the state, represented by both Reaganism and its
attendant conservatism. The locus of that hostility for most Black youth
was the ever-increasing unemployment rate and a bipartisan criminal

justice apparatus that was embodied for most Black folk in the figure of the police. The convergence of these attitudes was portrayed by the sensibilities of Black youth in Spike Lee's *Do the Right Thing* (1989),[20] which came a few years after much-publicized police and vigilante killings of Black youth, many of whom were products of hip hop culture or who belonged to that particular demographic. As the theme song of that film, penned by Public Enemy, suggested, the only thing left to do for the hip hop generation was to "Fight the Power."[21] Public Enemy's emergence also indicated that, by the 1980s, the locus of the movement was shifting a bit to the peripheries of the ghetto. Its members were Long Island residents who met as college students and were inspired by their Black Studies courses. Although this alone did not mean that they were "privileged," it did represent a movement of a unique form of Black cultural consciousness to different sites, ones that were often not prepared for them.[22] Howard University was one such place.

Yet another influential voice for Black college students was Boogie Down Productions, the brash voice of Black youth from hip hop's Bronx birthplace. Initially composed of Scott La Rock, D-Nice, and KRS-One, the group's "My Philosophy" was a watershed dispensation on the meaning of Black identity and group preservation.[23] KRS-One's ability to navigate both the meaning of ghetto and gangster life, while detailing the ways in which that life could also be and produce levels of consciousness, became a model for how to reach youth thought to be disaffected and, thus, "truly disadvantaged."[24] That this art could emerge from a segment of the population thought literally to be disposable gave the music resonance for those living within, and making sense of, such lives. This was not without deep and vexing challenges, and the murder of Scott La Rock represented that side of the coin. But it also indicated the belief that the development of this mode of hip hop was perhaps *how* such challenges had to be addressed.[25] Hip hop had to provide a language to deal with death, oppression, love, and joy. In this register, as many have argued, this moment did not produce the sort of dichotomy between conscious and nonconscious rap that would plague hip hop in the next decade. If it was hip hop, then it *was* conscious. For those for whom hip hop became a grammar for explaining the world around them, to make a distinction would be to engage in tautology. And this was why it was such an inspiration and more.

The political importance of message rap applies to gangsta rap as well, a mode some have erroneously opposed to the former. One could get into an extended argument about the meaning of "the political" here, but it suffices to say that the oft-quoted dichotomy that posits message rap on one side and other forms of rap on the other (depending on whom you ask, candidates could be "gangsta" or "party" rap) completely misses the significant ways that Black cultural expressions implicitly articulate and affirm political realities. The signifying traditions inherent in *all* of rap expresses an often underanalyzed politics of opposition that was and continues to be critical to Black youth consciousness.[26]

Ernest Allen, Jr.'s tripartite division of message rap includes one strand that concerned the convergence of elements of message rap with subsequent evolution, gangsta rap, perhaps best crystallized in the music and evolution of Ice Cube but inclusive of a range of voices. For Allen and others, this was a convergence within these forms that troubles the attempt to label one (a)political and the other *not.* While Allen argued that the politics were bereft of realizable political outcomes, it is important to remember here that the bravado, the boldness, and the courage of Black youth constituted a critical political posture.[27] In order to truly fight the power, one had to express a certain level of confidence. What it portended was the development of a generation of youth unwilling to staunch their anger while struggling to funnel it into a vessel that would establish a more "formal" political movement.[28] Bold confrontation with power manifested in major political protests and demonstrations, but also—and perhaps most important—power was confronted by simply *being* one's unvarnished self—in public and in private. It was the need to project an authenticity, a realness, that one must recognize as central to presaging whatever movement activity was to come. "Reality" emanated from the message, but "keeping it real" was also a statement about recognizing and uncovering truths that remained out of sight or muted by other kinds of "politics."[29]

These political sensibilities would engender an orientation that would take the form of both protest as well as self-awareness. This formulation of fighting the power would also be understood as an intellectual confrontation, as declarations that we must "do the knowledge" became the mantra of the culture. If we were to take Allen's division of message rap at face value, clearly the approach of Public Enemy, which he labeled "cultural-political" nationalist, inspired a deeper engagement with the Black Power politics of the 1960s—they, of course, saw their politics as extensions of the Black Panther Party. And while it has become somewhat de rigueur to reduce the Panthers to guns and confrontation, their political education apparatus would become a model for various movement organizations that were also inspired by hip hop. In crucial ways, the campus study group became the foundational model that would be replicated in Black student unions across the landscape and within Black or African-centered social organizations at historically Black colleges. In some ways, as Howard demonstrates, these formations would combine with nonstudent study circles already in operation on the level of neighborhood and community, many of which also met on campus.

"Do the knowledge" has yet a more specific provenance. What Allen calls "Islamic nationalism" spawned a range of rappers and rap groups like Eric B. and Rakim, Brand Nubian, Poor Righteous Teachers, Grand Puba, A Tribe Called Quest, Paris, and others that were inspired by the ways that the Nation of Islam and the Nation of Gods and Earths proclaimed the chosenness of Black people against the logic of inferiority required by the racial state. It was an attractive counternarrative that took Black people's condition to mean one of exploitation but also one of a destiny free of such repression; Islamic nationalism became a way of thinking and imagining liberation beyond what had been imagined *for* Black people. It was above all an explicit rejection of the "faith" of whiteness, the only and prevailing religious norm in the American cultural imagination. Although full of contradictions, in both of these variants study, or "knowledge," was central.[30]

It was out these contexts that "knowledge" became hip hop's fifth element. By the mid-late 1980s, Howard was not only home to many emergent and future hip hop artists and where many concerts and showcases would be held, it was also one of the sites of the debates about what it all meant. Questions of hip hop's political efficacy, the subject of many a book in the 1990s, were initially raised in many forums and conferences on campus, where young political actors sparred with each other as well as with the elders of the Black Arts Movement.[31] Such spaces were lively, for they allowed the hip hop generation to finally have their say, to put a philosophical and theoretical underpinning on the creative expression that now had the world in thrall. It was in the interstices of these debates, conversations, and confrontations that calls for organization would soon replace rhetoric, that action would manifest out of the inspiration of the lyrics. Despite the fact that the music was often charged with being bound by time-space constraints, the political expression it engendered would prove to be anything but ephemeral.

One of message rap's quintessential anthems, Queen Latifah's "Ladies First" (1989),[32] announced the presence of women's voices in a medium that many considered to be dominated by young male voices. Although Black and Latinx women—B-girls—were never actually absent from hip hop culture, the commercialization of the form tended to prioritize certain voices over others. Message rap was certainly not above such critiques.[33] What is interesting, however, about the song, which features the London-born rapper Monie Love, is not only how it demonstrates the need to grapple with what the women of hip hop had to say but also how those messages filtered through liberation struggles then being waged across the African world. Black gender politics were given concrete expression through depictions of on-the-ground struggles with the white supremacist regime of apartheid South Africa. The music video framed the emergence and power of women's voices with portraits of a genealogy of African American women freedom fighters before ending with an image of Winnie Mandela. Along with these images, we see footage of the marches and the violent reprisals faced by freedom fighters in South Africa, which provided powerful evidence of the *meaning* of resistance while simultaneously garnering awareness of the realities being faced by Africans at a critical location in the Black world and in global Black consciousness. In many ways, one could conclude from this video that any notion of Black liberation propounded by message rap would have to contend not only with the fact that women were central to that struggle but also that the larger African world provided the conceptual basis for how we might imagine how to struggle and what to struggle for.

Amandla!

The evolution of the Reagan administration Africa policy, not to mention its Central American policy, was also a spark that inspired student activism across the country and globe, which solidified into one of the most significant student movements of the twentieth century: the anti-apartheid movement.[34] Queen Latifah and Monie Love were able to place South Africa as the center of the Black liberation struggle because of the scores of Black youth who were brought to consciousness of the anti-apartheid struggle in that period. One of these critical voices in this effort was Lisa "Sister Souljah" Williamson, whose work of not only raising awareness but also in participating in various struggles to change these conditions was both inspirational and deeply connected to the work of many of the eventual leaders of the 1989 protest at Howard. Souljah's activity was a consequence of her work in an organization called the National African Student Youth Alliance, which held forums around the country.[35] At Howard, the anti-apartheid fervor, however, was complicated by various tensions that had always characterized questions of political struggle on campus, among them the role and relationship of the university vis-à-vis the official foreign policy of the United States. Yet it nevertheless deserves consideration as one of the nodal points upon which the protest of 1989 would intersect.

In this vein, as well, it is important to note that Howard cannot be extracted from Washington, DC, and the range of activist communities that sprang up in the city during the vibrant 1970s. Formations such as the DC Black United Front, the Drum and Spear Bookstore, the Centre for Black Education, NationHouse, and the African Liberation Support Committee, among many others, found in certain Howard communities (as well as in other universities, such as the University of the District of Columbia, then called Federal City College) space to organize and extend their work.[36] Of these, perhaps none were more critical than the Southern African Support Project (SASP), a network of initially Black women activists led by one of the leaders of the North American delegation to the Sixth Pan African Congress, Sylvia Hill, as well as Sandra Hill, Cecelie Counts, Kathy Flewellen, Adwoa Dunn, and Karen Jefferson, and eventually men like Joseph Jordan and Ira Stohlman. Centered in the broader DC community, their work was aimed at generating awareness around the impact of United States policy on southern African liberation movements and often utilized Dunn and Jefferson's bases at Howard to host events and house critical conversations.[37] By the late 1970s and early 1980s, the SASP had recruited students to help publicize events that featured southern African students, film screenings on African liberation movements, and community forums with leaders of nationalist movements such as Julius Nyerere, Oliver Tambo, and Moses Garoeb.[38] While the concern for southern African issues at Howard dates back to at least the 1930s, the presence of the SASP, the work of the African Studies and Research Center Outreach Program, African Studies professors Robert Cummings and Robert Edgar, E. Ethelbert Miller and the Afro-American Studies Resource Center, and Ronald W. Walters's involvement with TransAfrica made the university a lively setting for debates and work toward eliminating apartheid and settler colonial societies in the Frontline states long before the explosion of the divestment movement on larger white campuses in the mid-1980s.[39]

The roots of the question of divestment can be traced to liberal anti-apartheid organizing around the issue of "ethical investing" and "shareholder responsibility." At the center of these concerns were church-affiliated organizations as well as denominations like the United Church of Christ, which, along with Leon Sullivan's work at General Motors and his eventual authorship of what became known as the Sullivan Principles around corporate responsibility, was the public face of the struggle to challenge American business practices. Also focusing on the issue of divestment was the American Committee on Africa, an organization inspired by the earlier Council on African Affairs. The influence of the Congressional Black Caucus's Charles Diggs upon the House Committee on Africa led to the development of TransAfrica, which would be added to this mix by the late 1970s. Together these forces were able to place pressure upon universities, corporations, municipalities, and other institutions to create policies to withdraw funds and investments from the "business" of apartheid South Africa. Energizing this movement was the election of Ronald Reagan and the subsequent inauguration of the policy of constructive engagement with the South African regime. It was the pressure of the student movement, the development of direct action protests at the South African embassy with the Free South Africa Movement (FSAM), and the long struggle of pro-Africa lobby organizations that eventually secured the Comprehensive Anti-Apartheid Act in the United States, which finally enacted the long-sought sanctions against the apartheid government in 1986.[40]

The divestment movement was a critical incubator for progressive activism around questions of racism and imperialism at elite U.S. universities when it exploded in the spring of 1985.[41] It, however, did not

generate a protest movement at Howard University. Robert Edgar specu-
lates quite convincingly that, because Howard's endowment was so small
compared to those of other universities, divestment would not have un-
duly harmed the university's finances. It was "taken off the table" as a
strategy, in other words.[42] Instead of demonstrating on campus, Howard
students found ways to remain involved in other ways.

The most obvious entrée into the movement was the Free South Africa Movement, as it was inspired and organized, although not exclusively, by figures associated with the SASP and TransAfrica, many of
whom, as noted, had ties to Howard. On Thanksgiving Eve in 1984, Congressman Walter Fauntroy, Randall Robinson, and Mary Frances Berry,
a then Howard professor, staged a sit-in at the South African embassy.
With them was Eleanor Holmes Norton, a movement veteran, who was
tasked with engaging the media. The direct catalyst for this action was a
combination of events including the reelection of Ronald Reagan in the
United States and the protests in South Africa against its new, but inadequate, constitution, protests that often ended in violence and the imprisonment of political leaders. The embassy demonstrations that ensued
became the extension of a new movement that galvanized thousands of
volunteers, including many celebrities who scheduled appearances so
they could submit to arrest for protesting outside the building.[43]

After a debate about the nature of the protest, Howard students participated, although not at the level of other university students. On February 28, 1985, an ad hoc committee of faculty and students sponsored
"Howard Day at the Embassy" in a show of solidarity with South Africa.[44] Student participation in the embassy protests hinged on a range
of factors but most critically was their sense of the appropriateness of the
tactic of protest and their sense of political consciousness as it was being
forged in the crucible of their intellectual development. In other words,
coming as it did at the vortex of their political maturity and political
struggle, students' activities in *this* kind of political action were inconsis-
tent in the beginning moments of the protests.[45] As the year's struggles
across the country intensified, a few more students were inspired to
participate, and by the fall, the Undergraduate Student Assembly co-
sponsored an organized protest with TransAfrica framed as "Howard
University Against Apartheid" at the embassy on November 1.[46]

Another form of anti-apartheid work was the organization of programs. Since community organizers considered Howard a strategic location to house discussion, debate, and consciousness-raising, this necessarily affected the students on campus and, just as significant, the surrounding DC Black community. Leading many of these discussions were Howard students from South Africa representing the Pan Africanist Congress (PAC) and the Black Consciousness Movement (BCM), which was considerably important to the ways that they framed the question of liberation.[47] Howard students would often use "Azania" to refer to the country, a convention of the PAC and the BCM.

A quick roster of South Africans invited to address Howard students, faculty, and the community during the mid-late 1980s included Thabo Mbeki, Dennis Brutus, Maki Mandela, and Desmond Tutu—whose daughter, Mpho, was a student at Howard at the time—was honored with a special convocation.[48] There were other forums that included artists and activists from the African American community, perhaps the most significant being the singer Phyllis Hyman and Sonia Sanchez, who discussed the meaning of South African liberation to their work and the conception of global Black freedom.[49] Countless other forums featured SASP activists and Howard professors such as Edgar and Walters, as well as PAC representative Nana Seshibe, and they demonstrated the continued concern of ensuring that shifting student populations remained vigilant to the goings-on in Southern Africa. In addition, the multiracial DC Student Coalition against Racism and Apartheid maintained a Howard representative on its executive committee throughout the life of the organization. It is therefore not particularly shocking that Howard University has maintained a critical and strategic connection and partnership with South Africa to this day.[50]

Despite the complex conversations it often engendered, Africa was on the hearts and minds of Howard students, particularly those who grounded themselves in political activism and cultural reclamation. And if Africa was on their minds, the critical struggle of the South Africans was central to how many Howard students came to know and understand their relationship to the continent. It was a conversation that required a certain sharpening of one's analysis, one's conception of social and structural change. Revolutionary South Africans like Steve Biko would become part of the pantheon of Black exemplars that students would draw upon to claim Blackness as that which was to be preserved. More than merely an issue of identity, the anti-apartheid struggle became a model for how to place pressure upon power structures in ways that were direct and confrontational. It presaged the same brashness that was manifest in hip hop expression.

This was a message made more explicit in a song and music video by Stetsasonic titled "A.F.R.I.C.A." (1986).[51] Inspired by 1984 presidential candidate Jesse Jackson's South African activism, which was no doubt inspired by TransAfrica, the MCs of Stetsasonic were moved to raise awareness of the anti-apartheid struggle within the hip hop generation. In interesting ways, this song bore the imprint of the kind of activism pioneered by the SASP and TransAfrica, which understood the regional implications of apartheid, a politics that was much deeper and more complicated than simply challenging apartheid's violent excesses, which had become fodder for television cameras. Unlike those attracted to the anti-apartheid movement for humanitarian reasons, it appears from the music video that Stetsasonic had engaged the struggle against apartheid in concert with what Clarence Lusane calls the "dominant ideological trend" of the hip hop generation: black nationalism.[52]

The lyrics included declarations of Africa as motherland and evoked, "red, black, and green"—significations that foreshadowed the pro-African consciousness that would come a few years later. While the song's chorus spelled out "Africa," it focused upon the southern Africa Frontline states of Angola, Zimbabwe, Tanzania, Zambia, Mozambique, and Botswana, in addition to the South African township of Soweto, and the ways in which both South African and U.S. foreign policies were deepening the crises felt by Africans in this critical region. The track demonstrated an awareness that Africans worldwide required a conception of freedom that brooked no liberal compromises with white supremacist settler regimes, the United States included. Only the self-determination of oppressed peoples would carry the day. Serving as mostly an educational vehicle, the music video featured Jesse Jackson's condemnation of U.S. support of South African policy, showing how young Black people were both supportive of Jackson and utilizing hip hop music to engage the issue of apartheid in compelling ways.[53] As such, the imagery connects all three elements of Black student consciousness discussed in this chapter.

Black liberation was increasingly imagined as a Pan African political movement that linked South African apartheid to the U.S. post-industrial/neoliberal racial project and then sought to dismantle it. And many would imagine the presidential campaigns of Jesse Jackson along similar lines.[54]

Hope Alive

When Jesse Jackson ran for the Democratic Party's presidential nomination, it brought together more than a "rainbow coalition" of the "locked out"; it also represented an attempt to engineer a Black-led insurgency from within the Democratic Party, one that sought a new kind of social democracy. Jesse Jackson's 1984 campaign and the follow-up run of 1988 were experiments in a new way of politics. The 1984 campaign in particular and the movement that it stimulated was a test of America's capacity to think freedom anew, to imagine ways of eliminating human suffering across the nation and world. Against the neoliberal logic of the sanctity of the market's ability to manage the good life, Jackson advocates argued for a robust commitment to the central state as the force that would redistribute economic and social power to address the ills of society. Against the often disastrous foreign policy initiatives of Reagan's Cold War, Jackson's agenda called for a decrease in military spending and a more humane use of American military and diplomatic power. The movement argued that America should be open to dialogue with those regimes it had dismissed as incorrigible and abolish its propensity to solve problems through force. Where the Reagan era had silenced the public critique that argued that pervasive racism still held sway in every corner of American life, Jackson's voice represented those Black communities—as well as other, nonwhite constituencies—that continued to experience the inequities that originated from the race question. His was a plea to craft a politics based on the oneness of the human family that simultaneously struggled to resist the mythical oneness inherent in American exceptionalism. Culling together perhaps the most ideologically diverse group of strategists from the Black community—veterans from the National Black Political Assembly as well as more *and* less radical organizations—Jackson pushed forward a political agenda to the left of anything the Democrats had seen since the New Deal coalition.[55] It was a testament to the power of the neoliberal consensus to produce inequality that, at the height of its ideological power, a robust insurgency developed that had to be reckoned with. Their time had come.

Amiri Baraka's ruminations on Jesse Jackson's presidential campaigns demonstrated the hope that many had invested in the Democratic presidential campaigns of 1984 and 1988 and the challenges that befell those hopes. In charting the evolution of the relationship that Jackson forged with the party, particularly in the latter run, Baraka evinced a sense of loss, one that also revealed the limits of not only the party structures but the very structure of American politics itself. While covering the 1988 Democratic National Convention for *Essence*, Baraka began to again draw the contradictions between American party politics and truly democratic processes, between Black-led insurgency and simple cross-racial alliances, and between the concept of a supposedly transcendent "common ground" that could generate a coalition politics that nonetheless eschewed a deeper ideological reckoning. Reacting to Jackson's speech, which attempted to forge party unity around such contradictions, Baraka intoned: "You mean both the slave and the slavemaster are right? Both slavery and freedom are right? Is this what is required to qualify for the nomination as president of the United States, double talk and submission to the will of the mighty?"[56]

Five years earlier, few could see this turn. Baraka, and others, were supporters then of what they believed to be a watershed moment in the movement toward a more just, or even radically realtered, America.[57] Among those who felt both this hope and the eventual disappointment were the Black youth who had ardently supported Jesse Jackson. Their experiences and varying levels of involvement in the campaign became critical to the enlargement of their political development. Because of Howard's unique position, both intellectual and geographically, its students were exposed to and contributed to these valences of hope gripping Black America. Perhaps, as Baraka implies, in the end it was hope against reason, but it constituted a consequential moment, and one that nevertheless demonstrated insurgent possibilities and openings in local political movements. The movement campaign was for many involved, a veritable insurgency that attempted to make good on its assault against Democratic Party structures and the norms that drove the neoliberal status quo. Many important community and local-level formations emerged under the broad rubric of the "rainbow coalition" to continue the work of this emergent insurgency.[58]

If 1984 was the "insurgency," then 1988 became the pivot toward "inclusion." The political scientist Robert C. Smith offers that the shift in the latter campaign revolved around the Jackson team's attempt to trade its more insurgent demands in exchange for the banality of traditional brokerage politics.[59] The irony was that this occurred amid Jackson's more successful showing, though, as Baraka's comments suggest, perhaps it was a function of the system itself. Although Jackson had won major states in the North, like Michigan, the demands to undo the rules that had marked the 1984 convention were noticeably absent. Even as his delegates pushed for the eventual nominee, Michael Dukakis, to select Jackson as his running mate, many of them decided against forcing the issue once Jackson was snubbed. More damning, members of Jackson's team joined an unchanged Democratic establishment in exchange for the proverbial mess of pottage that had been nothing more than a rehash of the empty promises of Democrats for decades.[60]

Despite these eventual disappointments, the excitement to be found at the ground level generated a force that many believed to be the beginnings of the movement that might finally break open the neoliberal duopoly. During the 1984 primary season, the "locked out" emerged unexpectedly, buoyed by the rhetoric of Jackson amid the tepid platitudes of traditional voices like former vice president Walter Mondale and the yuppie appeal of Gary Hart.[61] As other candidates representing antiwar and nuclear-freeze positions dropped out, Jackson's candidacy gained in appeal for those white liberals attracted to those political issues. Poor white farmers in America's heartland were also attracted to the campaign, as it tailored messages about economic distress to speak to the hollowing out of the agricultural industry. The traditional "others" of American citizenship—people of Asian and Latinx extraction, gays and lesbians, and the anticapitalist Left—also lent their support. Although his campaign never received the support of the white feminist movement, Jackson appealed to Black women of various class distinctions. By most accounts, however, the most fervent supporters of the Jackson campaign effort were young voters. College campuses became sites of important organizing efforts to advance Jackson's prospects.[62]

In the fall of 1983, the Howard University political scientist Lorenzo Morris conducted an informal poll of students' enthusiasm for a potential candidacy, which then registered very little excitement. But after Jackson declared his intentions to seek the nomination, Morris observed that students became attracted to his charismatic disavowal of the Reaganite politics of the era and began to believe that he could actually disrupt the political spaces of normative electoral politics. As a result, they rapidly mobilized in support of the campaign, which was becoming indistinguishable from a larger movement.[63] The role of Howard scholars in the campaign architecture is critical. Not only were they in an advantageous position in terms of location—as Jackson's headquarters were located on nearby Sixteenth Street in Washington, DC—the historical linkages between Howard intellectuals and Black presidential politics yielded much collaboration, as well.[64] Ronald W. Walters, who had been teaching at the institution since the early 1970s, became the deputy campaign manager of issues, becoming one of an important core of Howard intellectuals that directly supported the effort. As Morris indicates, classrooms acted as informal focus groups and forums for debate. Howard scholars were also employed to generate position papers on various issues ranging from foreign policy to health care. It is no accident then, that the most important volumes produced assessing the impact of Jackson's candidacy emanated from scholars working at the university.[65]

Naturally, their students would come to support it as well—but in their own way. As early as the August 1983 March on Washington commemoration, Howard University Student Association president Nathaniel Jones, speaking at the gathering, urged the student population to contribute to the flowering of a national student movement to "uphold human and civil rights," a call that was echoed by activists within the Political Science Society.[66] Student-led organizations like the National Organization of Black University and College Students (NOBUCS), which had long protested the lack of attention paid to Black educational institutions under Reagan, were no doubt attracted to Jackson's brand of left-liberal politics, as well as the Black nationalist significations it also engendered. Students involved in political organizing on campus noted the crucial stakes that Jackson's Blackness—both political and racial—

evoked. These concerns and the speculation about a possible Black president were debated in the pages of *The Hilltop*. Students thought deeply about the meaning of symbolic politics and were able to make the connections between Jackson's civil rights past, his activist present, and the new thinking about electoral politics his very presence stimulated. Echoing the ideas of earlier analysts, an editorial in the September 2, 1983, edition argued that Jackson's run might bring to the fore specific issues that other candidates might not have endorsed, forcing such concerns into "the open."[67]

Jackson, who had been a frequent visitor to campus (his daughter Santita was enrolled at the time), included the university and its students in campaign stops and informal discussions. The Howard Inn, where he often lodged, became the de facto location for press conferences that directly addressed Black political concerns. These were added to the normal election-year forums, except, of course, that this year was different, the stakes a bit higher. After Jackson's announcement, the Liberal Arts Student Council's first annual summit quickly became a space to discuss and develop strategies in support of his candidacy. At one event, the National Conference of Black Mayors and a grouping of journalists convened on campus to discuss the meaning of the candidacy; while students were clearly concerned about questions of the economy, the elected officials discussed the possible impact that Jackson's run might have on voter registration.[68] This event occurred the day after Louis Farrakhan appeared as a guest of NOBUCS, offering his own endorsement of Jackson. For Farrakhan, the issue was about reviving a sense of Black unity and fortitude, and echoing some of the sentiment of the Black Power era, he suggested that "Jesse Jackson is your last chance to make America work for the masses of Black people."[69]

Perhaps energized by both local and national fervor, other Howard students decided to work directly in voter registration efforts, political education and awareness, and on the campaign itself. Christopher Brown, a political science major and president of the Political Science Society, who had earlier voiced concern over political apathy, helped organize a voter registration effort in Washington, DC, imagined to be directly concerned with raising support for Jackson. This sort of work was supported by a separate campaign by the Howard University Student Association, which added five thousand people to the election rolls, according to their figures.[70] It was for these active students imperative that Jackson, whose campaign had become mired in controversy by the winter months, win that spring's Washington, DC, primary. Along these lines, a formation called DC Students for Jesse Jackson collaborated with the Women's Network to organize a fundraiser that was held at Howard on April 1. There, Jacqueline Jackson, the candidate's wife, and Jackson supporter and civil rights heroine Rosa Parks addressed the crowd of two thousand. Parks's comments drew particular emphasis on the historic possibilities that Jackson represented.[71] The organizers' efforts were rewarded when the majority Black DC vote was easily won.

For Howard students, then, the nomination battle of 1984 was significant in raising their political consciousness and, for those involved, their experience in political organizing. According to a study by the Howard communications scholars Oscar H. Gandy and Larry G. Coleman, a significant segment of Howard students (one-third of their sample) became involved in electoral politics, and a majority demonstrated a keen interest in political campaigns, as a direct result of Jackson's run.[72] As it was for many Black youth, the campaign marked a significant turning point in their lives.

While there was a natural drop-off in the novelty of a Black presidential candidate, the continued misery that Black people felt under the Reagan regime would begin to foment more interest in Jackson's presidential campaign efforts.[73] By Jackson's 1987 announcement that he would again seek the Democratic nomination in 1988, students had been engaged in a range of political activities both on and off campus, including fighting to make Afro-American Studies courses a requirement, organizing for national student advocacy groups, and working on the anti-apartheid movement. Although these issues were pressing for many students, Jackson's scheduled appearances were widely anticipated on campus.

In the fall of 1987, students involved with a new formation called the National Black Student Unity Congress invited Jackson to appear alongside Farrakhan at its annual unity conference. This national organization was an attempt to organize Black college students to address issues facing them on campus, but it was also meant to foster an "intergenerational dialogue" with Black activists.[74] In the run-up to the event, however, students in the congress began to perceive a growing split between Jackson and Farrakhan. The congress's president, University of Pennsylvania student Conrad Tillard, believed that Jackson's pivot toward the "mainstream" was endangering his ability to speak directly to the need to champion "the cause of black people."[75] They would be disappointed, as Jackson canceled his appearance. In an editorial, *The Hilltop* castigated Jackson's "bad move," arguing that this national conference of Black students was a missed opportunity to not only secure the Black vote but to also demonstrate that one could be a viable mainstream candidate and at the same time speak to Black people's interests.[76]

As Jackson's most successful run of victories during either campaign unfolded in the winter of 1988, Black students nationwide became the targets of racially motivated incidents on campus. Howard students worked to raise awareness of these events, demonstrating a solidarity befitting a university community that had for at least a decade worked to create an intercampus activist base.[77] Unlike Jackson's earlier run, many students who organized forums meant to address the Black political condition in 1988 did not necessarily center Jackson's campaign. While he canceled his appearance with Farrakhan, Jackson months later appeared at the Howard Inn to discuss the drug issue, an admittedly critical issue, but also a valence issue that was utilized to pivot to the center.[78] Despite these challenges, the 1988 campaign was for many students a signal moment, and for those who voted, their support for Jackson was never in much doubt.[79] For students who had lived about a third of their lives under Reagan's regime, Jackson's politics were a breath of fresh air. And for many it was proof that Democratic Party politics were not enough.

After it was all said and done, Jackson's campaigns shifted the notions of what could be possible. Although the movement shifted from "insurgency to inclusion" in the end, the Democratic Party and electoral politics in America writ large would—in the words of both Frances Beale and Cornel West—"never be the same."[80] In forcing the nation to listen to Black America in ways that it had not, in venues that it had not, the Jackson campaigns effectively exposed the contradictions at the heart of the triumphalist civil rights narrative that had propped neoliberal and neoconservative politics. The response of the Democratic Party was to incorporate and contain such political rhetoric, showing little concern and directing few resources to address the conditions that necessitated it. College students—particularly those who were coming into the fold of the broadly conceived nationalist movement—had desired so much more.

PART II

1989

4

A Force

Force equals mass times acceleration. The word force carries meaning not only in Newtonian physics, but it also carries meaning to our organization; and in more ways than one. In physics, force is a vector, which simply means that it has direction as well as magnitude. The magnitude of our FORCE rests in the masses we strive to accelerate. But toward what goal? What is the direction of our particular FORCE? The FREEDOM ORGANIZATION FOR RACIAL AND CULTURAL ENLIGHTENMENT accelerates the masses (of which we are an integral part) toward the goal of total freedom from oppression.
—Black Nia F.O.R.C.E[1]

Black Nia F.O.R.C.E was the product of a tradition of student activism. Even as it sometimes was not "conscious of itself as a tradition,"[2] the foundations for this student group were in both the contextual political environments discussed in the chapter 3 and a formidable genealogy of Howard-based activity, both broadly conceived and specific to the 1980s. A useful point of entry into the discussion of Black Nia F.O.R.C.E's emergence, then, is to think about the genealogy of activism at Howard in the immediate years prior to its founding in the winter months of 1988. For they existed because this tradition existed. And because they existed, a protest happened.

In the decade and a half following what some might consider the 1968 high watermark of the student movement, a critical portion of Howard students remained staunchly nationalist and Pan Africanist in political orientation. It is difficult to offer one explanation for the continuity of this sort of energy, though there are a few factors that should be examined: the deepening inequity—what pundits called "the malaise"—that characterized American society in general, which, as discussed previously, is always racialized; the continuing struggle against colonialism in Southern Africa, which, as also discussed earlier, spawned groups with a presence on campus; and the development of the "Black university" concept that brought a coterie of scholars of the Black Studies movement to campus under the leadership of Vice President Andrew W. Billingsley during the early portion of that decade.[3] All of this resulted in an attempt by students to develop a greater capacity to understand and participate in these particular movements concerning the African world and to imagine the African future.

We might trace this evolution of Howard student activism through a brief focus on two organizations founded on campus in the mid-late 1970s: Ubiquity, Inc., and the National Organization of Black University and College Students (NOBUCS). Both groups were critical to continuing the sort of modes of engagement that had characterized student activism in the preceding decade. However, what they both faced was an environment for organizing that had seen the increasing marginalization and repression of Black movement activity by both the state and the "professionalization" of the movement by Black elites. Although this did not eliminate *all* of the work being done, it critically inaugurated a shift that would be consequential to how students perceived struggle and how they imagined the place of ideology in the pursuit of particular visions of a liberated future. Given the political shift of these moments, it was common for questions of revolution to give way to questions of personal responsibility, electoral politics, and a form of community engagement that would have been comfortable to even the Great Society reformers.[4]

And then there were those who maintained a focus upon making revolution, which inaugurated the rancorous but necessary battle for ideological clarity.[5] During this period, Washington, DC's Black cultural spaces became one of many sites in the African world that featured confrontations pitting adherents of an ideological conflict that has come to be known as "revolutionary nationalism" versus cultural and/or bourgeois nationalism. These clashes had important ramifications for the trajectory of the Black freedom struggle in the latter half of the twentieth century. That said, it would be imprecise to draw a sharp line of demarcation between these tendencies, as many individuals would prove the fluidity of these ideological formations. Still, the ways that they framed questions of political economy, the idea of racial capitalism, the role of historical consciousness, and the function of culture and its relationship to identity, gender, and sexuality represented key differences that have continued to inform current iterations of the Black freedom struggle.[6]

Having not quite resolved the tensions that resulted in the sharp disagreements (and much worse) of the late 1960s, nationalist activists from across the country organized an important conference at Howard University in 1974 themed "Which Road toward Black Liberation?" There they attempted to clarify the stakes of arguments that sought to posit "race-first" agendas and those inspired by Marxist-Leninist and Maoist thought that sought to understand the critical nature of class, especially as they manifested themselves in the anticolonial struggles that had galvanized the African diaspora by the middle of the decade.[7] This conference was held during the year that Amiri Baraka famously "changed his ideology," and it was at this conference where Kwame Ture would begin his decades-long process of organizing the All-African People's Revolutionary Party, which embraced a brand of what we might call "race-first, Pan-Africanist socialism."[8]

These ideological trajectories were present on campus not only because it was a hub of what was then called Chocolate City but also because so many of the activists and ideologues had found homes on the faculty, staff, and even the administration of the university. Their students would thus be influenced to develop their own organizational structures to advance the struggle. And so Ubiquity, Inc., and NOBUCS were born. Confronted by a need to reconnect to traditions of African culture and the contemporary urgency of Pan African political struggle, each in their own ways would creatively attempt to think beyond questions of liberal reform and along what Ronald W. Walters called "the two-line struggle." Walters and other faculty members like Jeff Donaldson and Joyce Ladner were extensions of what Robert Vitalis has labeled the "Howard School" of the earlier period and important connections that students had to the Pan Africanist movement during that decade.[9]

Chartered on campus in 1973, Ubiquity, Inc., was closely aligned with the dynamics of the Howard student movement and the larger Kiswahili-inspired cultural nationalist tradition of the late 1960s. Founded by Donald Temple, its presence on Howard's campus brought an Afrocentric energy, which ultimately resulted in its ability to foster a sense of community and service to the larger Black community. For

Ubiquitarians—as members of the group were called—the quest for Black liberation was grounded in the ideals of the Nguzo Saba.[10] Freedom now, or *uhuru sasa*, became its rallying cry. For Temple, the idea was not to build a new sorority or fraternity but a "family" concerned with such activities as tutoring children in neighborhood schools, working with imprisoned community members, and organizing social and cultural events on campus.[11]

The National Organization of Black University and College Students was founded in 1977 at Howard University as an advocacy organization supporting the interests of historically Black colleges and universities (HBCUs). As a network of students attending Black colleges, NOBUCS boasted a membership nationally of over nine thousand students by 1979. Among its many lobbying efforts was its fight to increase the Department of Education funding for HBCUs. It developed a major effort called "National Black College Day," which featured a march in Washington, DC, and later morphed into a week, and it supported issues such as the economic boycotts led by Jesse Jackson's Operation PUSH (People United to Save Humanity) and the Free South Africa Movement. Because of the decentralized nature of the organization, individual chapters seemed to embrace issues that ranged the ideological gamut.[12] But what is certainly clear is that Howard's chapter of NOBUCS tended to evince a revolutionary nationalist/Pan Africanist position, which could have been mistaken for the positions earlier championed by the Revolutionary Action Movement, the Black Panther Party, and the Student Organization for Black Unity.

By the end of the 1970s and with the encroaching conservatism of the 1980s, newer questions would arise—questions that would again place a "race-first" orientation front and center. The emergence of Reaganism and the explicitly white supremacist conservatism that it portended was the perfect foil under which particular forms of nationalism that had been repressed and disavowed as "reactionary" and "bourgeois" in the years prior would reappear. Without question, such critiques continued, but it was also true that the political traditions often unfairly associated with these labels helped to generate movement activity.[13] Howard was one place where this would ring true.

Perhaps the major force responsible for the nationalist zeal then present on campus was the rebirth of the Nation of Islam under the leadership of Minister Louis Farrakhan. Farrakhan's mid-1970s assumption of leadership came after a moment of retrenchment for the group that was quickly reversed through Farrakhan's charismatic appeal by end of the decade.[14] The Nation of Islam was again what it had been to Black folk disaffected by the American dream-nightmare in the time of Malcolm X's prominence. Ideologically, the Nation posited that racism was the intractable feature of American liberal democracy, and thus nationalism was the only way to ensure Black survival. Of course, this time it was a nationalist identity that was inflected by and through the hip hop movement, with Clarence X's Nation of Gods and Earths being the chief beneficiary of this particular variant.[15] A major organizer for this group (known as the Five Percenters) and the Nation of Islam, as well as the corresponding secretary for NOBUCS, was a student then known as True Mathematics. Hailing from South Jamaica, Queens, New York, True would become the main go-between connecting Howard University student activists to the work of the Nation of Islam and the persona of Louis Farrakhan, who would become a mentor to many. Throughout the 1980s, Farrakhan was a consistent speaker on campus, sometimes speaking two or three times a year to a filled Cramton Auditorium. True Mathematics—renamed Haqq Islam by Farrakhan—was also the person who helped introduce the leader of the DC mosque, the physician Dr. Abdul Alim Muhammad, to the Howard student community. Muhammad was known all across campus, and through Haqq Islam's influence and connections, he was able to secure university space to teach a class throughout the decade, which helped bring an alternative for students who were more inspired by Farrakhan's teachings than they were by the university's curriculum.[16]

These nationalist forces were joined by another: the aforementioned All-African People's Revolutionary Party (A-APRP). If the Nation's nationalism was considered bourgeois or conservative, then such charges could not have easily applied to the A-APRP and its critique of political economy as the engine through which racism operated. Founded by the first Ghanaian president and prime minister, Kwame Nkrumah, the A-APRP had as its chief organizer Kwame Ture, himself a graduate of Howard University and a constant presence on campus. Its major influence came from the basic message that Ture brought in his yearly messages to Howard students: "Organize, organize, organize!"[17] And organize is what Howard students did. Pan Africanism gave them a political grammar with which to connect the issues of Black life in the United States and beyond with the anti-apartheid struggle of South Africa. One of the critical figures who would emerge as a influential member of Ture's All-African People's Revolutionary Party was Howard Newell, who would eventually serve as president of the Howard University Student Association (HUSA) in 1982. As HUSA president, Newell spearheaded the major Administration Building sit-in and rally in response to the attempt to expel *Hilltop* editor in chief Janice McKnight that spring. The tactics of this protest, of course, resembled the 1968 Administration Building takeover and would also directly inform those of the protest to come in 1989.[18]

While nationalism and Pan Africanism, by all accounts, were the most influential ideological forces for Howard students, there was an attempt of the radical, anticapitalist white Left to gain a foothold. The major group occupying this space was the Spartacus Youth League—an offshoot of the New Left Trotyskite formations—which saw the nationalism of groups like NOBUCS as inherently reactionary. This group followed a long tradition of attempts to incorporate Black working-class communities as the foundation for national and global class struggle.[19] Howard students, despite the protestations of Left organizations, were not inattentive to class contradictions—they were at Howard and were aware of the historical legacy it represented, after all. It was just that the approach of the A-APRP was what resonated more. For Islam, and others, the posturing and antics exhibited by the Spartacus Youth League showed that it was not grounded in how Black student activists understood the world and never really posed a threat to those nationalist sensibilities then pervasive in the student activist community.[20] And importantly, neither did the emergent conservatism of the Black middle class—embodied by the elevation of figures like Reginald F. Lewis as *the* exemplar for certain Black college students as well as the liberals to the *right* of Jesse Jackson's politics.[21]

Islam's emergence as a respected force on campus eventuated in his appointment as program director of the Pan Africanist HUSA administration of Christopher Cathcart and Manotti Jenkins. Both Cathcart and Jenkins were NOBUCS members and Howard Newell protégés who were embroiled in various forms of student activism before deciding to run for elected office á la their mentor. In a *Hilltop* interview exploring their platforms, then–vice presidential candidate Jenkins responded to the question of his "ideology" by saying, "What I believe is Pan-Africanism."[22] Recognizing the saliency of their approach, *The Hilltop* endorsed their platform.[23] In a later interview after they had assumed power, President Cathcart declared the ultimate warrant for their administration's platform: "I'm an African . . . we have a common culture—an African heritage that is rich in tradition, rich in culture, rich in struggle."[24] Cathcart and Jenkins's tenure became the bellwether for the long-pursued strategy of taking the movement directly to the students via the power of student government. It was grounded in a push to use the platform to increase the awareness of Howard students who were not necessarily previously involved in such work and to provide spaces for them to actively contribute—filling what Cathcart called "a cultural void."[25]

Most prominent for Cathcart was the attempt to increase student involvement in the anti-apartheid struggle and to amplify their voices in the struggle to establish Afro-American Studies courses as a requirement for graduation for all students—both were yearlong struggles of this administration, which held office during the 1984–1985 school year.[26] Their activism and their model spawned the work of prominent and influential student leaders who came later, including Wayne Carter, Ona Alston, and Fritz Jean. For these leaders, the next step was developing the ability to build stable institutions that would facilitate the achievement of a greater purpose for life after graduation. It was ultimately about utilizing their experience as activists to discern routes to Black economic empowerment and to think about the Black experience as connected to the larger African world. While such work was effective, it would require constant refinement and replenishment by each generation of students, as Frantz Fanon would have us remember.[27] In order to reproduce a steady flow of new blood and ward off the "terminal" nature of student activism, Islam and others remained present on campus even after their own graduations.[28]

Beyond the organizational politics and contradictions that played themselves out on campus, many Howard University students would embrace variations of both historical materialist and Pan African nationalist ideologies—many less concerned to see them as distinct and opposed—in their pursuit for a just world. The "high eighties" ushered in a moment that rendered such pursuits necessary. Black life for Howard University students was, for many, of a piece with African life in the world. While it has become customary to create a hard-and-fast class line separating the elite college student from the larger masses, such, if it were ever so, was certainly not true for the Howard student of the late 1980s. In either case, class is not necessarily *the* marker for the kinds of consciousness that would be demonstrated and lived by those students. Neither was it unimportant. For Black students at Howard the unfolding of the 1980s would further reveal not only the necessity of such radical, antisystemic, and/or subversive movements, it would also provide ample opportunities to test their salience.

United

While the groups discussed above help explain the general tenor of Howard student activism, there are still more direct genealogies out of which Black Nia F.O.R.C.E was birthed. Out of the buzz still emanating from the attempted ouster of *Hilltop* editor Janice McKnight and the resultant protest in 1983, a group bearing the name Black United Youth emerged. Led by students such as Todd C. Shaw and Steve X (Stephen Jackson), they participated in the movement to create a national holiday for Martin Luther King, Jr. That subsequently led them to protest Doug "The Greaseman" Tracht, a shock jock who had advised whites to murder another four Black Americans so that they could benefit from an entire week of holidays.[29] While there were many instances of the group participating in activities like the Greaseman protest, Black United Youth was notable for its adherence to weekly meetings, where it focused on political education, often in small numbers. Study acted as the engine for the vehicle of their activism.

The connection between this somewhat eclectic group founded in 1983 and what would become Black Nia F.O.R.C.E requires an understanding of the very specific ethos of the freshman class of 1986. The men of that class were by all accounts noted for their extreme bravado, no doubt generated by their embrace of hip hop, as many of the most popular students—those who threw the best parties and had the best dance moves—were from the hip hop–infused Tri-State area. In many ways, this also generated a situation in which those from these areas along with those from the many cities that were strongly represented beyond the East Coast created what can best be described as a series of cliques (or crews) based on both regional affiliations and/or interests.[30] Although there was some overlap, there was the New York Posse, Osage Crew (Philadelphian students), Lou Phi (an assortment of so-called misfits brought together by circumstance), the Gentlemen of Drew Social Club (a campus organization whose origins preceded this class), groups representing cities in the Midwest and West Coast, and the athletic teams.[31] They manifested in large measure to both relieve the burden of seeking brotherhood in places beyond their new residences in Charles Drew Hall and George Washington Carver Hall and of having to navigate the world on and beyond campus alone. As such, these formations functioned as both social and real protection against the multiple dangers that might face naïve freshmen away from home for the first time. And yet there was more at work.

For these young men, the need to project a *cool* was about more than dealing with the average pressures faced by freshmen at many other institutions. The stakes were a bit higher because of the outsized cultural influence that Howard had upon the Black world. One had to be cool while also carrying on this legacy of excellence. But the reality was that such pressures were not immediately clear. It was to the guidance of organizations like Black United Youth that we might give at least part of the credit for channeling a bravado—that often went awry—to more productive usages.

A junior member and noted entrepreneur by the name of Aaron Johnson connected members of this freshmen class to the organization. One evening, Johnson, who sold T-shirts with radical messages and figures, was attempting to make sales when he ran into a discussion group of these freshmen men in Drew Hall. At the center of this session was Ras J. Baraka. Later pulling him aside, Johnson, an eventual organizer in Kwame Ture's A-APRP, convinced Baraka to join the Black United Youth. Baraka brought along a friend named Carlisle Sealy. The recruitment of Baraka, already a magnetic and charismatic force, into the Black United Youth was a strategic move that resulted in an increase of that organization's membership, but that increase did not come from the bases that represented the other side of Baraka's and Sealy's social lives.[32]

The son of Amiri and Amina Baraka, Ras was destined to be the person he became to the Howard community. On his son, Amiri Baraka would comment:

> Though they all have traces of myself and hers (Amina) . . . Ras, whom I stayed up all night with, plotting the historical metaphysic of his name, has such a striking physical resemblance it provides the other comparison. And when he plays at the trumpet, reminding me of a would-be hip little dude with an imitation-leather "gig bag" hippety-hopping across High Street—it's too much.[33]

While Ras Baraka's upbringing provided the necessary grounding, he would still need to find his own voice as well as escape many of the other temptations that would inevitably arise and distract someone born and reared in Newark, New Jersey, and inured to a certain way of living.[34] Nothing about his political evolution was automatic. The world of 1980s Northwest DC amid the political struggles that were both faced and ignored on campus provided a viable space for intellectual and ideological development. Coming into his calling would mean having to grasp the meanings of what his classmates faced and to find the language with which to help them make sense of it themselves. Baraka's background connected very well with those who had the sort of Tri-State cultural influences that tended to dominate certain areas of Howard social life, and the quest to connect it to a deep consideration of social and political reality would eventually become one of his strengths.[35] While he certainly found time to party and show off his perfect "wop," Baraka also apprenticed with an important group of campus and DC-based community workers and activists, fusing together his bourgeoning skills with a critical engagement with these long-distance runners of the Black freedom movement. He would soon add more broadly national figures like Lisa "Sister Souljah" Williamson, Kevin Powell, Conrad Tillard, and others to his growing circle of comradeship.

Carlisle Sealy was a New York native of Caribbean heritage. A high school athlete, Sealy came to Howard on a scholarship to study engineering. While attracted to the clique known as the New York Posse, Sealy was also more narrowly part of a group of engineering students who were somewhat isolated from the normal run of shenanigans in

Drew Hall. Yet after joining the football and track teams and making connections with students beyond the New York set, Sealy became a "people person," able to bring diverse groups together. His initial attraction to Howard, however, perhaps grounded the work that he would do once there; it was the Blackness—the ways that it manifested and the legacies it embodied—that drew Sealy to the work. Known as a brilliant student, Sealy would manage to bring a deft knowledge of the campus, transcending the narrowness of clique life, to elevate the organizing efforts of all groups of which he was a member. Along with Baraka, Sealy was also impressed with the ideas and approaches to the problem of white supremacy as explained by the psychiatrist Frances Cress Welsing and the Nation of Islam's Abdul Alim Muhammad. They both sat in on each of their informal classes on campus, both bona fide nationalist institutions in the undercommons of Howard University.[36]

In Black United Youth, Baraka and Sealy learned the importance of linking the vibrant energies of their Howard personas to the work of thinking and acting to change society. From these foundations, they would also join Ubiquity, Inc. These older and established on-campus formations were decisive influences in that they helped motivate and inspire Baraka and Sealy to do something other than just be in the spaces and scenes, the "party and bullshit" that dominated the social lives of their classmates. They also knew that introducing that lifestyle too soon to the cliques might be ineffective. The need to relate to this cadre would require something other than the kinds of organizational cultures characteristic of the Black United Youth and Ubiquity. The freshman class of 1986 would require another kind of structure, another formation.[37]

Apathy

The foundations of Baraka and Sealy's project to birth this new formation were their critiques of what they called the "apathy" of their freshmen brothers. At a certain point, they both came to possess the belief that the dangerous activities and choices being made as Black male college students warranted self-evaluation. In "apathy," they had found a concept that might bring them into a greater consciousness.[38] This idea of personal responsibility, distinct from how they would understand the outside forces endangering Black life, was inspired by the models of

the Nation of Islam and other Black nationalist traditions that acknowledged the evils of white supremacy while concluding that there were
some things that had to be done for ourselves.[39] Out of these reflections
Baraka and Sealy began to host "apathy discussions."

Initially convened in dorm rooms, the apathy discussions were
geared toward developing Black political consciousness in ways that
drew a comparison between what Black youth were doing in the 1980s
and in the immediate historical precedent. For these students, born at
the height of the Black Power era, this self-examination began with the
question of how they would contribute to or extend their parents' legacy.
"Apathy" became shorthand for the reasons that they had fallen short of
the lofty heights of the Black freedom movement of the sixties.[40] How
could they, in the wake of the erosion of the gains made and the deepening of Reaganism, not be inspired to build a movement? The only
explanation was that they had become too comfortable with the status
quo and that comfort would make them unable to understand the ways
that the fight waged by their parents and their parents' parents was not
at all complete. It would be necessary to wake up from this deep apathy,
before it was too late.

Ranging over the spring semester of 1987 to the beginnings of the
next fall, these meetings were largely convened and presided over by
Ras Baraka. At their height, some of these sets managed to cram fifteen to twenty students in one dorm room. As they gained in popularity,
they would move to the more accommodating dorm lounges, even attracting people who were not a part of any of the cliques. In the discussions, Baraka would expound upon the need to "do something," and it
was his familial connection to the movement and his charisma that lent
his voice credibility. None of these, however, could compare to his brilliance and his ability to turn a phrase. Although the fight against apathy
was not merely rhetorical, it was Baraka's oratorical abilities that were
responsible for drawing the crowds. He possessed the ability to speak
extemporaneously, often dropping poetry in between his newfound in-
sights, fully engulfing the crowd.[41] Such skills would prove critical, for
there was still more to come.

If the premise of the apathy discussions was that this generation was
falling short of the standards set by the movements past, it was not only
necessary to articulate this but to begin to develop an analysis of how

to respond as well. This would result in what Sealy framed as a desire to build stronger connections to each other, to become "my brother's keeper":

> We would just bring guys together. Initially, it would start during the week. We would start Monday, Tuesday, Wednesday, and all of a sudden it kind of migrated to a Friday or a Saturday. Rather than going to hang out, we'd kinda just get together, maybe we'd get together and have some drinks, but we'd be talking. And so, you know, Ras was very big on bringing things to the table to talk about . . . off the top . . . "Okay, where are you from? Where are you trying to go? Who else are you gonna help?" So those apathy discussions were a result of us [resolving to say,] "Don't be comfortable about where you are. Try to excel and do more."[42]

What these discussions accomplished, then, was to begin the process of instilling a more profound purpose into the workaday habits of attending class and being students, by positing that they might develop a social duty to each other, to help each other survive college as a first-order premise for surviving America. And from there, newer horizons would emerge.

Awareness

"Students Work for Awareness," read the headline of the first *Hilltop* story to mention the creation of Black Nia F.O.R.C.E.[43] And yet the meaning of what awareness included, how one came to that place, and what to do next were all at this moment of creation more questions than they were solutions. The group came into existence at the convergence of a critical inflection between the need to address the question of apathy as well as a desire to seek a greater knowledge of the conditions that produced Black suffering. And it was this latter concern that would come to be framed as "awareness," the raison d'être of the organization. This conception of awareness maintained that knowledge of the world beyond the interior dynamics of Black sociality required both an understanding of history and a political education and that these were essential tools in the fight to become and to overcome. The need for self-determination and identity were critically imagined as produced by, but not solely productive of, the external world, a context.[44]

Bringing many of these conversations to bear was a new formation called the National Black Student Unity Congress. In the mold of
NOBUCS, it sought to generate a cross-campus student movement. Its
inaugural convening was characterized by Jesse Jackson as the most important meeting since the founding of the Student Nonviolent Coordinating Committee. The second congress was held October 22–25, 1987,
at Howard, which was strategically chosen by the planning committee
of Fritz Jean, Conrad Tillard, and others because of its centrality to the
movement.[45] Along with student presentations, scheduled events included panel discussions and lectures from Sonia Sanchez, Tony Brown,
Sonia Kidd, Ronald Walters, James Mtume, Louis Farrakhan, Amiri
Baraka, and, as discussed in chapter 3, Jesse Jackson, who disappoint-
ingly canceled at the last minute. The closing dinner featured a tribute to
the Trinidadian-born scholar Tony Martin for his historical scholarship
on Marcus Garvey and the Universal Negro Improvement Association,
one of the chief inspirations of the group.[46]

Louis Farrakhan's keynote address held forth upon the theme "Seizing Power in the 21st Century" and located the foundations of the question of race within the logics of power. Connecting the problem back to
a spiritual core, he asserted to rapt applause that the ultimate meaning
of Black struggle was not simply to seize political and economic power
but to reimagine how humanity might be ordered on the possibility that
hierarchies of difference might be abandoned. Freedom was not a matter
of reversing white supremacy or simply basing power on its logics; it required instead a different way of being in the world. These themes would
have been familiar to many of those present, but for others, particularly
younger and apolitical students hearing the minister for the first time, it
would have sparked a generative reckoning.[47]

The high point of the conference, however, might have been the appearance of Public Enemy. Months earlier, the group's album *Yo! Bum
Rush the Show* had appeared, marking the rappers' arrival as critical
voices in the hip hop movement.[48] But it was in their presumed role as
"political activists" that many older activists found their message wanting. It was one thing to shine a light on the inequities of America, but
it was wholly another to develop a movement toward a liberated future.
Bill Stephney, Public Enemy's manager, participated in a conversation
with Amiri Baraka, Jamaican dub poet Mutabaruka, and musician James

Figure 4.1. National Black Student Unity Congress pin. April Silver Collection, private collection. Photograph by the author.

Mtume, where the former two challenged the new generation of engaged artists to become more active in political struggle. Stephney responded by arguing that this was not to be their role as artists and that the question for those drawn to activism was to develop an apparatus that was not wholly reliant on musicians as *the* movement.

Challenging Amiri Baraka was Lisa "Sister Souljah" Williamson, who, along with Haqq Islam, had helped to bring Public Enemy to the conference.[49] She defended Public Enemy and, by extension, the hip hop generation. Her words became one of the inspirations that would help form the attempt to build something permanent, something larger than the apathy discussion model that was then percolating on campus. According to Jeff Chang, who recounts this tale in his *Can't Stop Won't Stop*, these were the beginnings of a generational rift over the meaning and purpose of the music of the times.[50] Indeed, a few months later, many of the young activists and artists would meet outside of the presence of those elders to discuss the state of Black America and develop a way forward.[51]

Watching Souljah's confrontation with his father, Ras Baraka, who helped organize the conference, was undoubtedly noting the arguments and resolving to build from this moment. Likely because of his deepening relationship with Islam and Souljah, Ras was given the job of cobbling together Public Enemy's security detail, the basis of which was the dorm-room meeting group that was already searching and groping for something that they could do to forward their generation's contribution.[52] This would be the first time they appeared in public together, in makeshift uniforms—blazers and berets, and in formation.[53] Observing and dialoguing with members of the Fruit of Islam—then a visible presence at many Howard events, given the frequent appearances of Farrakhan—had provided them the rudiments of drilling, a feature of the group that would prove to be critical. According to Rich Byers, who was part of the security team, Baraka saw this initial appearance as the beginning of possibly doing "something bigger."[54] This would prove to be prophetic. From that show of unity and the conversations generated from the conference, the first meetings of Black Nia F.O.R.C.E would convene.

A week later, one of the turning points that also began the process of moving the cliques and apathy discussion group toward a more permanent organization involved an incident of police violence. The confrontation occurred on Halloween 1987 in the Georgetown neighborhood. Many of the members of these groups took part in a night of partying, joining thousands of others that converged upon this section of the city. At the end of the night, which all recall may have included many untoward activities, a group of about fifty of them encountered two plainclothes police officers roughing up two Black men. They intervened. A physical altercation between the students and the police ensued. Before it was all said and done, a few men in the group were arrested, while most of the others escaped.[55] According to Kevin Williams, an eventual member of Black Nia F.O.R.C.E's executive board from New York, this event helped many of the crews see in broad relief that the current path that they were treading would only lead to their destruction. Curiously, however, there was no critique of state violence or police brutality. It was read more along the lines as an instance of the need for self-examination, and the question for Baraka was whether they understood their own power. The quest for a deeper awareness of *external* power would come later.[56]

In the weeks after the Halloween incident, the dorm room meetings became logistically impossible. Baraka and Sealy—together with Charles "Chuck" Webb, a New Orleans native, who would go on to become the logistical glue of the three—decided to move the meetings on campus. They chose Frederick Douglass Memorial Hall, Lecture Room 116. There, one night near the end of the semester, the Sons of the Panthers were born.[57] This moniker, Baraka's idea, was a clear gesture toward the ideological and organizational influences of the Black Panther Party. In the early moments of the organization, both the Nation of Islam and its commitment to discipline and order as well as the Black Panther Party and its radical postures and programs determined the orientation of the group. However, for one important reason this name would not work.

Present at this late November meeting was a lone woman student named Gail Sharps, who insisted that the name reflect the actual gendered makeup of the group. And so it underwent a change to the Sons and Daughters of the Panthers.[58] Although the initial naming was not, as Sharps remembers, the result of any intentional misogyny, it was important for her that these young men realize that the question of gender balance be addressed at the organization's birth.[59] While the base of the organization was composed of cliques like the New York Posse, Osage Crew, and Lou Phi, Sharps's presence was the result of the attractiveness of this new organization's politics and practices to women organizers and thinkers, as well as her likely presence at the National Black Student Unity Congress. Although she was alone at this particular gathering, many women students would soon join her, first as a trickle, and then a stream, with women like Lisa Bynum, Sheri Warren, Alicia Westbrook, and Alice Westbrook, who had become members by the winter.[60]

Perhaps the new name was a bit clunky, or unwieldy. So the fledgling group, at that time featuring several dozen members, went back to the drawing board. One story of the official naming of the group has it emanating from the minds of Sealy and Baraka, who suggested "Black" to represent identity, and "Nia" for purpose, likely the result of their being influenced by Ubiquity and its reading of the Nguzo Saba.[61] And then there was "force." This part of the name actually came from an attendee who, after providing it, never returned to the group. However, his contribution was profound. Baraka remembers him giving a disquisition on the meaning of force: "He had a whole thing about force being a vector that it had both direction and power and we were trying move the mass. . . . Our job was to move the masses in the direction that we want them to move in. And everybody said, that's what we was talking about. That moves."[62]

The next step was to choose what each of the letters of the acronym would signify. Byers recalls that the initial rendering was "Freedom Organization for Racial and Cultural Equality" and that such a framing was rejected. Baraka argued that equality with whites should not be how the question of Black liberation should be approached. Although a debate ensued, the group finally settled on the word "Enlightenment" for the "E." And this is what stuck: Black Nia F.O.R.C.E (Freedom Organization for Racial and Cultural Enlightenment).[63] The name clearly spoke to both of the rationales for the development of organization: apathy and awareness.

Room 116

For Chuck Webb, the goals of the new organization would not manifest without the ability to create a logical structure and system for its activities. Webb, who labeled himself as somewhat of a "misfit," characterized his initial Howard experiences as being grounded with his affiliation with Lou Phi. The clique became his entrée into the scene, establishing his credentials as an organizer. But it would be through engaging and hanging out with Baraka and Sealy that he would be brought along to a greater consciousness. Once there, Webb would dive headlong into the affairs of the organization. One of Webb's many duties was making sure that there would be a place to meet.[64]

They chose to meet at Frederick Douglass Memorial Hall, Lecture Room 116. The story of this was peculiar. Unable to officially book the space since the group never sought or desired to be recognized as an on-campus student organization, they chose to essentially commandeer it. Their chosen time, Friday nights, became so well known that eventually university officials either assumed that they had gone through the proper channels or simply bent to their wills.[65] The net result was that, over time, Friday nights in Douglass 116 became known campus and community wide as a settled time and space.

It was there that the name of the organization and the first officers were chosen. The leadership core was built around Baraka, chosen as the executive minister; Sealy, the minister of administration-external; and Webb, minister of administration-internal. Among the other officers, important to the organization was the minister of defense, which during the first few months was occupied by various members of the original cliques, before Aaron Lloyd, and then Kevin Williams, provided some stability to the position.[66] As can be inferred, the makeup of the executive board was premised on the Black Panther Party's Central Committee, at least in terms of the names given to the positions.[67]

The Friday night meetings also had the flavor of the Nation of Islam, at least in terms of structure. In order to instill a focus, men and women agreed to sit separately on either side of the dual-columned room.[68] The form that each night took included a recitation of Kevin Powell's Black Pledge of Allegiance, a business portion, and ended with Baraka's "teaching." In this, the organization allowed its best recruiting tool, Baraka's words, to headline its most important organizational activity at that time. In these talks, the focus was on an eclectic mix of topics. Baraka had by that time become a national speaker on Sister Souljah's circuit, the GET BUSY tour (General Education in Training Blacks to United and Save our Youth), with stops on college campuses around the country.[69] Back home at Howard, Baraka roused the organization, opining on everything from African history to white supremacy in the educational system to interpersonal relationships. These Friday night meetings were also sites of debate, where everyone got the opportunity to speak either in response to, or to generate departures from, whatever topic Baraka had brought. As such, it was not simply a space where everyone sought to listen to a sermon, but a dialogic setting. It eventually grew to include "Jazz and Poetry" nights as well, as many members were practicing artists.[70]

Just as it was critical for the Black United Youth, study would be essential for Black Nia F.O.R.C.E. Because the base of the organization was growing, there needed to be some level of organizational discipline and unity, and reading together helped to forge this. However, these practices, along with other attempts to discipline the organization, led many initial members of the cliques to abandon the group.[71] This was precisely the fear that led Baraka and Sealy to create a distinct organization. While there was no formal reading group as existed in the Black United Youth, nor a trial period as existed in Ubiquity, the methods for instilling a sense of commitment were still too much for many of the initial cliques. Despite these defections, there was also constant growth, likely driven by the pursuit of knowledge. Together, members would read classics like

The Autobiography of Malcolm X, as well as works that were coming to the fore as a result of the Afrocentric movement, such as those of Anthony Browder, Yosef Ben-Jochannan, and Maulana Karenga. However, the group's "bible" was Baba Zak Kondo's *The Black Student's Guide to Positive Education*.[72] Many of the topics contained in this work became the basis for the discussions on Friday nights. Throughout the life of the organization, these Friday night meetings remained a space for discussion and an open disavowal of the normal activities that would have occupied college students at that time. One, of course, could still go out *after* the meeting, but whatever was discussed in these spirited meetings would have likely been in the foreground of their minds.

In *The Hilltop* story announcing the group's formation, Webb, Baraka, and members Alicia Westbrook and Tony Jones discussed the meaning of this new outfit, emphasizing that what made their work distinct was its clear and open embrace of Black "disciplinary love" and self-determination. Asked about their influences, they replied that they were Martin Luther King, Jr., Malcolm X, and Louis Farrakhan. And this demonstrated again, as a hallmark of the era, the attempt to forge a strategic unity out of the various ideological strands resonant in the Black community, with nationalism clearly constituting the major, rather than minor, note. The article also reported that Black Nia F.O.R.C.E's program of unity and struggle was to be achieved through study and economic organization. It was these concerns that drew as many as one hundred people to the Friday gatherings, and this was to be the work that Baraka declared would "put our generation back on its feet."[73]

Ideologically, the group espoused a nationalism that was attentive to the ways that race structured American and global society, but over the organization's life, this approach would be extended to also critique the relationship between race and imperialism. An awareness of political economy, then, would come to energize the nationalist impulse that guided the group, an impulse that would find resonance and inspiration with the cultural nationalism that defined hip hop by the early 1990s and the economic self-determination that would come to define what Michael Dawson calls "community nationalism."[74] The ability to creatively extend the ideological traditions of both the Nation of Islam and the Black Panther Party, among other precursor organizations, marked Black Nia F.O.R.C.E's significance to youth struggle during an era in

Figure 4.2. Black Nia F.O.R.C.E Drilling. Photograph courtesy of Akanke Washington.

which many other youth organizations were ideologically aligned with liberal and white leftist approaches to the question of race.[75] Among the critical manifestations of this was its reassertion of Black political and cultural identity as necessary for self-determination and liberation. One of the ways that members marked themselves as distinct was their dress, consisting of all black tops and bottoms with tams. The idea here was to turn heads and generate conversations. And it tended to work.[76] Another way to generate attention for the group was to convene informal speaking engagements. Baraka would often lecture at the flagpole on the main yard or in front of the Armour J. Blackburn Student Center. Many of these lectures attracted attention from those students who were perhaps less willing to give up their Friday nights. As such, when the unexpected call came to participate in more drastic actions, there just happened to be a base of support outside of the organization proper.

Despite its growing membership and often standing-room-only meetings, in these early moments the organization never sought official recognition.[77] The resources used to mount their activities would come from sympathetic administration officials, like the director of the Blackburn Center, Roberta McLeod, and from their affiliation, both formally and informally, with other organizations, including HUSA. At one point Fritz Jean, HUSA president and the force behind the National Black Student Unity Congress gathering, became an attendee at the meetings and close ally.[78]

Members of Black Nia F.O.R.C.E were also involved in tutoring services at Gage-Eckington Elementary School, Ujamaa Shule, and NationHouse Watoto, as well as at local housing projects and community centers. Representing one of its clear principles, the idea behind this decision was to both close the gap between Howard University and the local DC community and to reverse the miseducation of Black children. These connections would also become critical and necessary when the moments to participate in direct action presented themselves.[79]

It is important, finally, to note that many members of the organization did not join *in order* to participate in direct action. Many of the elements of the organization—such as study, participating in lectures, training and drilling, and other preparatory activities—were associated with the idea of "nation building," an idea connected to the kind of Black nationalism that focused on confronting problems internal to the Black community, rather than state power and its representatives directly. Unlike many of the influential student organizations at Howard listed above that sought to engage the state through protest, Black Nia F.O.R.C.E in its infancy stood resolutely on the principles of self-determination.[80] As they closed the book on their first few months of existence, new levels of growth were in the offing.

Transition

The summer of 1988 was important for the group. Rather than spending the vacation at home, many of the original crew decided to work along with Sister Souljah at a summer camp sponsored by Benjamin Chavis in

North Carolina. It provided them an opportunity to fulfill many of the ideals of the organization while also deepening the bonds that they had developed with one another. It was also a chance to forge the logistical skills necessary to mount and manage large-scale projects. In addition to this work, Baraka spent that summer on the lecture circuit with the GET BUSY tour and attending the Democratic National Convention, where his father was famously barred from entering.[81]

Although she did not participate in the summer activities, one of the best organizers within Black Nia F.O.R.C.E was April R. Silver. While she shared the New York origins of many of its members, Silver had spent the last half-decade of her life as a resident of Los Angeles. Returning to the East Coast would have felt like home, and coming to Howard would have felt the same, given its differences with the L.A. scene, especially the multiracial settings where she had attended secondary school. Less attracted to the upper-middle-class, "bourgeoisie" elements of Black life at Howard, Silver found the communities of students that would serve as the foundation for Black Nia F.O.R.C.E a welcome presence. A natural leader, Silver became involved in the leadership of organizations like the California Student Association and the Alpha Sweethearts, even as she productively and constructively bumped heads with the male leadership of Alpha Phi Alpha.

During this period, Silver also met and invited the poet Sonia Sanchez to a series of meetings on campus. She had met her son, Morani, in one of her English classes and from there built a strong relationship with the both of them. These meetings featured conversations around key and often underread texts like Martin Delany's *Blake*,[82] and they took place in the aptly titled Blackburn Reading Lounge. They would prove to be formative experiences for Silver, as would a budding relationship with the renowned poet and director of the Afro-American Studies Resource Center E. Ethelbert Miller. Hearing Sister Souljah and Ras Baraka speak at various events convinced her to check out the Friday night meetings in Douglass 116. And that would spark a deep and lasting commitment to the mission of Black Nia F.O.R.C.E.

It was so deeply felt that Silver, on her own accord, disseminated homemade flyers printed at her off-campus job, inviting students to join the organization. The transformation that she was feeling in this space was meaningless if it remained personal and individual. She sought to build the organization in order to generate a collective transformation of the student body and the Black community.[83] For her, as it was for many Black women, these transformations were often literally worn on their bodies and their hair.[84] As a fellow member of the freshman class that came in the fall of 1986, Silver would join Gail Sharps, Sheri Warren, Alice Westbrook, Alicia Westbrook, and a growing population of women in the organization. After about a month in Black Nia F.O.R.C.E, Silver picking up the apathy theme wrote in *The Hilltop*:

> For Black students, responsibility accompanies an education, and of course that responsibility is to further develop our race in all things meaningful. Unfortunately, some will argue a self-centered point that they are only responsible for themselves. I submit to them that if our ancestors had been as selfish with whatever opportunities they had, then today, there would be no room for such [an] arrogant and shallow mentality.[85]

She would soon learn what it meant to be responsible for thousands.

The triumvirate of Baraka, Sealy, and Webb eventually took notice of Silver's work. But what happened next was very puzzling to many members of the group. By the fall of 1988, Baraka had decided to step down as executive minister. For many who had identified the organization through the persona of Baraka, the decision made very little sense. After all, what would the organization be without him at the head? But what happened next was even more puzzling. Baraka and Sealy decided to put forward Silver's name for the post. Silver, while known among the circles she engaged, was not the obvious choice to succeed Baraka. According to Webb's account, the selection of nominees was somewhat contentious. Everyone at that meeting had expected that, even if Baraka would not be the nominee, the natural order of things would be for either Sealy or Webb to take over. But both refused to accept nominations, and as Webb refused, he nominated Silver, which was seconded by Baraka. This was enough for the membership to accept the plan. April Silver became the next executive minister and was leading meetings by October.[86]

For a woman in leadership, things could have been made very difficult. However, this was an era in which women throughout the Howard student body had exerted themselves in really important ways, and it was also a legacy that can be traced to earlier moments of student activism.[87] While, as Sealy remembers, they were not thinking about whether she was a woman and were more concerned about her skills, none of this would have prevented unchecked sexism, organizational or not, to potentially compromise her tenure. It was true, however, that one of the planks of Black Nia F.O.R.C.E was an insistence on the equality and protection of Black women, although it was a constant and evolving struggle.[88] In any case, there were some quiet doubts about Silver's leadership skills, given the fact that she was the complete opposite of Baraka. Quiet and reserved, she in many ways did not possess the stereotypical, brash hip hop style of leadership.[89] Whatever their motives and despite whatever doubts existed, Silver turned out to be an excellent choice. In her first few months, there would be enough events to test her mettle. And her resolute response to the new demands on her skills undoubtedly produced a monumental shift in the history of Howard University.

5

The Confrontation

So in education, now Howard becomes attractive to white
supremacy. And from merely influencing and controlling
through the "head Negro" university policy more and more
the rulers will want to swallow H.U., like a butter cookie. But
the students Ras told us about were hip to all this!
—Amiri Baraka[1]

Commenting upon the international dimensions of the struggle to
destroy the system of enslavement, Frederick Douglass uttered words
that have become immortalized: "Power concedes nothing without a
demand."[2] Just as it would have been to those for whom Douglass spoke
and for the legions who have taken these words to inspire more recent
iterations of struggle, to demand is to also imagine. Imagination often
and perhaps should always govern how we think about what might
structure our freedom and all it must mean. And so it was imagination
that underpinned the force that swept through Howard University at the
close of the 1980s. To imagine that a university, languishing under the
weight of a complex history, could in fact change, could in fact be the
dream sequence of our freedom—this is what emboldened and enliv-
ened the moments of confrontation that occurred on March 3, 1989.[3]
And it was only the beginning.

The Spark

It was Aarian Pope's vocation to imagine, for she was an artist. A sophomore from Harlem, Pope had joined Black Nia F.O.R.C.E (BNF) out of
a desire and a need to connect with the kinds of students that reminded
her of the sorts of political discussions she had experienced in the company of her large family. Glenroy Atkinson, Pope's father, was one of
eight children and was deeply immersed in the local and global meaning

of Black struggle. Eventually becoming a poet, Pope represented a family that was quintessentially Harlem—the Garveyites, the African diasporic influences, the jazz, the Black church.[4] So finding a group of Howard students who were also concerned about Black politics and struggle was immediately familiar.

On a Tuesday evening in February, Pope heard a loud voice summoning her to the community telephone of Meridian Hill Hall, the off-campus Howard dormitory adjacent to Malcolm X Park on 16th Street. Her father was calling, and the message was urgent. A prodigious reader, he had seen the stories that had appeared as early as the first of the month announcing the appointment of Lee Atwater to the board of trustees at Howard.[5] Worried, he asked Aarian if she had heard about it, and if so, "What was BNF going to do?" But it was news to her, and—as she would soon find out—it was news to many of the others. And here is where the spark came. One could not be engaged in the work of awareness, the veteran public servant and organic intellectual explained to his daughter, without maintaining an understanding of the things happening around the very spaces they inhabit as students. For universities themselves are constituted by the consequential political trajectories that endanger us, and thus vigilance is always necessary. As was something more. Hanging up the phone, Atkinson urged BNF to do something. Knowing required action.[6]

Those words moved Pope to feverishly pepper her friends with the news. It was as if she was roused by a force. On the following Friday, February 17, she formally raised the issue of Atwater's appointment during the regular meeting of BNF.[7] Aaron Lloyd, the soon-to-be minister of defense, and a few others had remembered the controversial campaign advertisement, but there were others who did not.[8] But whether they remembered or not, it was clear that everyone needed and many desired more information. So as was their custom, the group set out to study. Who, in fact, was Lee Atwater? And why had he been appointed to Howard's board of trustees? Those basic concerns would lead to intense questioning and, then, to a confrontation.

Researching Atwater uncovered a number of unsavory features of his political life. First, the group came to know of his mentee-mentor relationship to Strom Thurmond, the racist U.S. senator and opponent of Black civil rights. Second, they had added details to what they already

knew of the racist electoral strategy that Atwater had employed to ensure that the Republicans maintained control of the executive office of
the United States. They then became aware of his stance on civil rights,
his support for the nomination of the conservative jurist Robert Bork
to the Supreme Court, and his lobbying work on behalf of apartheid in
South Africa.[9]

To the question of why Howard University would embrace him, the
group began to see that what motivated those board members who recommended him was, in large measure, the potential benefit of having a
key figure in the Republican establishment—the Republican National
Committee Chairman, no less—in a strategic position to affect and influence university decision making, particularly when that party was in
possession of the presidency. University officials from Vice President
Carlton Alexis to Member of the Board Thaddeus Garrett expressed this
view, and they were not without support.[10] Black Nia F.O.R.C.E's research sought to reveal the nature of Atwater's politics, but it ended up
also revealing the nature of Howard. It caused them to question how
certain actors perceived the destiny of the university.

With officials willing to embrace figures like Atwater, where was
Howard going? And, of course, also, where *should* it go? Again, as it
was for every generation, the question became: Could Howard be a university that was for what the students imagined was the function and
purpose of Black educational institutions? What did it mean to be the
"Mecca"? What it could not be, they came to decide, was a university
that courted and accepted within its most significant decisional structures someone who was clearly racist and willing to utilize those beliefs
to influence questions of power. Although many other Howard students
accepted that these sorts of issues were complicated by many factors,
there were among them those who felt much like the members of BNF,
that this was a step too far.

A week before Aarian Pope raised the issue at the meeting of BNF,
The Hilltop reported that there were many in the Howard community
who were both angered by the appointment but also willing to take a
wait-and-see approach. Among them were the student leaders, Garfield
Swaby and Daniel Goodwin. Swaby, who was the president of the Howard University Student Association (HUSA), told *The Hilltop* that he had
received "negative feedback" from students, but he also stated that "it

may be a plus to have him on the board," given the university's federal appropriation. Goodwin, the undergraduate student trustee, similarly stated that this could turn into a positive if Atwater's appointment could "generate more funds."[11] *The Hilltop* disagreed. In a blistering editorial that ran in the same edition, the editors denounced the decision, arguing that the "Howard community should be ashamed of our administration." Contextualizing President James Cheek's actions as unnecessarily accommodationist, the actions of a "modern day [Booker T.] Washington," the authors of the editorial disagreed with the position that this creator of the "most racist strategy in a national presidential campaign in the twentieth century" could be transubstantiated into a strategic ally of the university.[12]

An irony that fully reveals the contradictory features of the university is that much of the intellectual thrust for the idea and study of Black politics, centered upon unique ways of understanding the political behavior and ideological development of Black communities, had actually originated, in part, at Howard University.[13] That members of BNF as well as other student leaders were close to the professors who helped produce this epistemological shift away from "mainstream" understandings of the study of politics would prove to be consequential.[14] It would be these ideas that would help shape their understanding of the relationship between the overt racism of the GOP via Atwater and the question of Howard's financial security. One of those figures, Professor Alvin Thornton, could see the "logic" of the decision but emphatically condemned the racism of Atwater's campaign strategy, amid the campaign's chorus of denials, intimating that the university needed to take a moral stand. Thornton also placed the university's action in a larger context— the result of a concerted attempt by the conservative intelligentsia to generate an "alternative leadership" out of the ashes of the assault on the 1960s dispensation of liberalism. This was an often unacknowledged strategy of Reaganism on the direction of Black politics, a tactic that would have benefited greatly from Howard University's endorsement.[15]

Professor Joseph McCormick polled his students as to their understanding and knowledge of Atwater and his recent campaign strategy in his Urban Government Politics and Administration course. Few knew of the story, so he spent a few classes demonstrating the impact of the southern strategy on the Black community and national politics. It was, in fact, his student Derrick Payne who would go on to compose *The Hilltop* editorial that derided Cheek and Atwater. For McCormick, the idea of outreach by the Republicans was strategic, but their use of Howard was shallow; if they wanted Black support, they should "go out into the Black community and earn it."[16] Much like Thornton, McCormick saw the gesture as a means for securing the ongoing conservative "constitutional revolution" and as evidence of the "politics of dependency" that had structured Black American relations with the "politico-economic order."[17] Another professor in the department, the well-regarded Ronald W. Walters, told the *Washington Post* that he and his fellow faculty members were "incredulous," stating that it was "inappropriate to turn and reward the guy who kicked [Blacks] in the pants."[18]

The students interviewed for the *Washington Post* story, like M. Kasim Reed, again demonstrated that, at this point, there were students who supported the appointment, characterizing it as "very strategic." The eventual mayor of Atlanta, Reed became an outspoken opponent of the protest, leveraging this stance to become an influential member of the board himself. But the managing editor of *The Hilltop*, Alonza Robertson, asserted what was the opinion among students who would join BNF in dissent, stating that the university's appointment felt "just like a slap in the face to me."[19]

In the two weeks between Pope's notification and the eventual direct action, spaces convened by BNF became sites of vibrant debates and strategy sessions concerning this issue. After it appeared that the university was simply going to push forward and ignore the rising levels of dissent, the question of participating in a more radical action was raised. As a gauge on the level of anger that this appointment generated, one need only remember that BNF, generally speaking, did not necessarily participate in direct action, nor had it particularly been founded for that purpose. But as BNF members learned more and more about the recent legacy of Atwater, the predominant concern was the ways in which his presence on the board might compromise those sacred spaces, those undercommons that had been created at Howard to allow for the kinds of work that BNF was doing. More, the question of whether this might compromise the view of Howard that saw the intellectual thrust of the university as a bulwark against white supremacy also became a critical issue to be debated and addressed.

Thus, at their regular Friday meeting a week before the university's Charter Day celebration, Ras Baraka, perhaps echoing the sentiments of the group, raised the necessity of launching a protest. It was the only way to protect the institution and their view of what it should be. After accepting the responsibility to continue to collect and disseminate further information on why Atwater had to be opposed, members went to work over the weekend to develop perhaps their most ambitious initiative: to organize the entire student body. This represented a historic decision, one that required a significant level of organizing savvy. But for BNF president April Silver it was the same desire for self-determination that defined their organization from its inception that would inform this substantial undertaking.[20]

Glenroy Atkinson's spark was becoming a flame. Maybe the protest action would have been inevitable without his intervention, but it is likely that it would not have become what it did. However it happened, what was most critical was that the vision for Howard that the students in Black Nia F.O.R.C.E had would not allow them to accept the decision made by the board. For them, it could not stand.

The Coalition

Realizing that they could not mount this effort alone, BNF members began the weeklong process of campus outreach immediately. The effort to reach the entire campus was as broad as possible, including students who would not have been drawn ideologically to BNF, such as the Black Greek letter organizations, other competing factions and crews, the athletic teams, state and national clubs, and the aforementioned student leaders. Silver and others strategically designated individuals with preexisting relationships with these groups with the responsibility to inform them of the issue and seek their support. In addition to this grassroots outreach, there were plans to issue a formal letter to the major student organizations by the following Monday.[21]

On Sunday, February 26, there was a Progressive Student Movement (PSM) meeting in the School of Engineering, in which BNF members were urged by Baraka to participate. The Progressive Student Movement, founded in the mid-1980s, was a smaller rival organization to BNF, headed by Paris Lewis (Malik Zulu Shabazz), who would eventually achieve renown as the leader of the New Black Panther Party.[22] Much like BNF, PSM was made up of many individuals who were also known quantities on the party scene and who would exhibit a pro-Black consciousness as a result of the politics of hip hop. In many ways this constituted the source of the PSM/BNF rivalry. But crisis often creates possibilities for strategic unities. In this setting and in other informal meetings, BNF's need to connect with other students around this issue became a key strategy, even when it meant working with groups with whom their past interactions were unfriendly, to say the least.[23]

On Monday, at a meeting in the Undergraduate Library, members of BNF gathered again to update each other on the progress that they had made over the weekend. Present at this gathering was junior Sheri Warren, who had quickly become a crucial member of BNF, serving as Silver's right hand. She remembers being frustrated at this particular meeting, for despite much anticipation and conversation, it was sparsely attended. Whether this was because the organizing had not gone forth as planned or whether members were busy organizing as the meeting was occurring is hard to say. But creeping doubt might have begun to emerge.

Warren's work within the organization stemmed back to its earliest moments. A brilliant student from the Bronx, Warren had a childhood dream to attend Howard University. Overcoming crushing poverty and other familial struggles, she made it there and early on plunged herself into campus activities. Present at the creation of BNF as one of the first female members, Warren, a veritable hard worker, was elevated to a leadership position with Silver's election as executive minister, and she would prove instrumental to the planning and execution of the protest even as she juggled a number of off-campus jobs in order to make ends meet.[24] The low turnout at this preparatory meeting, then, might have discouraged a less committed collection of figures. But Warren, Silver, and others redoubled their efforts and recommitted to organizing an action, one that had to be swiftly consummated in order to embody the forceful response they desired and, quite frankly, needed in order to budge the university's administration. It was so urgent for, at this stage, the question of what exactly they were going to do had not yet been decided.

Whether the formal letter to the other on-campus organizations ever materialized, it would soon prove inconsequential as outreach took other more organic and spontaneous forms. The leadership and rank and file of

Black Nia F.O.R.C.E transformed campus spaces into incubators for the protest. Unofficial meetings took place in informal settings, such as dorm rooms, hallways, and the cafeteria. And it was perhaps in these moments where ideas that would eventuate in the "plan" began to emerge.

There was also the possibility that students in these discussions had been made aware of the immediate preceding protest actions on Charter Day. It had happened twice thus far in the decade: the disruption of the proceedings in 1983 to denounce the university's expulsion of *Hilltop* editor Janice McKnight and the picket line calling for the Afro-American Studies course requirement in 1986, organized by Black United Youth's Todd Shaw and the Afro-American Studies Push Collective.[25] And even if no one knew of these immediate Charter Day protest precedents, there would have been some who would have been told of the 1968 Charter Day protest and subsequent takeover of the Administration Building through their parents, institutional memory in the form of faculty and staff, and the previous year's mock protest led by HUSA to historicize the event.[26] Therefore Baraka's recommendation the previous Friday was not one that was devoid of historical memory. The question was not *if* something would be done on Charter Day but what form it would take, what sort of protest would be deployed.

While the members of the executive committee focused on campus outreach, the base of the organization—the freshman class of fall 1986— began to meet simultaneously and secretly to forge a plan. A group of twelve men, led by Baraka, had secured the floor plan of the Administration Building (A-Building) from a sympathetic source. Under the cover of night on the loading dock of the School of Engineering, they met to discuss what taking control of the building might look like.[27] The idea of an occupation was risky, given the many possibilities that could ensue in response. But the reality was that this option continued to provide the most drastic means for addressing an issue that the university seemed unwilling to debate or discuss.

According to BNF member Jam Shakwi, the plans for what eventually became the Charter Day protest were hatched in these talks, as was the preparation for the subsequent takeover of the A-Building. Shakwi, a sophomore from New York, was part of a group of men and women who had been consistently training and learning how to execute security and self-defense functions. It was a role that fit him well. An athlete,

Shakwi had performed similar functions as a roadie with various hip hop groups prior to coming to Howard as a student. Shaped and formed in the crucible of the Bronx of the 1980s, he had also acquired the sort of sensibility that made moving with purposeful and considered force and aggression more natural than not. By the time he joined BNF this special set of skills and the attendant sensibilities they required found a place in the struggle.[28]

Black Nia F.O.R.C.E members who had provided security for Public Enemy a year and a half earlier worked to develop an organized security wing that was responsible for instilling order for events and for providing defense and protection for the group's leadership. Their paramilitary training included Saturday morning workouts that featured obstacle courses at neighboring parks, where members like Shakwi, Sergeant at Arms Darnell Dinkins, Women's Minister of Defense Makita Shabazz, and Men's Minister of Defense Louis Camphor would prepare the organization for executing effective security and countermeasures for protection.[29] This was also the foundation of the organization's drilling practices, a feature of their influence, and direct contact with the Fruit of Islam. As such, both tactically and physically, they were prepared to engage in an operation like a takeover. The only question was whether the strategy of occupation would be agreed upon by all, whether it was indeed time for such an action.

In the meantime, another speakout featuring Ras Baraka was planned for that Wednesday, where he urged students to understand the nature of Atwater's politics and its threat to their conception of the university. With attendance at these speakouts growing, the ongoing outreach efforts began to show results. The following day, a major meeting took place in Douglass 116, where a list of demands was drafted. After a long night of discussions in which the demands were settled, an agreed-upon action was in place. Or so it appeared.[30]

While it was not yet a finished product, BNF formed, along with three other groups—the student National Association for the Advancement of Colored People (NAACP) chapter, HUSA, and PSM—a group that would soon bear the name Coalition of Concerned Howard University Students.[31] At the front of this group were April Silver and Sheri Warren from BNF, who were spokesperson and organizer, respectively. They were joined by Swaby, HUSA Vice President Robert Turner, and Zenobia White, the head of the NAACP. Rounding out the group, which eventually participated in negotiations with the administration, were BNF members including William Simms and Cody Coleman; strong supporters Michael Lewis and Van Johnson; a cadre of students who represented the other constituent organizations; and organizers like David Porter and Anthony Joseph, who had opposed Swaby and Turner in the previous year's HUSA election.

If the objective had been campus-wide collaboration, then by Thursday night it had been achieved. Black Nia F.O.R.C.E had reached its goal of making the action broadly representative of the student body, forging a unity that had heretofore been difficult to imagine. While there were many students who continued to harbor reservations and outright condemnation of what was to come, and while not everyone who agreed on action agreed on tactics and strategy, the meetings that led up to Charter Day were enough to develop a coalition that would prove to be effective. It is likely that without this effort, the protest might not have occurred or been as effective as it was. In that sense, the mission of every progressive force from the Nonviolent Action Group to Christopher Cathcart and Manotti Jenkins's HUSA strategy was once again realized through BNF's organizing—a large segment of the student body had been brought to the precipice of action.

The Demands

The grievances of the students—by now, including students who were not yet (or not going to be) formal members of BNF—were collected in a document that would soon be presented to the administration.[32] The seven demands in this document were strenuously debated and perhaps represented a strategy of galvanizing students who were less concerned about Atwater's appointment (addressed in the seventh demand) or did not understand its possible dangers. While Atwater was a clear issue for progressive students on campus, six other demands may have helped generate the attention of students still on the fence, as they represented issues that clearly concerned questions of Howard student life and the direction of the university. The organizers of what would become the Coalition were also very clear that the question of Atwater's appointment and these other on-campus issues were fundamentally related. They were two sides of the same coin, evidence of Howard's failure to provide an optimal on-campus experience for the majority of its students. A flyer disseminated during the protest argued that "the appointment of Lee Atwater to the Board of Trustees is indicative of a lack of Afrocentric consciousness and vision prevalent throughout the administration." This generated a set of concerns about Howard's ability to meet "the needs of the students and African people world-wide."[33] It was, in other words, an attempt to call again for the remaking of Howard into a Black university. But now it would be the hip hop generation's chance to frame that meaning.

No doubt inspired by their reading of scholars like Zak Kondo, the first demand was for the "promotion of a more Afro-centric curriculum by building up the African-American studies department through the recruitment of noted and respected scholars, and increased funds to the department." In accordance with this demand, the students contended that "the establishment of an African-American studies graduate program" would "strengthen and legitimize the department."[34] This demand, of course, placed the 1989 organizers squarely within the Howard tradition of student engagement and, quite frankly, the larger history of Black student activism. Black Studies was the basis and foundation for the very convulsions of the university that have occurred in the past few decades, a transformation that remained, by the late 1980s, compromised by a range of factors and today remains undone.[35] On this question, Silver, when she was profiled in *Black Networking News*, argued that, "with Afro-centric teaching, people would have a greater sense of self. . . . For example, Shakespeare or Chaucer are required in the English Department. Why not [Zora Neale] Hurston or [James] Baldwin? We need must-take courses on Kwame Nkrumah, on what Kwanzaa means, on Malcolm X. If these were mandatory, structurally set programs, then Howard would truly be a Black institution and Afro-centric."[36]

Black Nia F.O.R.C.E members were aware of the emergence of Afrocentricity as a conceptual project in the work of Molefi Kete Asante owing to the presence of his work on their reading lists. But what further inspired this demand was the desire for Howard University to create this sort of curricula for the university, directly benefiting from the unique perspectives generated at the Mecca of Black education.[37] A year prior to the protest, the founding of the first doctoral program in the discipline at Temple University set the stage for a unique opportunity for Howard to contribute to the cultivation of the idea of Black Studies by establishing its own program. In many ways, given the sort of faculty who were still present at Howard, many of them products of the "Black university" and Black Studies movements of the 1960s, that opportunity, they felt, could have immediately shaped the evolution of the discipline in generative ways.[38]

The second demand was for Howard to "establish a university wide program that would allow students to receive academic credit for community service. This will stimulate our involvement and interaction in the community."[39] This was both connected to the mission of Black Studies and a key cog in the practice of BNF as evidenced by its already established initiatives that provided tutoring services in the surrounding DC community. Further, the connection that Howard students forged with the community was critical to the nationalist consciousness that stood at center of the protest. There was the need not only to relate to the community as service providers, but also to relate as co-workers in the formation of a Black collective identity that would translate into better lives for both parties. The idea of receiving credit for community service was not new to the academy then, and it would become more prominent in the decades after the protest.[40]

The third and fourth demands were tied to the financial situations faced by Howard students. These were, of course, complicated by a range of factors, including a decade of stagnant and then declining federal student support for higher education. The simultaneous tuition increases and declining state aid, which over the next few decades would cripple the student aid system, precipitated a crisis that continues to persist. For Black students, this would have doubly jeopardized their abilities to afford a higher education given the assault economically on Black communities.[41] The average Howard student—despite many of the stereotypical associations with the Black bourgeoisie—was simply not flush with cash, and many of them actually extended their matriculation for two or three additional years, solely for financial reasons.[42]

In order to compete with the market-oriented shifts dominating the higher education landscape, private institutions also began to increase their tuition. Howard was following the trend. Perhaps it was also the case that the university, recognizing this, saw an opportunity to address its cash flow needs by gesturing toward figures like Atwater, who might be situated in spaces to help alleviate some of this pain. This would have been in line with the university's earlier engagements with the Reagan administration. It was interesting, to say that least, that, despite such financial peril, protesting students *still* could not countenance the move to embrace Atwater, whether his appointment to the board of trustees was a stroke of strategic genius on the administration's part or something more sinister. The students did not trust that the quality of life on campus would be resolved by what they saw as tainted funds. Moreover, the demand also included the issue of human resources; what had made the issue more difficult was the treatment of students by the staff in the financial aid office. The third demand read: "Effective changes in the financial aid process: a. Increase in financial aid staff to facilitate the processing of student aid. b. Decentralize the financial process (separate graduate and undergraduate processing centers). c. Improve the treatment students receive in the financial aid office (hostile attitudes). d. Complete and process all loan applications by a stated deadline." In an effort to stem the rising costs of attendance, the fourth demand made stated that Howard should "strike out the proposed 15% tuition increase."[43]

Another quality-of-life issue that was acutely felt among Howard students was life in the residence halls. In the university's housing there were issues surrounding safety, infestations of various pests and vermin, the breakdown of elevators, and other related issues with the physical plant that caused an enormous strain on students. Howard's dormitories, like the Harriet Tubman Quadrangle and Charles Drew Hall, were decades old by 1989. While many of the students involved in organizing the protest lived in repurposed buildings off-campus like Sutton, Eton, and Meridian Hill Halls, the general quality of life in these buildings left much to be desired as well. Noting the problems with the water quality and security in the dormitories, Silver remarked, "I'm not saying we should live in houses on the hill. But we need to live in environments that are conducive to studying."[44] With the erection of the Howard Plaza Towers beginning in 1988, there was some indication that things were beginning to look up, but perhaps this was too little, too late, as they were initially geared and targeted toward graduate students. As an issue that all Howard students could relate to, the fifth demand called for "guaranteed improvement in the general maintenance of Howard University Housing."[45]

The last of the collection of demands that intended to improve campus life was centered on the safety and security of students. It is necessary to view this particular demand—that Howard "enhance the effectiveness of security" by increasing "the number of officers" and their "wages"—as part of the general attempt to build and fortify community not only with those who were off-campus but also with the officers themselves.[46] The second demand—"Establish a university wide program that would allow students to receive academic credit for community service"—was designed to break down the barriers between the university community and the wider DC community. In some cases—for instance, seeing students as targets for crimes of opportunity—the need for the sixth demand—"Enhance the effectiveness of security"—was a consequence of the desires underpinning the second. While there were adversarial moments in BNF's relationship with campus police, it was more consistently a relationship that generated respectful engagement. Going back to the fall semester of 1986, these relationships were cultivated in the wake of the violent confrontations with DC residents that freshmen men often faced on campus and in the surrounding community. Further, BNF men often interfaced with the campus police as they performed security functions on campus themselves. They could identify with their challenges as well, many feeling that they were unfairly treated by the university along with many other staff members. As a consequence, campus police gave the student protestors quiet support.[47]

Finally, the language around the chief issue—the seventh demand—read: "The immediate removal of Harvey Lee Atwater from the Board of Trustees of Howard University because his interests are not consistent with the mission of Howard University."[48] It is necessary to pause and consider what "mission" could mean here. The September 1988 revision of the mission of the University declared that it sought "to provide an educational experience of exceptional quality to students of high academic potential with particular emphasis upon the provision of educational opportunities to promising black students" in a collective quest "for solutions to human social problems in the United States and throughout the world."[49] But could this be read in multiple ways? Any consensus around this question would be achieved only through direct engagement, but would the university be willing to listen to students?

HU STUDENT DEMANDS

We the students of Howard University demand a more accountable administration which will support a more Afro-centric curriculum. In addtition, we demand an administration that identifies completely with our concerns!

In an effort to bring about the above changes, we submit the following demands:

1. Promotion of a more Afro-centric curriculum by building up the African-American studies department through the recruitment of noted and respected scholars, and increased funds to the department.

    a. The establishment of an African-American studies graduate program. This program will help strengthen and legitimize the department.

2. Establish a university wide program that would allow students to receive academic credit for community service. This will stimulate our involvement and interaction in the community.

3. Effective changes in the financial aid process:

    a. Increase in financial aid staff to facilitate the processing of student aid.

    b. Decentralize the financial process (separate graduate and undergraduate processing centers)

    c. Improve the treatment students receive in the financial aid office (hostile attitudes).

    d. Complete and process all loan applications by a stated deadline.

4. Strike out the proposed 15% tuition increase.

5. Guaranteed improvement in the general maintenance of Howard University Housing.

6. Enhance the effectiveness of security: increase the number of officers, and increase their wages.

7. The immediate removal of Harvey Lee Atwater from the Board of Trustees of Howard University because his interests are not consistent with the mission of Howard University.

NOW IS THE TIME!

Figure 5.1. "HU Student Demands," March 3, 1989. April Silver Collection, private collection.

The Direct Action

On Friday morning, March 3, *The Hilltop* ran a story announcing the plan of action. Whether it was purposeful misdirection or lack of coordination between those responsible for media engagement, the story only gave notice of a scheduled sit-in at the Charter Day Convocation later that morning.[50] But V. Jimale Ridgeway, a transfer student from Buffalo, New York, remembers that there were simultaneously different plans for what exactly was going to happen. The previous school year, she had transferred to Howard from Niagara University after attending Howard's homecoming festivities. Also inspired by the depictions of life at historically Black colleges and universities (HBCUs) in Spike Lee's *School Daze* (1988),[51] Ridgeway immediately found student activism to be her calling, meeting Haqq Islam and organizing with the AFL-CIO's student group before finally finding Black Nia F.O.R.C.E. She recalls that the direct action was to encompass three components: an outside protest, a sit-in, and finally, a takeover. While Sheri Warren remembers that she and Silver were not previously apprised of the final component, that climatic ending would not have been a shock.[52] Perhaps riffing upon the cultural motifs of BNF's "Jazz and Poetry" night, the revolt was both planned and improvised.

The Charter Day Convocation at Howard is a formal occasion, replete with university ritual and regalia. European classical music punctures the air, and the pretense of an almost ecclesiastical sense of purpose and direction come together to mark the moment of remembrance of the university's founding and the recalibration of its mission. After and underneath the processions, speeches, declarations, and singing of alma mater is togetherness, a sociality bound by "Truth and Service," the university motto created by the former dean Kelly Miller in 1910, that itself inaugurated a "new Howard."[53] These rituals produce a reckoning with, and embrace of, a nostalgia marking the ceremony as a near-sacred event.[54]

But this also explains why it was so often chosen as a site of protest. The dissonance would be too difficult to misrecognize. The gap between nostalgia and reality required that a light be shone. As the choir took its place, preparing to again sound the ritual remembrance, the dissonance between their planned song and the Public Enemy–inspired Black students provided a sharp metaphor for what was to come. Twenty years prior, it would have been framed as the removal of the Negro and the birth of Black folk. Alas, student protest is a cycle.

But the plans for a takeover of this Charter Day had one noticeable hitch. One of Black America's most identifiable and respected figures was to deliver that year's Charter Day address. William "Bill" Cosby's televisual art had been for the 1980s Black elite, a sort of model for how to generate a measure of cultural autonomy while also gesturing for and desiring inclusion and equality into the American national project. Cosby's politics, however, never required any real disruption or challenge to the prevailing ethos of American universalism and its attendant racial logics (something many members of BNF would in time come to know). Despite these contradictions, for the vast majority of the Howard community, it was an honor to have Cosby address the university.

This was the height of *The Cosby Show*, a television show that embodied the aspiration of a sizable segment of the Howard University student body.[55] It was a dream of social mobility in an age of extreme social dislocation, or the American dream in Blackface. And to boot, it starred Howard graduate Phylicia Rashad as Clair Huxtable and demonstrated through positive images of a Black family that had made it that America could also be ours. It was a fictional story that became real and possible in the imagination of those who accepted this Blackened version of American exceptionalism. Although it was perhaps an exercise in political delusion, even those who rejected the pretensions and elitism that shrouded its message might have found much to identify with in certain portions of the show and its attempt to cleave together an ideal.[56] Moreover, BNF members knew Howard student Carl Anthony Payne, the actor who portrayed Cockroach, on the sitcom. For Rich Byers, the connection to Cosby came even earlier than the famous show: "Bill was in my favorite movie, *Let's Do It Again*, and before I'd discovered Richard Pryor, you couldn't have told me that anything was funnier than the album *More of the Best of Bill Cosby*."[57]

There was also, of course, much for Black college students to identify with in its spin-off, *A Different World*, then in its critical second season.[58] This show was experiencing a shift in direction led by Debbie Allen, also a Howard graduate and Rashad's sister, who, unlike Phylicia, had participated in the 1968 A-Building takeover. Under Allen's direction, *A Different World* directly challenged normative understandings of what college education looked like, creating a near-authentic depiction of HBCU life that found deep resonance with Black viewers.[59] There was the danger of losing support, then, for those who did not want to spoil Cosby's appearance, and there may have been many more who felt that a donation the size of his recent gift to Spelman College was imminent and thus would be in jeopardy.[60]

All of this was discussed in the Thursday night meeting in Douglass 116. And all agreed that the messaging was to be clear: This is not about Bill Cosby. Silver remembers that the prevailing feeling was: "We loved Bill Cosby." But they also saw him as a potential ally, as they did not expect him to side with the administration despite the fact that he was their honoree. And even if he did, they also were clear that their issue was more important than his honor—they loved him, but not more than they wanted to transform the university by challenging its embrace of what Baraka had begun to call "Atwaterism."[61]

That morning, as BNF members and the broader body of committed students made their way to Cramton Auditorium, the site of the Charter Day ceremony, there was a mixture of nervous tension and anticipation for what was for many of them their first direct action. One thing was very clear, and that is that there was broad support, with over two thousand students ready and willing to follow the lead of the budding Coalition, and many more besides, like the medical, professional, and graduate students who showed up and supported the action in their own ways.

Arriving at 10:00 A.M., an hour before the ceremony was to begin, students raised a picket with signs outside declaring, "Just Say No to Atwater," "Get Off the Phone, Process Our Loans," "Bill, We Love You but the Truth Must Be Known," and "How Far Will Howard Go for a $?" Then they brought the picket closer to the doors, where they began to sing and chant, "No to Atwater, Not the Man but the Issues." As the level of energy rose, the singing and chanting foregrounded a move into the lobby as soon as the doors were opened to let attendees into the ceremony. At the beginning, only a few BNF members entered, but eventually the lobby was filled, as many of the men who had originally founded BNF led. From the lobby, they made their way into the auditorium itself. And this is what created a groundswell of momentum that was simultaneously fortified by the freedom songs that they borrowed from earlier struggles and the chants that they had updated for this one. There in the crowd, April Silver and Ras Baraka would address the students who began to fill the space. On her role, Silver stated shortly after the protest that the leaders "were microphones. We were servants of the students. . . . It was not about egotism or individualism."[62] Silver, Baraka, and the others who articulated the issues of the students would follow as much as they led.

By about 10:40 A.M., the sit-in had begun in earnest. All fifteen hundred seats in Cramton Auditorium were filled with students, with many more standing in the aisles.[63] While some stood, some sat, and some waited for the ceremony to begin, the dominant influences in those moments were those who knew that a forceful response would be necessary. They continued to sing. They continued to chant. And then it began with a signal. The plans had changed—or the true plan had been called into action. This year, the Charter Day ritual was not to be. At that signal, members of BNF and others, who Shawn Houston labeled "go-guys," people who were only called upon only when "you['re] ready to go," bodied the campus security guards, preventing them from intervening in what was to happen next. The target was the stage, where the dignitaries had taken their positions. Everything was its in prim and proper place, and then it was subverted. Rich Byers remembers moments of sheer chaos: "Kids were running and screaming everywhere. There was actual violence. Things were crashing onstage and people were being pushed." In his description, he even used the word "riot."[64] Whether things rose to that level or not, the dichotomy between what Charter Day represented and the business that these students came to handle was sharp. As Cosby sought to intervene and address what may have appeared to him as pandemonium, Silver, who moved next to him, calmly whispered in his ear, "Mr. Cosby, we respect you, but you're going to have to leave the stage."[65] From there, Silver's personal security detail escorted her to the podium.[66]

Silver's ascent to the podium displaced Cosby's, both literally and symbolically. Thrust into the spotlight, Silver's leadership was put to the test. It was also to be her first major speech to the campus community. This was a role the previous executive minister Baraka relished and in which he throve, but it was one that did not come as naturally to Silver. Although nervous, she was cool, for it was a nervousness that was not paralytic. It was a large undertaking, but Silver remained composed largely because she "trusted the research that we had done. I trusted the role of the organization. I trusted that this was a moment in time. I trusted that we were guided, that we were guided in a very serious way."[67] As she took over the stage, she calmly stated: "This is our convocation. We are not letting things like Atwater on the board define this university. We are not stopping until Atwater is off the board." She continued, "This is our convocation. When we know what we have to do, nothing can stop us." Anticipating the concerns that might emerge about disrupting Cosby, she stated, "We are not here to protest Dr. Bill Cosby. We love him, we will let him speak, but we have to make sure that you understand we are taking control of this." She continued: "The university exists for the students, not the other way around. This is step A; we're not stopping until Atwater is off the board."[68] In those words, Silver beautifully captured the spirit of the student's concerns while also intimating that there were other plans that might be afoot.

In these moments, as the energy began to rise, those students who had not been privy to the plans to take over the ceremony were alerted that something bigger was on the horizon. A freshman student from Long Island named Akanke Washington—who was not yet a member of Black Nia F.O.R.C.E but who certainly on the way to playing a prominent role in the organization—remembers that, as Silver was escorted to the microphone, the room was engulfed in the intense spontaneity of the moment: "I thought we were gonna have some signs, walk in a circle outside of Cramton and be like, 'No, no, no.'" As things escalated, she and others were quite literally ushered into a moment of decision of whether to stay or go. "At some point it was just movement. . . . I don't know who was at the front that said, 'We're gonna just go.' But at some point it was just movement. . . . I just know the crowd went that way and I [also] went that way." As the stage was being taken, Silver was joined by one hundred students or so on the platform. It was a tense moment, as few knew what was to come, and many who were not aware of any plans to take over Charter Day were confused. Yet, as Washington indicated, they still moved: "I never doubted that I was gonna do whatever Nia Force laid out."[69]

One could of course read this as a "follow the leader" moment—and that it was. But as the popular saying within BNF went: "Force equals mass times acceleration. [We] want to be the force to accelerate the masses."[70] For Washington, it was a cautious following, as those moments of spontaneity and unity "didn't erase questions."[71] Yet this trust also might have emanated from a resolve that was ultimately more than a thoughtless following of individual, charismatic identities. While there were many who simply moved because the crowd moved, that movement also was called into being by a dialectical relationship between mover and moved, rather than simply a hierarchal one. It was a leadership that was ordained and summoned by the very followership it inculcated, by the spirit force to which it was beholden. And they were all destined to see what the end would be.

Although the moment became too fluid to actually allow him to speak, Cosby's reaction to all of this was generally positive. Taking no offense, he conceded the space to students, affirming that protest was their right: "I feel that students have a right to do what they're doing now, to make their statement." On the issue itself, he believed, "Worse demonstrations have been held about lesser causes."[72] As his limousine rode away, he rolled down the window and gave the protesting students a thumbs up.[73]

President James Cheek was less willing to think along these terms. But rather than having the occupying students physically removed, the administration simply canceled convocation and then convened a small ceremony to confer the honorary doctorate in the adjacent Lulu Vere Childers Hall. From there the annual luncheon in honor of the awardees ensued in the nearby Armour J. Blackburn Student Center. Electrified by both Silver's speech and the successful interruption of one of the university's most important events, the momentum of the BNF-led Coalition only grew. As the administration attempted to carry on things as usual, the leadership—followed by a train of one thousand students—led a short march to the Blackburn Center, where they promptly took it over while chanting "We Want Cheek!" Surrounding the luncheon, they demanded an audience. Unnerved and visibly angry with the students, he relented, allowing five of the students to enter. Silver faced him publicly, asserting: "We come in peace, no confrontation. You have to concede to the power of the students." Clearly surprised by the students' insistence and boldness in disrupting the luncheon, Cheek agreed to meet with them in the morning, a solution that Vice President for Student Affairs Carl Anderson helped to facilitate.[74]

In between the meeting and the end of the Friday march, there were moments of potential bedlam. As news cameras descended on campus, unaffiliated students attempted to burn the university's American flag, which flew on the flagpole at the center of the Yard. Kevin Williams and others intervened, warning, "Yo, don't do that. [The] media [is] all around you. You cannot set this flag on fire."[75] But they did replace the flag with the red, black, and green colors of "the African flag of libera-tion," showing the clear nationalist influences that were representative of the protesting students.[76]

There were other lapses in judgment, owing to the very "go-with-the-flow" nature of the day's events.[77] In other words, it would have been very difficult to see whatever order there was in the evolution of events. There was something, however, to be said about the style and posture of BNF and their ability to handle and contain such issues, preventing them from undermining the credibility of the protest in the eyes of the students who would come to participate in the next cycle of events. It was not always so well oiled, but the paramilitary training that they had acquired was now being put to good use.

That night, the regular meeting of BNF went forth. There, Silver con-gratulated everyone for showing up organized and ready to sacrifice for their cause. But it was also clear in that meeting that things were not even close to being over. In their resolve to move forward, members stressed the need to remain orderly, strategic, vigilant, and above all, safe.[78] There was a clear emphasis both on ensuring that responsible and effective leadership of the protest emerged from BNF and on creating the conditions for radical change. And with that, the events of March 3, 1989, came to a close.

The Meeting

At 7:30 A.M. the following morning, members of BNF's security team began to converge upon the A-Building. Once they arrived, the leader-ship of the coalition was escorted into its meeting with the university's administration. Before entering the conference room, they gathered in prayer. And then for six hours they conferred, while outside a picket began to form, taking on much of the character of the previous day's energy.[79] Discussing many of the demands, Cheek and his leadership, as well as Board Chairman John E. Jacob, found them somewhat reasonable. But on the one demand that had guided the entire protest, that of Lee Atwater's removal from the board of trustees, Cheek was unequivocal.[80] He could not be removed. So the students, undeterred, walked out of the A-Building. But their return was imminent.

6

Occupation

I knew what they did in '68, and to me it was just our turn.
That's how I always looked at it. It came full circle. . . . We
were just like them. We were establishing, they had established, that cycle had come. Howard has a tremendous legacy, but our era—it's just lights. It's shine upon shine.
—Tunji Turner[1]

At the convergence of what we could describe as the binary opposition
of the two visions of Howard that has served as somewhat of a theme of
this story was the question of order. If one's vision required that Howard
become the model for a kind of politics of acquiescence to power as the
more enduring practice of survival, then the appropriate tactic for securing that vision was management and control—the endorsement of law
and order. If, however, one's vision required that Howard be something
other than it ever was, if it required that it draw upon a deeper register of
radical potential, then the necessary tactic might require making those
whose job it was to maintain order next to impossible. For it was order
that had to be disrupted to allow for the creation of a new form, a different vision to emerge. What Howard University should be was a battle
between the pragmatic and practical versus the ideal and fantastic, and
it was this sense of struggle that was pressed into the consciousness of
those who would instill order and those who were not cowed by order's
call to cease and desist.[2]

For three days, the Coalition of Concerned Howard University Students and more than three thousand students, led by Black
Nia F.O.R.C.E (BNF), driven by the ideals of earlier struggles, and
inspired by the immediate influences of hip hop and Black nationalism, occupied the Mordecai Wyatt Johnson Administration Building (A-Building) in an attempt to enact their vision, disrupting the
university's order. That they chose a takeover rather than continue to

merely protest is significant. It represented an attempt to claim space that was supposed to be already theirs, space that they felt was being taken from them and utilized for purposes that ran counter to their political interests and spiritual calling. To protest was to beg for consideration, to plead their case. To take over was to seize power and to ensure that what was done in their names reflected *their* vision. If it were a question of whom Howard belonged to, or if there were views in common among differing political beliefs, these would have to be struggled over, rather than assumed. But the takeover signified that this debate, this coming together and struggle over the question of the university's mission, could not include outright racists and racist institutions, for what, after all, could a Black university be if it allowed such figures a seat at the table? And while, yes, there were immediate precedents to A-Building takeovers, it was a tactic that was profoundly risky, as events would soon bear out. Those risks, however, were not greater than what the students felt were *their* ideals, the truer ideals of the Mecca.

Confronting the instantiation of order is never to be taken lightly. The dictates of the settler states in which Africans were forced to labor required systems of enclosure, territorial boundaries that had to be policed, and the United States and its predilection for the protection of private property was the quintessential model for this formation. Occupying ongoing occupation could mean the worse, for Howard was not (yet) liberated space.[3] The challenges that ensued over the three days were the results of these contradictions. What would it mean to imagine that Howard could *be* liberated space—and a force for the liberation of Africans around the world? For the students who took over the A-Building, it meant the potential for harm.

Clearly, the takeover was meant to draw attention to the appointment of Lee Atwater and to prevent it from going forth. But it was also more than this. It had to be. The story of the 1989 A-Building takeover is one that is shaped by, and significantly shaped, a generation of youth who would bring struggles over identity, nation and state, and culture into the last decade of the twentieth century, and in so doing, they would provide a vibrant resistance to the neoliberal status quo.[4] Above all, it was, as April Silver remembered, "a divinely ordered" moment.[5]

Saturday and Sunday

After the lengthy meeting with the administration on Saturday, March 4, BNF leaders met with the core of the organization. Retreating to Douglass 116, they met to debrief and consider what had just occurred. They had learned that the university was unwavering in its belief that Atwater's appointment would stand and that James Cheek and John E. Jacob felt that board membership, in any case, should not be the concern of students.

There was also the appearance that the administration's concern was procedural, rather than ideological. While President Cheek would later come to declaim any involvement in Atwater's selection, his influence as a prominent Republican was in line with the appointment and the GOP's outreach campaign. On the board, the leading Republican was the clergyman and consultant Thaddeus Garrett, a senior advisor to President George H. W. Bush both during his campaign and in his administration as well as on Bush's shortlist for a deputy ambassadorship to the United Nations. It was Garrett who nominated Lee Atwater, with the support of Cheek and all but one dissenter, who feared the university's political independence would be compromised. And it was Garrett who had in the media reports dismissed student concerns and resistance as naïve and out of place.[6] But he was not made available to the students to discuss the ins and outs of the board's thinking. Although it is likely it would not have mattered, hearing the board's side of things, at least, would have given the students the administration's official rationale for Atwater's selection to the board. In any case, BNF members moved to discuss the only thing left to consider: the question of a follow-up action.

It was likely here where the plan of taking over the building—an idea that had been percolating among some members at the secret School of Engineering meetings—was first raised among the entire body. Ras Baraka and many of the men who had participated in the earlier "apathy" discussions, together with the newer leadership of BNF—composed of April Silver and Sheri Warren—quickly agreed that taking over the A-Building should be the follow-up act, and the plan moved forward. There seemed to be little debate about the impropriety of participating in an illegal activity. In fact, the decision was so quickly consummated that it was made in the absence of a group of essential members who had briefly stepped away.

Four members who had played a prominent role in the organization were not present when the decision was made. Two of them were the recently appointed co-ministers of defense Aaron Lloyd and Kevin Williams. The others were one part of the founding triumvirate, Chuck Webb, and key member Russell Carter. After standing outside in formation for the duration of the meeting with the administration, the quartet decided to get a quick bite to eat. In the time that they were gone, they were surprised to learn that everyone (else) had agreed that a takeover was the appropriate action. Kevin Williams, a native of Long Island and member of the freshman class of 1986, Lou Phi, and an original member of BNF, was initially taken aback, as such a decision was made without the influence and input of the ministers of defense: "I just remember being mad at Ras, like, 'Yo, for real?'" While it was a source of perhaps minor frustration, it never became a major issue. More frustrated by the lack of movement from the administration, Williams and the others decided not to break the achieved consensus.[7]

Yet it is important to note that, if members like Williams and Lloyd—who were cognizant of the landscape and systems at Howard and had been training and running security for at least two years, were initially apprehensive about the takeover—it would have taken very little for the average Howard student to experience feelings of doubt and skepticism. Apparently not present at the earlier secret meetings, they did not have the same amount of time to mull over the risks. Lloyd remembers feeling somewhat uneasy and even asking Carter in the moments before the takeover, "Yo, what if only like fifteen people show up?"[8] So while BNF members were prepared physically and organizationally, which gave them confidence and a deep resolve, these did not fully eliminate moments of hesitance—although the latter, for obvious reasons, was never articulated in public.

Those doubts would be quickly subsumed under the weight of preparation. The first order of business was to address the material needs associated with such a mission. While not everyone thought of other necessities like food, there was widespread focus on securing tools and equipment. A group, including Louis Camphor and Shawn Houston, piled into V. Jimale Ridgeway's car and drove out to Hechinger's hardware store. Armed with Ridgeway's mother's American Express card, they went on a quest to buy chains, locks, and other equipment that they would need to lock down the A-Building. The acquisition of this equipment was part of the plan to develop security and safety strategies for the occupation. Leading in this effort were people like Williams, Lloyd, Camphor, Jam Shakwi, Darnell Dinkins, Makita Shabazz, and others. After buying what they felt would be an adequate amount of equipment to control access to and from the building, they came back to campus to help pass out flyers.[9]

Designed by Michael Lewis, a vital member of the negotiating team, the flyers insisted upon the connection between the array of student demands and the board's decision to appoint Lee Atwater. Interviewed later by the *Washington Post*, Lewis spoke for the group when he stated, "We are prepared to hold the building as long as possible, physically and mentally, until demands are met," and that Atwater was "opposed to the Black agenda."[10] The group was also strategic in another way. As they disseminated the flyers, organizers called on students to meet at 9:00 A.M. only for a rally at the flagpole at the center of campus, a few yards away from the A-Building.[11] While it was perhaps leaked to the administration that a takeover was being planned, they did not want to openly state their intentions or reveal the time that the takeover was going to occur.

There were also personal crises to deal with. Beyond the normal strains and stresses of being a college student—such as the fact that the protest happened during the midterm period—key members experienced both mental and physical setbacks that were significant. Webb had recently lost his grandmother. As BNF was building up its outreach efforts, he was in New Orleans with his family. And there was even a question of whether he would return:

I didn't want to come back. So my mind is gone. My grandfather told me to come back . . . [Later] we're doing some type of test. I remember telling the teacher, I walked into her class. And I told her I wasn't taking it. She said, "Yes, you are." I tore that paper up and walked out. And she promptly failed me. I don't think I went to another class that year. My head was gone.[12]

Why We Don't Want Harvey Lee Atwater (Co-Chairperson of the Republican National Committee) at Howard?

He has consistently opposed the agenda of African People, examples of this are:

I. Opposes Civil Rights Legislation
   A. Civil and Voting Rights Act of 1964-65
   B. Civil Rights Restoration Act
   C. Affirmative Action and Set Asides

II. Opposes the appointment of African-American Judges and endorsed the appointment of Judge Robert Bork.

III. Supports the racist apartheid regime of Azania (South Africa).

IV. Protege of Strom Thurmond, a well know racist Republican Senator of South Carolina.

V. Master-minded the racist use of the Willie Horton issue to exploit and contribute to the rising tide of anti-Black sentiment of American people, which facilitated the election of former klansman David Duke to Louisiana State Legislature.

VI. Lee Atwater's purpose in becoming a member of the Board of Trustees is to strengthen the Republican party by exploiting an increasing economic class division within the Black community.

The appointment of Harvey Lee Atwater to the Board of Trustees is indicative of a larger lack of Afrocentric consciousness and vision prevalent throughout the administration. Previous and ongoing issues that have been overlooked are:

1. Inept processing
   -Financial Aid
   -Housing

2. Security
   -lack of security
   -ineptness
   -low wages

3. Curriculum
   -inclination towards Eurocentricity

Because of the reasons stated above, we demand the immediate removal of Harvey Lee Atwater from the Board of Trustees and the accountability of the administration to the needs of the students and African people world-wide.

Note: This protest is a non-partisan effort by concerned students and there is no disrespect intended towards Dr. William H. Cosby, Jr.

Figure 6.1. "Why We Don't Want Harvey Lee Atwater (Co-Chairperson of the Republican National Committee) at Howard?" April Silver Collection, private collection.

Webb's considerable skills had always been a boon to BNF, so they would be necessary to the success of the protest and a critical loss if he could not be his usual self. While it would have been a difficult undertaking even under normal circumstances, Webb was able to persevere, even though he "felt disconnected from the organizing" of the protest.[13]

Hailing from Long Island, Aaron Lloyd was a fan of hip hop but described himself as politically "naïve." After meeting Baraka and participating in the apathy discussions, he became an early member of BNF. After a year, he was appointed to the position of minister of defense. In the preparation for the takeover, Lloyd worked into the night, helping to identify the pitfalls and dangers BNF needed to avoid in their attempt to take the building. It was a convenient fact that he had previously worked in the A-Building and was aware that they needed to avoid the building's U.S. Post Office since it was technically "federal" property. Lloyd was also central to training defense captains who were in charge of carrying out particular functions, many of which would have arisen in the moment and could not be foreseen. But on Sunday night, he fell sick. Lloyd had sickle cell anemia, and that night he experienced a medical crisis that would hospitalize him the entire length of the takeover. As he lay in Howard University Hospital, he would have to provide support in other ways.[14]

On Sunday night, Silver placed a call to Sonia Sanchez, who reminded her of the long-view political significance of their action. In her conversation, Sanchez prioritized two things. She first emphasized the need to cultivate mass support, walking Silver through methods for achieving that end. Her advice included building positive relationships with the media, political activists, alumni, and faculty who had relationships with the community. While it was clear that many of these figures had quietly supported their actions, Sanchez's role was to place Silver and the students in direct contact with many of them, including Jesse Jackson; 1968 protestors Paula Giddings and Anthony Gittens; Benjamin Chavis, who was then the National Council of Churches vice president; and the attorney Donald Temple.[15] Along with sympathetic faculty like Alvin Thornton, Ronald Walters, Eleanor Traylor, and others, the support of well-known Black leaders would be key, and the group would rely on their ability to shape their message to the outside world.

The second crucial takeaway from this conversation was a reminder about the ultimate integrity of their position. Sanchez offered a kind of fortification and reassurance that they would in fact be on the right side of history in what they were doing, that it was imperative that Howard be what *they*, the students, imagined it to be.[16] She reminded Silver that integrity would always be more important than money. And with that reinforcement and resolve, doubt was on the way to being fully extinguished—in April Silver and in everyone else.

Monday

Made up of four main floors, a ground floor, and a basement, the A-Building is one of the epicenters of Howard University's campus. Built in 1957, the space was to be the new location of the university's administrative offices, which had previously been in Founders Library. Along with housing the offices of the executive suite, it was also the location for human resources, financial aid, registration, and admissions. As the university bureaucracy grew, more and more functions were added, making it even more central to the university's operations. In addition to the post office, it also included a loading dock and was equipped with multiple rooftop access points. All in all, it was a difficult building to secure and hold.

Moreover, recognizing that it was chokepoint for the basic functionality of the administration, the students decided to take it over at a time when critical activities in the academic calendar, such as graduation processing and financial aid, were just getting under way. Symbolically, it was traditionally the source and location of much of the bureaucratic pain that the average Howard student would experience, including the place where the dreaded financial aid interactions took place. For the burgeoning Coalition, it was also the site of the contentious meeting with the administration that ineluctably drove them to action. That they decided to take over the building on a Monday—the beginning of the week, as opposed to the end—was also strategic and critical. It could slow down or stall university procedures, like processing the university's payroll, thus forcing the administration's hand.[17]

At 7:00 A.M. on the morning of Monday, March 6, a group of BNF members who lived in Meridian Hill Hall walked to an Adams Morgan hardware store to pick up additional locks, chains, wire, and rope. It was a sight that must have invited suspicion to anyone who cared to pay attention.[18] Making their way to campus, they were to soon participate in a somewhat elaborate ruse to enter and then occupy the A-Building. The plan called for simultaneous actions that needed to occur for it to work. At about half past 8:00 A.M., a group of no more than fifteen entered the building in stages, feigning legitimate reasons for being in the building. In pantomiming visits to the financial aid office, their ruse perhaps unwittingly traded in irony.[19]

Outside, Ridgeway drove up 6th Street and parked her car directly in front of the building. Around 9:00 A.M., she walked to the main entrance and sought the help of the security guard on duty. Claiming that she had locked her keys in the car, she pleaded with him for help. Knowing that a stalled car at that location and at that time on campus would probably cause a headache, he fell for the "damsel in distress" routine and followed her to help. At that cue, the men locked down the front door with their locks and chains.[20] Throughout the building, they began to evict the staff—there were no administrators present in the building, and Cheek's absence was, of course, expected. Being careful not to appear as though they were holding anyone hostage, they simply let it be known that they were intending to take over the building and that the staff could stay or leave, but if staff chose to stay, they would be subject to the terms of the students. After seeing the equipment that the students began to pull out of their large bags, many of the staff decided that the students were serious and began to exit. After they left, BNF security disabled the communications apparatus and the systems that were in place in the staff offices by pulling telephones from the walls and unplugging computers.[21]

With the rally set to begin a few minutes later at the flagpole, students had begun to commandeer the building. Although campus police quickly removed the locks, they did not attempt to stop the students. With the exception of the outdoor entrance to the post office, which was being guarded by the university's security, the students oversaw all possible points of entry.[22] Whether it was a planned or not, the fact that campus police also chose this Monday to engage in a sick-out effectively smoothed the way to an occupation.[23]

Because of the freezing rain, the rally, which included an estimated one thousand students, was moved from the flagpole into the Armour

J. Blackburn Student Center. After the leadership gave them a rudimentary set of guidelines and training in nonviolent tactics, they marched from the student center into the A-Building, some of them carrying food they liberated from the Blackburn Center Cafeteria. While only a few hundred students actually entered the building at that time, as morning turned to afternoon, more and more would join. They were carefully screened—their bags and belongings were checked, and measures were taken to allow them to enter in thirty-minute intervals, but only with a student ID. By midmorning the students were in complete control of the building, and they hunkered down, while the organizers developed a plan of action until their demands were met.[24]

The command center of the organizers was set up on the west side of the building on the second floor. There Williams, Webb, Shakwi, Dinkins, Shabazz, and others handled the difficult issues regarding security that inevitably arose. It was a fluid moment, so there was much to decide and handle. As more students filed in, they decided to place internal controls and restricted movement to certain locations to student organizers only.[25] Their passcode was "The White Man Is Still in Charge," a humorous phrase that nevertheless represented a serious critique.[26]

The most pressing task of the security committee was to develop a system to maintain control of all points of entry. All entrances and exits into the building were assigned to BNF members, who, as discussed, had already acquired much experience working security. To man the roof, the committee assigned a group of men who were a mixture of core BNF members and others who were close friends of that group. They would become known as the "Rooftop Posse." And in many ways, they constituted the first line of defense.[27]

There were other committees that had to get to work swiftly. The most basic of needs was food. How would students who were themselves experiencing difficulty making ends meet provide food for an unknown quantity of students participating in an unauthorized activity? While there was some indication that there were plans for dealing with this by converting an area of nearby Douglass Hall into a food bank, by Monday there was not much follow-through.[28] The only sources of food was that which was brought in by students from the cafeteria, as well as from restaurants like Brown Rice, which had previously agreed to help. Chernee Johnson, the student in charge of the food committee, told *The Hilltop* that there was support from other local food chains, but as they entered, it was unclear if there would be enough to go around. Food taken from the cafeteria and the reliance on business donations were sources that could not effectively feed the numbers of students who would join the takeover. As the hours turned into days, the committee, which would grow to include all other forms of hospitality and care, would have to adjust and adapt quickly to accommodate a growing number of protestors.[29]

The leadership also decided to hold information sessions to educate students who were not fully aware of the details of Lee Atwater's politics. These sessions were held constantly throughout the occupation and were particularly important in educating students who might have been drawn to the protest out of curiosity or for other reasons.[30] It was also important to give students a sense of the risks involved in participating. Early on in the occupation, a student from Howard's School of Law gave a brief presentation on what might happen if the police came to arrest them. According to Williams, it did not have the intended effect. In fact, it spooked students who had had previous brushes with the law, knowing that they could be held if they had outstanding warrants or other issues. As a result, a few of them left.[31]

The leadership also decided to convene a committee that was in charge of entertainment. The idea here was to ensure that protesting students remained in high spirits. Fortunately, BNF was an organization of artists, so poetry, spoken word, and rap ciphers became the immediate go-to for this committee. Those who did not have original content recited poetry from luminaries like Langston Hughes. Rich Byers remembers performing a comedy routine: "I'd even taken the stage as part of one evening's entertainment, doing a skit I'd done many times before at Carver Hall where I riffed on Richard Pryor's preacher character, calling myself Reverend Cleveland Washington, parting my High Top down the middle and demanding donations."[32] In addition to the performance art, there were painters who displayed their artwork throughout the hallways. When not attending performances, the students brought games, televisions, and even toys; they were essentially having a good time. The temperature outside was chilly, but inside there was warmth, both physically and socially, that drew people together at least temporarily. The protest generated a camaraderie that was sorely needed, as it was in short supply owing to on-campus rivalries of many sorts.[33]

Another crucial committee was media relations. Many journalists, including some who the leadership had previously identified as sympathetic, had generated great interest in the protest with their initial reports on the Charter Day action. The combination of national figures like Bill Cosby, Lee Atwater, as well as others, naturally drew national interest to the story. The concern for the Coalition would be to ensure that the right message was getting out. Ras Baraka, who strategically declined to be the spokesperson for the protest at the negotiating table, was often present, providing rhetorical ballast to the protest via television and radio as well as to the print media. Baraka's voice was critical. Among the themes he tried to emphasize at the outset was that the protest was not aimed at a single man but at the systemic structures that his racist attitudes enabled as well as the question of the university's integrity: "We are here to oppose Lee Atwaterism. It is not the man Lee Atwater, but the ideology he represents."[34] Echoing those who had associated Cheek's and the board's overture to Atwater with prostitution, he declared: "This is not a brothel. The president of our school does not have to stoop to get government money like this."[35]

Baraka effectively countered some of the negative portrayals of the protest by other students, including those who were in charge of the on-campus Republican Club. The clarity he provided in articulating BNF and the Coalition's position cannot be underestimated, especially to a national media that was prone to seeing the university's appointment of Atwater as rational. Other members of the broad coalition that spoke to media included Silver, as well as Lewis, Garfield Swaby, and William Simms.

The most prominent and consequential of the media attention generated by the protest came from Cathy Hughes's WOL Radio. She promptly informed the local Black Washington, DC, community and surrounding area with news about what was happening on campus. She then graciously extended her airwaves to the protestors and provided round-the-clock coverage of the events. In so doing, Hughes's broadcasts essentially solved the food problem. Hosting an on-air drive that called for donations of food and supplies to the students, Hughes's intervention drew attention to the urgent shortfall the students would soon experience unless the community stepped in. Heeding the message, they responded in kind.

Meanwhile, classes went on, which meant also that midterm season continued. Some students created makeshift study halls and ensured that they kept up with their assignments and student obligations. Study was not disavowed, nor was it used an excuse to limit participation in the movement. A critical number of faculty members who supported the students were willing to sacrifice class time for the cause.[36] Joseph Jordan, an activist and professor in the Department of Social Sciences, who saw the era as a vibrant time in which students were inspired to be "enlightened radicals," was shocked to see his class was full. As he walked into his lecture room, he asked them, "How come y'all ain't out there?" Their response was, "You mean we can go?" He then responded, "If you gotta ask, you ain't rebelling."[37] That was, of course, the reaction of professors tied to the College of Liberal Arts. In some of the more professional schools, the responses were different. In the School of Business, for instance, some professors gave pop quizzes as a means to keep their students from becoming involved and to punish those who did.[38] As the days went on, some classes would grind to a halt, although the university never officially closed. On Wednesday, the protestors would call for a general strike of classes. But that was a long way away.

By Monday afternoon, the administration was weighing its options. In order to restore the A-Building to functionality, it relied on the law. The building was, after all, part of a private institution that had been illegally commandeered. Thinking themselves on firm legal ground, that evening university officials secured a restraining order that effectively empowered the city to enforce the removal of the students from the premises.[39] Assuming that the students would have no representation, the university used intermediaries to notify them of the restraining order. At 10:00 P.M., an "alumnus and attorney John Garvey, announced that the university's lawyers had placed a restraining order on the building which would go into effect an hour later." Garvey then repeated the warning about students who had had prior brushes with the law. A few students left, fearful of the repercussions.[40] Cheek's tactic might have also proven true one of the critiques that had been launched toward him at that time—that he was out of touch with the students. It is clear that he believed that the students would simply concede once they were notified of the injunction. It is also telling that at this point he chose not to directly communicate with the students. Perhaps he had heard enough on Saturday. But what the decision to involve the courts and the legal system also indicated was his lack of willingness or desire to take the students seriously, even as they had shown how far they were willing to go. The decision would prove to be dangerous and detrimental to his legacy.

That night, as scores of students entered for the first time, the rumblings began to filter in about a possible police raid. Interestingly, those reports were initially dismissed as scare tactics that the administration was employing to get them to surrender. But increasingly, they would be taken seriously. A plainclothes campus police officer had even breached the security. Making her way to the security team, she informed them of who she was and why she was there. She had heard that a raid was imminent and had come to retrieve her son, a student who was participating in the protest. This, of course, aroused suspicion, and Williams declined to allow her access to other parts of the building, thinking she could also be informing on them. In a bit of paranoia, others created a makeshift blindfold and marched her through before quickly being told to remove it lest any cameras caught such a picture. Fortunately, it was concluded that she posed no threat and that she was legitimately concerned for the safety of her son.[41] At 11:00 P.M., when no police officers showed up to eject them, the protestors felt a sense of relief. Around eight hundred students spent the night inside.[42]

Tuesday

And then everyone woke up from that first night to the sound of helicopters, inaugurating perhaps the most significant day of the takeover. The leadership was alerted to their presence by the Rooftop Posse, and greeted the the second day with a level of apprehension that was thick. If the rumors were true—and the helicopters were evidence that they indeed might be—then the leadership found itself wholly unprepared for an adequate response. The Rooftop Posse, a motley crew of BNF members and supporters, was the first line of defense. On the roof during the protest were Matt Middleton, Sean "Puff" Combs, Akil Kamau, Rob "Brother" Wright, Kamal Harris, Oscar Solis, Bo Martin, Darrell Clark, Eric Trapp, and Deric "D-Dot" Angelettie. Together they made plans to defend the building from a siege from above. They were also critical in providing watch, as they could see better than everyone else not only the helicopters but also the police maneuverings, command stations, and paddy wagons stationed down the street, awaiting them.[43]

Inside, the security team had assembled all of the strongest men together to try and defend themselves from a siege from the ground. The football team that had been recruited by Baraka and others to join the protest would be used strategically to secure the internal doors to the hallways. Over the course of the day, upward of one thousand students— many rejoining the fray and most coming for the first time were situated in these hallways. As the campus police came later that morning to prevent others from joining, many hoisted themselves up into the building through the windows.[44] The numbers were rising even as things were appearing to get very dangerous.

That morning there were also truckloads of food that had appeared on 6th Street. In response to Cathy Hughes's call, the community showed up in force. Interviewed by the *Washington Post*, A. B. Mann, a construction worker, was moved by the actions of the protest and stated that "we got to help these kids. Hey, listen, I got a union card. If you're standing up, you're taking a chance. I'm taking the chance. Hell, they might as well have named David Duke or Botha of South Africa to their damn board." When he heard the call on Hughes's show, he loaded his Isuzu station wagon with donations from his neighborhood of "blankets, sheets, pillowcases, tubes of toothpaste, cases of soda, loaves of bread, and copies of the morning paper" and made his way from suburban Maryland to Howard University. After delivering his first load, he went on several additional runs to supply the students, who used ropes and pulleys to lift them into the building. Aarian Pope, Tessa Murphy, and others created a system for distribution that was located in the basement of the building. The donations were overwhelming. Pope remembers that, by the end of the occupation, community members had been moved to donate enough supplies to sustain them for an additional week or two.[45]

Akanke Washington was moved as well. She recalled the depth of feeling that overcame her when she saw half-filled jars of peanut butter and feminine products among the items that had been donated. To her mind, it signified that people were sacrificing what little they might have had to their cause and their movement. She recalls:

The community was donating. And this also warmed my heart. Because when I came to DC, [it] was the murder capital, and there was all of this beef between the campus and the community, and the DC boys was like the block boys, [so] there was all of this beef. And the message really was you should be afraid of the community, and when the community came out in full support and they were donating food, and just the things that were like, half jars of peanut butter, people were giving you whatever they had. They sent tampons. Whatever you needed, they sent everything.[46]

It was a show of support that reinforced the bonds of community among Black people on and off campus. Ultimately, this was what it was all about.

Baraka believed that it was crucial to survive the first night of the takeover in order for them to receive national attention.[47] They did, and the media came. The media trucks lined 6th Street as far the eye could see. Perhaps there was some thinking that, with so many cameras trained on the building, it would stop the police action that was rumored and feared. Only time would tell. Demonstrating the importance of what the takeover represented, national television news shows like Tom Brokaw's *NBC Nightly News* and Dan Rather's *CBS Evening News* had joined the local outlets covering the story. They were joined by the *Washington Post*, the *New York Times*, the wire services, and a host of other print media.

As the cameras focused on the building, other signs of an impending confrontation emerged. Kemry Hughes, DC's deputy mayor for youth services, hurried over to campus to provide assistance. However, when he arrived, he was not allowed in. There was a fear that he, too, was somehow an informant and that he would report back what he had seen. And he did, but not in the way that the students thought. Returning to his office, Hughes pushed the mayor to consider what could be a volatile situation and to do anything he could to defuse it.[48] Fortunately, the mayor at the time was Marion Barry, himself a former student activist with the Student Nonviolent Coordinating Committee (SNCC) and an exemplar of the widespread strategy to stem the conservative response to Black political progress by bringing Black Power into the mayor's office.[49] Hughes knew that Barry would more than sympathize with the Howard students. The issue was: Would his police chief?

This snowy Tuesday was filled with song and chants. When the occupying students read the newspapers that Mann had supplied and saw themselves making the news, they cheered. Garfield Bright, who was known for "always singing," remembered a pledge song he had heard growing up on the campus of Alabama State University, "I Got a Feeling," which utilized a melodic structure similar to the spiritual "Wade in the Water." He then repurposed it, and it became the protest's song: "I got a feeling / I got a feeling / I got a feeling / Atwater snuck in beyond our back / We ain't gonna take no shit like that."[50] It was an important maneuver, and it worked to ensure that spirits were high enough to drown whatever fears had arisen. But as the police cars kept arriving, it was becoming clear that a grave situation was brewing.

The early Saturday morning paramilitary training that every BNF member had had to participate in was thought to be necessary for self-defense and protection. The drilling exercises and marching that they exhibited on the Yard were thought to demonstrate that they had the capacity to organize and move as a unit. However much they trained, it is another thing to actually have to utilize those skills in what could have amounted to a life-or-death situation. This was precisely what was to come on the second day of the takeover.

At around half past noon, the DC police chief Maurice Turner ordered a siege, responding to calls from the university that the students were in violation of the court order. The invasion started with an attempt to land helicopters carrying SWAT teams on the roof, causing the Rooftop Posse to spring into action. They took fire extinguishers to spray the surrounding area, hoping that it would cause incoming officers to slip upon landing. Posse member Matt Middleton remembers that "it was like real messy, I just remember [it] being chaotic and slippery." Since they were in the thralls of a DC winter, the fire extinguisher material got cold rather quickly, making the surface even more slick. Yet this bit of resistance worked, allowing them to retreat inside, temporarily barricading the doors behind them. Middleton recalls that they were "just thinking, like MacGyvers, we were just trying to think of whatever we can think of to prevent them from coming into the A-Building. So it was a combination of being scared and panicked. But it was also a certain level of calmness because it was just about being focused and just being determined 'We not letting this happen.'"[51] The doors were eventually breached. Armed with teargas canisters as well as oil tanks, the SWAT team spread oil on the interior steps, making the staircases impassable.

Forced to retreat, the Rooftop Posse came all the way down the stairs to the main floor, where the students, who had been alerted to the police's presence, waited nervously, hoping that the defenses that they created would hold up. Their plan was to secure the front of the building and main entrance by placing women seated in rows in the vestibule. They supposed that the police would think twice about raiding the building with women situated near the front. Later Williams admitted that this was "a dumb plan" because it relied on the police showing a level of humanity in a situation such as this.[52] In complete disregard of the women's presence, the officers broke the glass doors with their billy clubs, launching flying shards of glass toward the women who were seated with their legs crossed at the door. Fearing the worst, Shawn Houston, the DJ Trouble Trev (John Stevens), and others placed their bodies on the line, covering the women to prevent the glass from causing more damage. Angelettie, another early member of BNF, came down from the roof and urged the students to remain calm and nonviolent, yelling, "We've got to remember Dr. King!"[53] For Jam Shakwi, this was a signature moment of the takeover. He remembers feeling that "that moment is when I fell in love with the fraternity of Black manhood and being a Black man. That moment."[54]

Houston, who was part of the Osage Crew from Philadelphia that joined BNF early on, recalls what made him move toward the women: "I see all them in there crying. . . . I just remember Sheri [Warren] and Akanke's [Washington] face. They was just looking at us. . . . Then you know, I actually thought I was gonna be the target. That's what I was prepared for. I was actually prepared to die there. . . . That was the first time in my life, for something that didn't involve money, or a family member, [but] for an ideal, to be willing to die for it."[55] Washington recalled that "there's just all of this noise. Then the smell. The smell coming down, I thought it was teargas at the time. . . . I thought 'Oh my God. They're sending in teargas.' On TV, it's the teargas first, then it's the bomb. I was just, I was really, really, terrified. And very afraid of what my family was gonna see on television."[56]

As the glass was flying, Shakwi and others returned upstairs to see if the officers were making progress. As they ran full speed ahead, the oily floors caused them to slide and fall. As officers filed in, the BNF members who had been training for such a moment knew that their pretense toward nonviolence meant very little to the officers, so they hatched a plan. From Shakwi's recollection, a few of them decided to go to the fourth-floor executive offices with a plan for them to come in from behind and subdue the first wave of officers, forcing them to meet with the forces on the lower floors that were awaiting them. They believed that they could successfully neutralize the officers by coming at them from opposite sides. After all, as the media reported, the officers were outnumbered ten to one. Fortunately, the question of how they were going to do so while dealing with the deadly weapons that the officers brought inside never materialized. The oily floors prevented them from gaining any momentum. As they slid across the floor, presenting the potential for serious injury, any plans for outmaneuvering the officers were spoiled.[57] They did not know it at the time, but another timely intervention would help prevent any further catastrophe.

At the beginning of the siege, everyone in the building was directed to the first floor. The leadership decided that they had to muster all of the manpower that they could in order to prevent the rest of the officers from successfully entering from the ground floor. While the women and men placed their bodies on the line at the main entrance, another group of officers were stationed at the stairwell that led to the first floor. They had come in through the ground floor, where the post office and loading dock were located—the very location that Lloyd had warned against controlling. Remembering that this location was vulnerable, BNF leadership placed between thirty and forty men, many of them football players, against the door, absorbing the force of the officers. As they pushed back one of the officers yelled, "Get the rabbit!"[58]

The "rabbit" was a pneumatic device that the SWAT team had brought to force open the door. Shakwi described it as an "electric battering ram" that "went against the door, and went against the wall in the hallway and the thing cranked and it would punch, it cranked and then it punched." As it cranked and punched, the men held on. They knew that, if the officers were allowed to come up through this way, "we were looking at another MOVE, Kent State, South Africa."[59] History had also demonstrated that most police killings of students on university campuses had occurred at historically Black colleges and universities (HBCUs), and it was one of the provocations for the 1968 Howard A-Building takeover. The students knew how vulnerable they were, that their lives potentially hung in the balance.[60]

Recalling what it was like in that moment, Washington remembered that "there was nowhere to go. All you could do was wait for them to get into that building, and I wasn't close enough because when they were breaking and pushing through that front door, I wasn't close enough to . . . dip out the front door. . . . If they are coming this way, can I dip that way? I wasn't close enough to get out that door, the stairs were blocked, and there was just like fumes. So [there was] nothing you could do but wait."[61] Bright, who, in addition to improvising the protest song, worked to man the doors leading to the stairwell, reflected on feeling a surreal moment that seemed to happen very quickly: "It was a weird chronology. It just happened so fast. . . . In that moment, everything felt like it was all at one time. You heard the commotion . . . and the canisters coming in there. . . . All these questions coming into my head. And wondering if everybody is alright."[62] In reality, the confrontation and siege lasted a little under forty minutes.

Another BNF member who ran security during the takeover, Killa Patterson, described the kind of psychological and spiritual feeling generated out of the rightness of their cause and the togetherness it inculcated. It was this sensibility that kept them grounded: "When you're afraid of something, but . . . everything else in you is greater than the fear, is greater than what you think might be coming. Like we can overpower this. Like we're bigger than this. This is just a small thing. So it wasn't a whole lot of fear. Because we were bigger." A student from Oakland, Patterson had always felt and been drawn to that which was "bigger." Finding it in BNF, she exhibited a common confidence among members of the organization, a steadfastness that stood up to their biggest foe.[63]

Chuck Webb was one of the men holding on. After absorbing blow after blow, he remembered that he did "not know how many more of these we could take." The door bent to the wills and force of order. But the spirit of resistance would not break. Only one of these would survive the takeover. After a particularly loud blast of the device, a voice pierced through the chaos. It was not immediately familiar because it belonged to Mayor Barry. He then began to yell to the officers deploying the rabbit: "Aye, aye, why y'all doing that? Stop that! Leave them kids alone." And with that command the siege abruptly ended. Barry had countermanded Police Chief—and eventual Republican candidate for mayor—Maurice Turner's order. As far as Webb is concerned, "Marion Barry saved our lives."[64]

For BNF and the other student protestors, it was something that they would never forget. There was widespread relief. Washington's feelings instantly shifted: "Oh, I'm not gonna die? My grandmother won't be upset."[65] Bright recalled that there were also "some people [who were] disappointed, like, 'Aw, we let they ass in.' We were trying to avoid this the whole time. How they get in?"[66] But ultimately, as William Simms asserted, they realized their strength in unity: "We came together, we stood strong, stood steadfast. Even when the police were at the front door there were many of us who believed that victory could come if we remained unified."[67] As one of their chants indicated, they were "too Black, too strong," to believe otherwise. And that Blackness was infectious.

It could have ended very differently. When Deputy Mayor Kemry Hughes went back to the mayor's office to alert the administration of the dangers that were brewing, some staff personnel initially brushed the threat off. To make matters worse, when President Cheek called the police chief, the mayor's office was apparently not officially notified. This may have raised red flags. Not wanting to have a massacre on his hands, Barry quickly sprung into action, arriving in time to prevent what could have been the worst. President Cheek was later quoted as saying that, as Barry arrived, he, too, had asked the officers to withdraw, fearing for the safety of the students. But it was Barry's dramatic appearance that has remained one of the more memorable moments of the siege. Obviously reflecting upon his encounters with police and white supremacists in the South as a SNCC organizer, Barry reminded the media, "I used to do this myself. If I were them, I'd probably feel that way, too."[68] He then spent the next two hours meeting with the students.

The cameras caught it all. The White House press pool had even asked President George H. W. Bush about the events of that day. Supporting Atwater, his campaign's number 2 man, Bush replied that he thought "it was a good thing he's on the board. I think it's a good thing he's gonna talk to these students, and I think that'll work out just fine."[69] Viewing this footage from his hospital bed, Lloyd spoke to the BNF members on the ground, updating them about how things were being perceived nationally and internationally. This might have influenced how they in turn engaged the media and helped inform the negotiations that were to come.[70]

As the images of police cars, helicopters, and the heavily armed SWAT team destroying the glass doors were broadcast across the world, it was becoming obvious that something was going to have to give. Moments after Barry called the police off, Atwater, cutting his losses, decided by that evening that the only face-saving option was to resign from the board. In a letter to Board Chairman John E. Jacob, he framed the opposition to his appointment as "counterproductive" and a "distraction" to the work he and President Bush had intended to accomplish in Black communities, while lamenting the refusal of the protestors to have a discussion with him about his views.

Sounding the themes of those who supported his appointment, Atwater regretted not being able to "help bolster" the "financial support" of the institution and bring more Black people into the "political process." Most picked-up upon was Atwater's attempt to frame his resignation as necessary given the possibility of violence against the students. His statement asserted that, "in particular, today's events at Howard demonstrate the possibility that someone could be injured in the protest. That I could not accept. I would never forgive myself if someone was hurt in one of these episodes."[71] Anyone with even a little bit of political common sense could see that this was clearly an attempt to salvage the GOP's project from the blow to its credibility struck by the Howard students.

Atwater, who did in fact meet with representatives from the Howard University Student Association (HUSA), apparently thought that the BNF leadership would also somehow be amenable to being spun by the strategist's tactics. But they refused to meet with him. Privately, Atwater felt that this snub was unfair; his biographer characterized his attitude as akin to "an innocent pawn in somebody else's game."[72] Even his letter of resignation included a carefully worded denial of the political validity of their critiques of the deeper and broader issues that he represented as well as a dismissal of the most radical elements of the protest. In his reading of the situation, their unwillingness to sit down at the table with a racist was framed as unreasonable.

In another attempt at spin, Atwater published an editorial in the *Washington Post* titled, "What I Would Have Told the Howard Students," in which he reiterated some of the same themes. Responding to a list of concerns HUSA vice president Robert Turner and other leaders had drawn up and presented in their meeting with him, Atwater stated that he "supported the Voting Rights Act extension," that he was for "affirmative action in its traditional sense," that he supported an end to apartheid "and the establishment in South Africa of democratic majority rule," and that he denied the veracity of the literature that claimed he did not support the Civil Rights Act of 1964, sarcastically stating that he was "in the seventh grade" when it passed.[73] As an anonymous student stated, this was not their point, arguing that "the way he acts *right now* shows how much he is against even that Civil Rights Act."[74]

All of these "explanations," of course, obscured the fact that these were exactly the public positions to be taken if the whole thrust of his Republican National Committee chairmanship was to convince Black Democrats to switch party support, a tactic that trustee member Thaddeus Garrett openly embraced.[75] It also obscured the ways in which the GOP's leadership was actively leading the judicial fight against affirmative action and for a conservative interpretation of civil rights and also obscured that Atwater's own lobbying firm had worked directly with Jonas Savimbi and the National Union for the Total Independence of Angola (UNITA) in the West's proxy war supporting the apartheid regime in South Africa. The letter ended with what amounts to a strategic obfuscation—one he had also used with the students he *did* meet with—that the William Horton issue was not about race. Further, Atwater claimed that he did not authorize the advertisements that featured Horton and that the issue of furloughs was more important than his race, which he again claimed, was not a factor. He even rightly pointed out that the issue was first raised by Democrats, which for many was beside the point but revealing of the fact that in the final analysis, this was all about politics—and in the most basic sense of the word. None of this passed the basic litmus test of veracity on the question of race and the historical uses of dog whistles. It also demonstrated that nothing of value would have come from BNF leaders taking a meeting with him. That the resignation was clearly a GOP political ploy was confirmed when this editorial was read into the *Congressional Record*.[76]

Atwater had earlier tried a different tack, posing the possibility of sponsoring a blues concert on campus. As an avid fan of the blues and a blues guitarist himself, Atwater would use this point repeatedly to smooth things over whenever he had a Black audience. He had even performed with artists like B. B. King and put on a major show to celebrate Bush's inauguration before opening a blues-and-barbeque joint in nearby Arlington, Virginia. It is unclear, though, why he thought this high-profile act of "I have Black friends" would work. It was as if he believed that Howard students, of all people, would be impressed by celebrity or that he would be introducing the Howard community to something that they were not aware of or had an any prior appreciation for. Or, perhaps most egregiously, he thought that Howard students would trade his blues credentials for the political price of Atwaterism.[77]

Perhaps it felt so because it was clearly a price the administration was willing to pay. President Cheek responded to the news sorrowfully, stating that he was "saddened" to hear of Atwater's resignation. It was also clear that Cheek sincerely believed that the protests would never work.[78] Interviewed by The Hilltop the week prior about what could possibly happen with regard to Atwater's position, he stated, "Nothing. He was elected by the full board." Cheek believed so strongly in the university's bureaucratic system of governance that the idea that the students would concern themselves with who sat on the board elicited a certain contempt. Regarding students, he stated that they were here to "pursue their studies." Forgetting his own activist history and his subsequent support of student activism at Shaw University in the 1960s, as well as the kinds of engagement they had with power, he told The Hilltop that when he was a student he "did not consider who was on the board."[79] He followed up this interview with his famous open letter a week later, in which he explained his side of things. Published in The Capstone, Cheek offered a softer tone but still articulated that "it was the Board's view, which I supported, that Mr. Atwater would provide a valuable entrée to the world of business finance. I am of the opinion that history will vindicate our judgment by his future actions—despite his resignation from the Board."[80]

And then there was Thaddeus Garrett, a "Lincoln Republican" who had also stuck with the party as it made its turn in the wake of the Civil Rights movement. In the weeks before the protest he confidently asserted that "[Atwater's] not going anywhere and those students had just better get used to it."[81] In a heated exchange with Daniel Goodwin a little over a week after his nominee to the board resigned, Garrett blamed students for the university's problems.[82]

Garrett and Cheek were miffed at the news, but it was met with both joy and a measured caution, when Mayor Barry returned to notify the students in the building of Atwater's resignation.[83] It was clear that the moment created the feeling of euphoria, for they had placed everything on the line and reached a goal that no one outside of them thought they would be successful in attaining. But the price of victory was eternal vigilance. Speaking to the students, April Silver reminded them that they first needed to get official notification of Atwater's resignation, preferably in writing. She then alerted them to the fact that their work was not over, intimating that all of the demands had not been met.[84] Patterson expressed their mood in this way, using a word that was consistently reiterated in the press:

> Jubilation. Everybody was happy in the A-Building. All these cheers and joy and everything. But . . . it was like, "This is just the beginning." Ras and April and Carlisle, all of them made it very clear. "This is just the beginning of stuff that we have to fight for and stop things from happening that shouldn't be happening." This is the beginning. And we were successful . . . because we stuck together . . . because we believed in each other. But it was just the beginning.[85]

"Jubilation" was the word that seemed to define the moment. And if this jubilation and sense of satisfaction were the immediate response, the long-term one was to ensure that everything that they put themselves on the line for would end up coming to fruition.

Kemry Hughes stayed in the building after the police had attempted to end the takeover. He met with the security committee and helped draw up a plan in case of an emergency. He also called the Department of Public Works to help with the cleanup effort, particularly to board up the front of the building where the glass had been broken. What Hughes also represented was the fact that the students had the support of Mayor Barry for as long as they needed it. They knew that as long as he was there with them, they would not have to worry about the police—or so they thought.[86] The support of Hughes and Barry also clearly helped the students in the next crucial phases of the takeover, which were the negotiations to come.

Later that evening, as the dust was beginning to settle, Cheek entered the building. By that point the administration had been embarrassed, as the media imagery of students struggling with the police hit the national nightly news stories. Those images of armed officers versus unarmed students recalled the juxtapositions of the Civil Rights era—nonviolent demonstrators against dogs and water hoses. Although Cheek was still unwilling to extend an olive branch, the purpose of his visit was to see firsthand what the students had done with the building. Williams remembers that Cheek demanded that his entire team accompany him inside. Refusing to allow that many policemen and staff to enter the building, the students eventually compromised, allowing Cheek and one other person, his security chief, to accompany him.[87] They then began what would prove to the first of many antagonistic attempts at resolution.

Outside of the building, everyone wondered if the takeover would soon be over. When Lloyd spoke to Williams again, he wondered if they knew that Atwater had actually resigned. When Williams responded that they indeed were aware, Lloyd asked them why they had not left the building, and he replied that they still had business to take care of. Among the issues that were left to hash out between the administration and the students was the question of amnesty. In fact, this question was the only check on the feelings of elation that night.[88] Reflecting this concern, Akanke Washington asked Darnell Dinkins, "'What does "victorious" mean?' He told me that 'Lee Atwater was going to step down.' [But] there were other things from our demands, [and] in that moment, those other things weren't included in 'victorious.'"[89]

To deal with the problem of amnesty, the leadership of the protest had retained the services of Howard alumnus Donald Temple, the founder of Ubiquity, Inc., and a staunch ally of student activists. According to Silver, it was Temple who recommended that they go by the name Coalition of Concerned Howard University Students. Before they went into the building, he advised them on what to be prepared for and what sorts of challenges might emerge. One of those issues became how to negotiate with the university to avoid criminal liability or university

Figure 6.2. The front of the Mordecai Wyatt Johnson Administration Building after the siege. Courtesy of Howard University Archives, Moorland-Spingarn Research Center.

sanction. They would add other demands, including an agreement that they would not be held liable for any damages to the building and other Howard University property, since it was the police who had actually done the bulk of the destruction. They also began talks to generate a mechanism by which students would be allowed to have some say in who was appointed to the board of trustees. Finally, they demanded that the university extend the withdrawal period for the semester to a week later to accommodate students who had participated in the protest.[90]

After Williams allowed Cheek in, he met with Silver and the others, where he was presented with the additional demands. But it was clear at that point that a resolution was not forthcoming. At a certain point, the negotiations hit a wall, and the student leadership decided to suspend the discussion.

Wednesday

On Wednesday morning, the protestors were graced with the presence of Sonia Sanchez, Walter Fauntroy, and Ralph D. Abernathy. While pledging her support, Sanchez spoke again to the long-view meaning of their action, affirming that its foundation was "the love of our people and our ancestors."[91] Abernathy, then in the throes of an illness, tried his best to connect the protest to the history of nonviolent resistance and the Black freedom struggle that he represented through his work as Martin Luther King's top lieutenant in the Southern Christian Leadership Conference (SCLC). Fauntroy, an SCLC veteran who was the DC delegate to the House of Representatives, also afforded the protestors the opportunity to interface with a movement veteran who was also connected to local and national politics. He would stay in the building to aid in negotiations.

Stewing from the Tuesday night meeting, Cheek issued a statement on Wednesday that basically agreed to the demands that the university would not bring charges against the students or expel any of them, but only if they agreed to leave the building by the end of the day. In a one-page statement that was distributed across campus, he ominously declared that, if they did not comply, he would resort to the very tactic he had supposedly dismissed as too dangerous the previous day. It read: "Any students or other individuals who persist in occupying any university building and otherwise disrupting university operations will be arrested and/or expelled."[92] The letter, however, did not instill confidence that Cheek's intentions were made in good faith. As the word spread inside, students began to get restless, and some felt that perhaps it was time to leave. The numbers, however, did not decline because BNF members, in particular, engineered a boycott of classes, which resulted in the movement of even more bodies toward the A-Building. As they went out onto the campus, Coalition leaders informed the media that the protest was indeed not over.

As the precipitation that had been falling across campus froze the ground, making the Yard icy, Shawn Houston and others interrupted classes with a question: "Listen, what are y'all doing in the classroom?" Turning to the professors, they stated: "Respectfully, the students got something that's going on that's bigger than the classroom right now. I need to speak to the students."[93] Rich Byers, who also participated in these classroom disruptions, remembers that

> it was so easy to get kids to ride with us. It was as if everybody had been waiting for just such an occasion to arise. All the kids from Douglass came immediately as if they'd heard there'd be free chicken. The kids from the School of Communication, never ones to miss out on the possibil-

Figure 6.3. Sheri Warren, Zenobia White, and Robert Turner address the media.
Courtesy of Howard University Archives, Moorland-Spingarn Research Center.

ity of speaking engagements, primed themselves then ran after us. The
kids in the Blackburn, already at leisure, some behind beers, some playing video games, were more reluctant, but came out of a sense of, if not
duty . . . at least another likely cure for boredom."[94]

While these students followed, others felt that the protest was in fact
doing more harm than good. It was not that difficult to find dissenting
voices—Houston remembers being told that "they were messing up the
school."[95] And even after the events of Tuesday, there were still many
who were concerned with students' disruption of the processing of registration and financial aid. Some expressed doubts about the credibility
of the leadership, especially after unsympathetic media sources began
to question their claims concerning Atwater. Finally, there were those
who were fearful of the repercussions of the takeover, the very real ones
Cheek had proposed in his letter.[96]

For Houston, who was close friends with Sidney Williams, a leader of
the campus Republicans who had appeared on television condemning
the protest, these were political differences that cut deep. Friends since

grade school, Houston remembered what he told him: "I said, 'When you look back at this you gon' be sorry which side of the equation that you were on.' I remember my friend, I don't think we spoke for about a year. And I wasn't even that kind of person."[97] When Byers and others got to the School of Business, they ran into this kind of resistance: "It was only at the School of Business did we encounter the least bit of resistance. And by resistance, I mean that we were stonewalled. I dunno; it was as if the kids in the School of B had been so thoroughly conditioned to deal with the unpredictability of the business world, had been schooled in the histories of depression-based suicides, market fluctuation, worldwide economic instability, that nothing at all could faze them."[98]

While the class disruptions ensued, other protestors reportedly disrupted by pulling fire alarms. As the administration prepared to create a satellite office across campus, one hundred and fifty students staged a sit-in there, preventing the university from creating a temporary solution to having their business functions shuttered. Signs that read "It's Not Over! Please Boycott Classes. We Have Not Achieved All of Our Goals Yet" could be seen on campus. Professors canceled classes. Some canceled exams. Others were furious at the tactics deployed to interrupt class and stated that those students who participated would still be responsible for work missed.[99]

The result of all this activity was the largest day of the takeover in terms of student participation. The estimates reached three thousand, with many more wanting and wishing to participate. They waited outside as leaders assured those who were inside to prepare for the arrival of perhaps the best-known guest, Jesse Jackson.[100] Perhaps hearing that Jackson was making his way to campus, Cheek thought twice about his threat to have the students forcibly removed. By the close of day, there was no sign of another police assault. So again, they hunkered down and waited.

Jackson was in Miami supporting the work stoppage of the International Machinists Union against the unfair labor practices of Eastern Airlines. While there, he responded to Sanchez's request that he speak with the students. April Silver remembers first talking to Jackson on the phone, who after a discussion about what they were facing agreed to come. He then told her that she needed to tell the media that "you invited me to come." Jackson, according to Silver, was trying to shape the optics of his appearance, while lives were possibly at stake. In his view, the optics would have looked better if he came in and played the savior role, rather than the way it actually happened. Silver recalls how this made her feel: "My naïveté. I couldn't hear him. What he was saying was that it would be to his advantage that the world believed that we invited him, when in fact he was told to call us." While it is unclear exactly what the media play was for Jackson, for Silver, it "was the death" of her innocence regarding the nature of national politics and activism.[101] Later speaking to the larger group, Jackson stated, "My job is to bring the cameras to you."[102]

If we are to believe the intimations from the Atwater camp, Jackson was attempting to play both sides. In his self-assigned role as referee and conciliator, he might have sought to appear as someone who could threaten the recalcitrant Democratic Party by leveraging the Black vote—the very premise of Atwater's Operation Outreach—while at the same time drawing upon the windfall of cachet he would receive by "saving" the students. In his conversations with Atwater, he apparently agreed to try to smooth things other with the students, stating that he would "take care of it with everybody, would make Lee look good, that he would tell the students that Lee had their best interests at heart, that Lee just wanted to do the right thing."[103] But when he finally did get in front of the cameras, he told *CBS This Morning* that the Horton advertisement was "not so much about furloughs, but about race inciting fears in white people and creating very painful feelings among African Americans. Unfortunately, Lee Atwater symbolizes the worst of that situation."[104] This was basically the "talking point" of the protest leadership. Fuming and feeling betrayed, Atwater vowed to never trust Jackson again.[105] Perhaps Jackson, too, was moved by the force that was generating the resistance to the politics of white supremacist reaction.

In any case, Jackson's arrival marked an important point in the takeover. He emerged at the A-Building at 11:00 P.M. on Wednesday and met with the student leadership, helping to facilitate the negotiation of their demands. Joining Fauntroy and Barry, Jackson and the students met with President Cheek and Chairman Jacob via phone. After helping with the negotiations, he visited with the other students, addressing students on each of the four occupied floors. In his speeches, he tried to instill a sense of purpose into their actions, telling them that victory was imminent and that they were setting a model for engagement and activism for their generation. At least on this score, Jackson was absolutely correct.[106] But many BNF members were not particularly floored by the "up with hope, down with dope" routine that followed. Taken aback, Houston remembers holding back laughter and thinking to himself, "Nobody's using dope in here, Jesse. Tailor your message."[107]

Retreating back to the second floor, the group prepared for what became the final stage of negotiations. Much like his work with local business with Operation Breadbasket in the late 1960s, Jackson and Donald Temple helped orchestrate a "covenant" between the student protestors and the administration.[108] The "Covenant between Howard University and the Coalition of Concerned Howard University Students" laid out eight agreements, each mapped onto the six remaining original demands and the four additional ones. The first two reflected the sticking points of concern of the past day. The first and second agreements read: "The University will not take any disciplinary actions (financial or academic) against the Coalition or individual students who participated in this specific student strike" and "The Coalition and the students who participated in this strike are released and discharged from liability for any damages to the Administration Building, offices, or Howard University property." The third agreement reflected the reality that the student trustee was already invested with the ability to nominate trustees but affirmed that they "shall not be prohibited from soliciting from the student body recommendations for nomination" to the board. The fourth agreement extended the date for course withdrawals to March 17. The fifth stated, "Students may develop and present proposals regarding the establishment of a graduate African American Studies department and program for academic credit for community service to the Faculty Senate for its consideration." This agreement spoke to the parts of the first demand and the second demand. In less-than-committal language, the sixth and seventh agreements stated that the university "will publish in *The Hilltop* a schedule regarding" the "established" plan to renovate and improve the dormitories and that it would "take every appropriate measure to increase security for the university and its guests." The final agreement read: "The University will take every appropriate measure to increase its financial aid staff to facilitate the processing of student aid,

Figure 6.4. Jesse Jackson addresses protestors. Courtesy of Howard University Archives, Moorland-Spingarn Research Center.

improve treatment of students by personnel, and complete and process all loan applications by April 1, or as soon as possible."[109]

At 3:00 A.M., they returned to the first floor and announced that a preliminary agreement was reached. They could now leave the building.

The feeling of jubilance reappeared. Silver described the mood as a "victory party."[110] The men of BNF even performed an impromptu step show before chanting and marching across the Yard. The "victory" was as much as about reaching the goal of having Atwater removed and an agreement to work through their other demands as it was about avoiding the worst that could happen. Houston remembers that they "came out, and everybody feels exhilarated. Everybody feels like family." But it was also measured by the fact that he felt that there were those in the building who had not stepped up when the time for sacrifice came: "Everybody didn't do the same thing." The feeling of family was premised upon the level of work and risk that was shared. This did not spread to people who looked away when it came time to place their bodies on the line: "You were there, but we ain't the same guy."[111] While there were those who warned against celebrating too early and, as Houston argues, those who had no business joining in the celebration in the first place, the unadulterated joy that defined the moment was too much not to notice and participate in. Williams remembers it was a feeling akin to being victorious on a battlefield.[112]

* * *

That Friday, in the regular BNF meeting, there was an extensive debriefing session in which everyone congratulated each other and noted many points of issue that needed to be continually addressed. They also knew that the preliminary agreement reached early Thursday morning needed to be enforced. There would be more negotiations. Some members expressed concerns about what they called "bandwagoners." With the success of the protest, many people would now be drawn toward the organization and what it stood for. They knew early on that they would have to learn how to deal with success and notoriety. Rooftop Posse member Sean "Puff" Combs even capitalized on this energy by selling T-shirts and posters commemorating the protest.[113] Finally, there was an immediate desire to correct the mistaken record of events that many press figures had articulated. As well, the negative reactions of columnists like Courtland Milloy and Cal Thomas contained falsehoods that presented problems that needed to be addressed.[114]

At this meeting, Ras's father, Imamu Amiri Baraka addressed the students. It was, of course, a significant visit. Sonia Sanchez had earlier supported them, and here was Amiri Baraka who came to be with them. But it was memorable for another reason. His words did not massage the significance of what they were doing. Recognizing the urgent and historical gravity of the undertaking, he stated, "You know they will kill you because they've done so for less than this."[115] In an editorial published later, titled, "Howard University 'Cap Stone,'" he placed the students' takeover in a larger context of the shift in the political economy and the role of Black labor in this transformation, arguing that the "education" provided to Black folk would be one that would cause them to "lower their sights."

Figure 6.5. "Students United Will Never Be Defeated." April Silver Collection, private collection. Photograph by the author.

For figures like Atwater, it would be necessary for Howard's elite to be brought into the fold.[116]

Friday's edition of *The Hilltop* contained a similar range of opinion. In addition to providing accounts of the protest and the day-to-day happenings, the editorial pages contained nine pieces, ranging from congratulatory to condemnatory, with much of the latter from students who felt that the action was naïve. Countering such opinions were those who felt that, at least for a moment, the protest was a victory for campus collective power. In "Ovation," the editorial board of the student newspaper reflected that the protest brought the student body "closer to unifying this campus." It thanked everyone from the leadership to students who were outside of the building but who supported the protest in other ways for inciting a "wave of political activism that should continue infinitely."[117] A political cartoon depicted Atwater symbolically booted out of the university, by the "United Students of Howard" as "apathy" flailed in the wind.[118]

Writing for *Essence*, junior Retha Powers affirmed that "we were supportive of one another. For the first time since I had come to Howard, I witnessed Greeks and non-Greeks, light-skinned and dark-skinned folks casting aside the usual campus politics." She argued that "we came as far as we did because of a recognition of collective power, followed by the assumption of the responsibility to use that collective power to effect change. It is imperative that we continue to draw on the courage and discipline that made our protest succeed."[119]

In her interviews with students, the Black journalist Jacqueline Trescott of the *Washington Post* found that they felt the protest awakened something that had lain dormant for too long. A senior, Marjorie Andrews, who came from a background of social activism, told her that "you get to the point where you expected things not to work. I was really surprised it went off." Her friend Quentina Johnson said that "we stood up because we love this black school." Some Republican students even felt the need to participate. In that camp was Bridgette Hector, who stated that before the takeover "students didn't understand the power they have collectively."[120]

With regard to the leadership, the sheer exhaustion took its tool. Sheri Warren remembers sleeping for an entire twenty-four-hour period. The rest was needed for more than simply the physical toll because Warren and others, unlike many who were in the building, knew that things were indeed about reach a higher level of intensity.[121] Then there were literally housekeeping items to address. Jam Shakwi worked through his exhaustion and led a group who was responsible for cleaning up the A-Building and distributing leftover food to area homeless shelters and community centers. Outside of what was done to the building by the police, it sustained very little damage. This, of course, was a testament to the discipline that was instilled by BNF into the management of the takeover. As this happened, others returned to Cathy Hughes's WOL airwaves to announce victory to the DC community.[122]

Jubilation quickly transformed into work. As classes resumed that Thursday, Silver and other Coalition leaders visited Capitol Hill, where Cheek gave previously scheduled testimony to the House Appropriations Subcommittee.[123] History was repeating itself, it seemed. Thrust before the Congress in moments of campus upheaval in the 1930s, Mordecai Wyatt Johnson forcefully affirmed the right of academic freedom, even if it meant the loss of the federal appropriation.[124] Cheek, however, was not forced to decide. Silvio Conte and Black Congressman Louis Stokes lightly grilled him on financial aid, security, and building and housing issues, while also addressing the enrollment figures for Black men and foreign students and the question of Afro-American Studies. These were issues that the students wanted addressed, and he spoke honestly to the challenges. Cheek, however, was never asked directly about the takeover of the A-Building, nor did he mention it, perhaps because Congress had already been alerted to many of those issues. Running into Silver as he left the hearing, she embraced him "warmly," stating, "We thank you for your cooperation. We're glad things worked out the way they did."[125]

This warmth did not last. In their subsequent meetings to iron out the details of the agreement, there was still a fear of reprisals. Sheri Warren remembers the moment when "we went into a room and it was set up like a boardroom. . . . Everybody's just sitting there. We had our demands, at this point. . . . I know we were definitely advocating that none of us get expelled because they were trying to put us out [of] the institution."[126] It appears that this desire to have them removed was grounded in a retaliatory measure as their movement was read by Cheek as almost a personal referendum on his leadership:

I remember at that last minute, Dr. Cheek, if he could have cursed us out into the ground, he would have. He had to hold it together in front of all those folks. I remember him yelling, saying that we didn't know what we were doing. Like basically, he was trying to convey that we were messing up the future, really that we were messing up, we didn't know what we were doing, we didn't understand how things were like connected, or whatever the case may be. And I remember the argument was like, "We do understand and we know that this man should not be . . . on the board." It wasn't a good meeting. . . . The overall tone was that we were young and that we should defer to them because we were young, and they knew better. And they were very upset, Dr. Cheek was very upset, which was confusing, because we also talked about the fact that he led a protest and did the same thing we did.[127]

In such fraught settings, they were able to agree on some measured actions to ensure that the university worked toward solving these issues.

While "officially" there were no expulsions, many BNF members felt that there was retaliation. V. Jimale Ridgeway recalls that Baraka and she were followed on multiple occasions, including in the dormitories. Others experienced academic retaliation, beyond those problems that were self-inflicted. And broadly speaking, there was a belief that the university shifted its recruitment from areas such as Newark, the Bronx and Brooklyn, and Philadelphia to avoid having to deal with students who were influenced by those elements that created groups like BNF in the first place.[128]

It was April Silver, however, who might have experienced the most severe forms of harassment. As the spokesperson for the protest, she became the target of the white supremacist right-wing element from which Atwater's campaign apparatus had derived an electoral advantage. For some time in the wake of the protest, she received death threats that were both written and voiced over the phone.[129] Amiri Baraka's words were quite prophetic. Responding to these threats, BNF security escorted Silver everywhere for months.

Of the positive reflections on the protest, those of David Nicholson, a Black book editor at the *Washington Post*, were also quite prescient. He concluded his long-form article, titled, "Why Howard University Exploded Last Week," by postulating that "the protest at Howard just might be black America's awakening from the long slumber of the Reagan years."[130] Many other veteran activists and Black leaders felt the same. Toni Cade Bambara, whose daughter Karma had reluctantly participated in the protest, sent a telegram directly to Silver reminding her of their goal and affirming their "determination to make Howard an institution deserving of your wonderful selves." Al Sharpton offered congratulations and the support of the United African Movement.[131]

Moreover, BNF and Silver received numerous invitations to speak at panels and conferences, including the Third Annual Melanin Conference alongside John Henrik Clarke and Yosef Ben-Jochannan. Some invitations, however, they turned down, such as one inviting them to appear with skinheads on the *Geraldo* television talk show.[132] To some commentators, the protest's leadership reflected a newness and promise in the form of Black women performing powerfully at the helm. But Silver and others disagreed with Jill Nelson of the *Washington Post*, who framed the protest in this way, asserting that Nelson had misrepresented the collective nature of their movement.[133] Yet her article contained a quote from Silver that demonstrated her understanding of the moment. She again emphasized the whole, rather than the head, stating that "you can't embody the spirit of thousands of students in three women. . . . We don't want what we accomplished to be an era, we want it to stay."[134]

It was that spirit that defeated the encroachment of Atwaterism on Howard's campus—for the time being, at least. The main thrust of Atwater's Operation Outreach was discredited, not by the political maneuvering of the Democratic Party, but by the hip hop generation, by Black youth who decided to end it. The white nationalist flood that resulted in the emergence of David Duke had a discernible foe in Black college students, who would soon show the world their power. Atwater would not live to see the bulk of the resistance to the politics that he had wrought. A year after the protest he collapsed while giving a speech in which he had planned to place Duke and Louis Farrakhan in the same category, again trying to declaim the influence of the Southern strategy on the open embrace of white supremacy in politics. Stricken with a brain tumor, he had a few months left to live. In those moments, he supposedly underwent a transformation, offering an extended mea culpa.[135] Whether sincere or not—with Atwater it would have been impossible to tell—the enactment of the dog whistle in politics and the larger politics of resentment that it engineered was a hole that an apology could never suture. What it started lingers into the present.

The A-Building takeover put BNF and its leadership in a spotlight both on campus and beyond. An organization that had been largely marginal to the campus mainstream, the group was now primed to transform for the nineties the meaning of student leadership and activism. This would, of course, mean continuing to address its own contradictions and challenges while working to add its generation to the long genealogy of resistance. On a national scale, the hip hop movement was beginning to find its activist and political voice, as this cadre sought to move out of the shadows of their parents' example and create a lasting monument to their own tradition of social and radical change. It would be clear that the ideological strands that had tied together Black political life would reemerge in their own lives, in the debates and struggles of this period. The protest brought together nationalist, socialist, and integrationist traditions under one roof, which would come to generate staunch disagreements in the years to come. Yet the resistance to Atwater's selection showed that conservatism in its many guises would be a critical limit to the variety of political questions to emerge from Black America in the nineties. In this way, the protest was redolent of this changing same—under what terms would Black America and the larger African world speak and ordain its own liberation? And now that this takeover forced these questions to the fore and pushed Atwaterism out of the door, where would the "Mecca" fall on these larger questions? The next stage of activity, the follow-up to the takeover of the A-Building, was to ensure that they continued to ask that question so that possible answers would be lived and realized.

In the days after the protest, the offices of the Howard University Student Association were flooded with calls of support and congratulations. Drawing upon the media's narrative, many who had called were looking to reach April Silver. They simply assumed that she must have been involved, somehow, in an official capacity with the leadership of the student body.[136] But they could not locate her there. While they could not know it, they were simply calling a few years in advance, too early for a prophecy that had not yet been realized.

PART III

Aftermath

7

New Howard

We were satisfied with what we had done, but we didn't celebrate what we had done. It was a part of what was supposed
to be done. It was really part of the work.
—Aarian Pope Punter[1]

For recent Howard graduates, the appellation "New Howard" has come
to signify their unfamiliarity with certain cultural or institutional
changes that define the experiences of its current students. Often over
the life of short five-to-seven-year increments, these perceptions of
change mark the differences in certain commonplaces thought to define
the truly authentic experiences of the Mecca—certain community and
campus landmarks, annual events, gatherings and traditions, and other
unquantifiable Howardisms—that have been lost over the years. Some
of these changes have to do with changes in leadership, but they are
often systemic. In recent years, gentrification has been most consistently
fingered as the culprit that has created a "New Howard."[2] At the annual
homecoming ritual, the occasion is accompanied by avocations of "Old
Howard" amid a quixotic search and yearning for that old landmark.
With the spirit of these memories in tow, we might ask if Howard actually experiences such sharp and drastic changes, and if so, in what ways.

"New Howard" and "Old Howard" also speak to broader concerns,
beyond the memories of campus life, concerns that center the university's mission and purpose in providing "educational opportunities for
Black students" and its professed emphasis on providing leadership to
"America and the global community."[3] What these nostalgic moments
actually conjure are reflections that neatly map onto how one envisions
the future lifeworlds of the "African diaspora"—a term that Howard's administration has increasingly come to use in the last two decades.[4] What
they obscure, however, is that everything at Howard is simultaneously
old *and* new—and has always been. Its "newness" is a product of the

largely external political changes that coincide with its history. Howard has been variously forced to respond to New Deal liberalism as much as it has been forced to adapt to neoliberal late capitalism. Its "oldness" is representative of an "official" university mission that has remained remarkably consistent: the reproduction of a Black bourgeoisie.

In this sense, as J. Lorand Matory's study *Stigma and Culture* relates, Howard's status as a university—responsible for transforming the descendants of what the dominant strata once considered chattel into what the descendants of that group would accept as productive citizens—is both unique as far as universities are concerned and in some cases deeply conservative in that it relies on a model of Western culture and learning that rejects the Black cultures associated with the very communities it represents. In so doing, Howard represents the "locus classicus" of the idea that universities incorporate and inculcate "stigma, competition, and hierarchy in the self-making" of one of the world's, and certainly of America's, most maligned cultural groups.[5] This "double consciousness" produces the sorts of responses to student activism that we encountered in the previous chapters and that Howard continues to embody.

Uniquely situated at the vortex of African American ideological and political culture, Howard has both produced and been pushed to competing ends of an ideological continuum that have represented themselves as solutions to these temporal, external problems, which have in turn shaped how certain actors have engaged the progressive or conservative nature of its perennial mission. That is to say, the idea of producing a Black elite might have been a step toward an emancipatory solution in the late nineteenth century, but by the late 1980s, those same methods might have made little sense if the perceived end was radical transformation. In much the same way, some "new" responses to challenges, such as the university's civil rights legacy, have come to be folded into conceptions of Howard's traditional mission and have simultaneously been affirmed across different Black political cultures.[6] The question for Howard at the turn of the decade seemed to be: Would the nationalist politics of the hip hop generation similarly transform the mission of the university? Could it similarly force new questions into the old model of elite education?

In some ways, the response to the triumphalist post-1989 dispensation of global ideology in the wake of the end of the Cold War found one of its "Black" variants at Howard University in the early nineties and the hip hop activism it housed.[7] The aftermath of the protest shaped this newness by forcing certain institutional changes. But the energy put in motion by the vision of the students behind the protest would struggle to address the traditionalism of "Old Howard" that often seemed to win out—even as the university was forced into supporting and honoring certain progressive visions.

A New President

On March 31, the Coalition of Concerned Howard University Students wrote a long letter of gratitude to the student body, thanking them for their support. Clarifying their greater intent, of which the protest was only a part, the statement emphatically read: "Our long-term goals are, in essence, to effect permanent and structural changes in the areas of academics and administration." The protest was not to be understood as a flash-in-the-pan response to issues that the administration had then dismissed as minor. The Coalition "realized that since we are trying to cause substantial changes that are traditionally unwelcomed by the 'powers that be,'" that everyone "must anticipate an evolutionary process that may not occur overnight."[8] Echoing this theme in an earlier opinion piece, Chuck Webb declared that what grounded the movement was a belief in the potential of "revolution," one that was in his estimation still in the beginning phases and still required "a conditioning process that reconditions the mis-educated." And it also still required unity, a prerequisite to any sense of empowerment.[9] The cameras were gone, but the work could not stop.

While the campus hosted *Washington Post* columnist Courtland Milloy to answer for his negative editorials related to the protest, the Coalition and its Black Nia F.O.R.C.E (BNF) base worked to hold the administration accountable.[10] After two follow-up meetings on March 31 and April 1, Coalition members announced progress on the immediate issues of financial aid processing and housing, but the targets for resolving these and other issues had not been hit. In an earlier letter to Undergraduate Trustee Daniel Goodwin, the Coalition recommended candidates to replace Atwater on the board—a list that included Bill Cosby, Sonia Sanchez, Reginald Lewis, Earl Graves, Maxine Waters, and

Randall Robinson. The letter indicated that they understood the process for student input on board participation had to go through Goodwin, but apparently a discussion on Atwater's replacement did not occur at the March 14 board meeting. *The Hilltop* reported that there was "little indication" the board would "appoint any of the student's candidates." Finally, by this time, the Coalition had drawn up a "concept proposal" for the Afro-American Studies program that was supposedly well received, but there was still no firm commitment from the board on moving forward.[11]

Since the takeover, three weeks prior to these meetings, the Coalition had been working to win faculty support for the African American Studies graduate proposal and the community service for-credit initiative, while researching the other campus issues and developing rationales for the candidates to the board that they recommended. In this, they had the support of alumni, some of whom began to organize. As things continued to heat up, the Coalition planned a major public forum with the administration for April 12, designed to openly discuss these and other issues. Going over the plans to convene a "Where Do We Go From Here" town hall during their March 31 closed-door session, Cheek was noticeably hesitant, possibly feeling that he would be treated unfairly at such an event. However, he eventually agreed—and, in what was representative of Cheek's tenure during this time, he and other invited administrators failed to show up twelve days later.[12]

At this juncture, the group felt strongly that Cheek's administration was not holding up its end of the covenant. Unhappy with the administration's lack of speed and perceived commitment to resolving these issues, the Coalition and BNF convened a state-of-emergency meeting two days after the forum fell through in order to address what was described as the "lack of cooperation" between the administration and the students. It was at this meeting that the students agreed to launch another protest.[13]

The Coalition decided to host a rally on Friday, April 21, at the center of the Yard, followed by what was called a "symbolic candlelight vigil" at the 16th Street home of President Cheek. The press release framed the action as "continued efforts by the Coalition against an inefficient administration." Outlining the progress—or lack thereof—April Silver stated that "if the students aren't allowed to be a part of the decision-making process then we will once again be in protest. It is sad that the students have to use our energies this way in trying to get the adminis- tration to listen to us because we realize our purpose is education; how- ever we do not want to be taken for granted."[14] At noon the rally began. A few hours later, at 4:00 P.M., protestors met at Meridian Hill Hall and proceeded to the Cheek residence.[15]

A group of around two hundred and fifty protestors walked the five miles to the house, packing the sidewalks of the neighborhood of Black elites known as the "Gold Coast." As they reached the home, the last house before the Maryland border, they circled the block twice be- fore settling outside. They were more solemn than rowdy. As they lit their candles, a few protestors, tired from the journey, sat on the lawn, prompting Howard security to attempt to remove them. The group re- sponded that, since the home was university property, they had just as much right to sit on the lawn as they did any other location on cam- pus. It was apparent that President Cheek was home, but he declined to address the protestors, only briefly making an appearance at the door. After a series of speeches from Coalition members, they began the long journey back to campus.[16]

Perhaps the incursion on his home was the last straw. The next day, Cheek announced his retirement, to go into effect at the end of the fis- cal year. It did not come as much of a surprise to anyone paying atten- tion. The rumors began as early as the week of the takeover. Raised at that Friday's BNF meeting, Sheri Warren noted that, if a resignation was coming, "so be it"—although the target was clearly Atwater, ultimately Cheek, too, could be implicated as a negative force with regard to their understanding of the university.[17] A *Hilltop* editorial on March 17 de- clared that "the writing was on the wall" for the Cheek administration, voicing what had become a long-standing concern over his absences and the feeling that he was out of touch, a concern that was acute even before Cheek delegated the day-to-day duties for university operations to Carlton Alexis. The editorial asked: "Why can't the man just have an open meeting with the students and faculty in Cramton?" and implored him to "come down from his mountain."[18] The Coalition had also no- ticed a *Jet* article announcing his acceptance of the ambassadorship to Cameroon. While the piece noted his numerous accomplishments over two decades as Howard's chief administrator, it failed to note his current embattlement. Moreover, it alerted everyone to his plans since the article appeared *before* he had actually announced his retirement.[19]

In an extended exit interview with the Howard publication *New Directions*, the outgoing president attempted to situate his handling of the protest amid his larger legacy. He first answered charges that he had lost touch by explaining his higher education bona fides and discussing the physical toll the presidency had taken on his health—he had literally collapsed and stopped breathing in his office a year earlier. It was for this reason that he had taken a step back, hiring Alexis, ironically his personal physician, to handle the operations of the university.[20]

The unenviable demands of the Howard presidency notwithstanding, Cheek's other responses were far more dismissive and colder than his statements in the open letter published two months earlier. He argued that the protest was not grounded in any "substantive issues," that it lacked true support, and that it was "manipulated from the outside." Part of what had vexed him so was the fact that he felt the students in the Coalition were not representative of the student government. Sounding like those who dismissed the civil rights workers of the 1960s as outside agitators, Cheek referred to the protest leadership as the "self-appointed, self-anointed" who essentially had no business uprooting things as "nobody knows where they came from, nobody elected them to anything." Clearly referring to BNF, he stated that he felt that the protest was somewhat of an insurgent action that did not reflect how the majority of the campus felt about Atwater's appointment. Responding to the reported figures of those who participated in the protest, he stated: "They didn't have that. What one really needed to do was to go around this campus and talk to students. I mean there were students who came in this [Administration] building and stayed an hour so they could say, 'I was there.'"[21]

While the lack of universal support for the protest may have been true, Cheek's claims that everyone at the university generally supported Atwater's appointment was revisionism. He revealed that he was shocked that the events on Charter Day took place "because that was not a grassroots student movement. You just think yourself now: Mr. Atwater was elected in January. If there had been passionate objection why was not *The Hilltop* filled with passion or letters from the constituency expressing outrage and so forth?"[22] On both scores, Cheek was mistaken. While the protest and takeover were clearly led and organized by BNF and there were strong alliances with student leaders like Michael Lewis and David Porter, the collaboration with representatives of the Howard University Student Association (HUSA) and other elected leaders was clearly identifiable. And it was also untrue that there was very little campus uproar prior to Charter Day. As shown in the previous chapter, *The Hilltop* was a vibrant space for critique of the issue, and the *Washington Post* had caught wind of the dissension on campus. But if these were his honest assessments, it was no wonder that the impasse that drove students to further action came to be. Unsurprisingly, the Coalition welcomed his retirement, as did other students, many of whom were observed cheering the news.[23]

Reflecting the dynamics discussed above, Cheek's long-run legacy has been largely affirmed as more than favorable, despite his handling of the protest and involvement with Republican Party politics. At his passing in 2010, he was remembered as a key to the "expansion" of not only Howard's physical plant but also of its national and international imprint and reputation.[24] It is true that, under Cheek, Howard became a more comprehensive research university, expanding its schools and colleges to become more than what he once called an "overgrown liberal arts school with a collection of professional schools."[25] His understanding of the mission of Howard University—particularly the meaning impressed upon him as the president who succeeded James Nabrit after the 1968 protest—was grounded in its ability to compete with other top universities by attracting the best students and faculty, producing groundbreaking research, developing the best facilities, growing its real estate holdings, and offering the most effective forms of service to the U.S. nation-state.[26] It is a meaning that still resonates for those who also see Howard in this light. Cheek's presidency has often been lauded as a model for subsequent presidents to emulate.[27] In all these measures, Cheek's contribution to the ledger is clear.

Today, even some former BNF members are more open to understanding the long-view maneuverings of Cheek's administration. In the *New Yorker*, former executive minister Jelani Cobb gestured toward the widely held opinion, "less stark" than his own, that Cheek's legacy and his attempts to secure the financial security of the university was, for some, much larger than the temporary issues that student protestors had with his administration.[28] One of the original BNF members, Carlisle Sealy, shared much of this opinion, while Jam Shakwi offered that Cheek's tenure perhaps had lasted too long, which led to the differences that had produced the protest.[29]

While Cheek's accomplishments cannot be gainsaid, the larger question of his legacy and his historical contribution perhaps should not be judged simply with account ledgers and balance sheets. It was a sort of moral and ideal vision that was the broader canvas on which BNF and members of the Coalition sought to illuminate the question of the future of Black education and Black politics. It was the same canvas that the student protestors deployed in 1968: Beyond dollars and cents, individual ambition and institutional growth, what is the ultimate purpose for our being here? Thus the kind of change they sought was—as Sheri Warren then asserted—decidedly ideological.[30]

There would be a new president, but what would that president bring to the table? As they prepared to enter into another school year, the student activists began to consider how they would have to help usher "New Howard" into existence in other ways. In the wake of the vigil and Cheek's subsequent retirement, BNF would have to move "from protest to politics" in much the same way earlier Black freedom movement activists had done, understanding Howard's campus as somewhat of a microcosm of a Black political landscape.[31] They, however, hoped for greater results.

A New BNF

The success of the protest and takeover generated many internal issues in BNF. The fear of reprisals never went away and was often justified. Black Nia F.O.R.C.E members experienced mysterious and concerning vignettes that signaled that things were certainly out of the ordinary. Apartments and dorm rooms were broken into, people were followed, and there were suspicions that phones had been tapped.[32] The recent history of COINTELPRO (the Federal Bureau of Investigation's Counterintelligence Program) was a constant reminder to be aware of the possibility of surveillance and repression. They constantly studied the history of its tactics.

The popularity of the protest also generated a wave of interest in new membership. Meetings in Room 116 had become standing-room only, and the question of how to balance genuine interest with what was also for many simply a temporary curiosity amid the possibility of inadvertently taking in informants was paramount. As minister of administration, Sheri Warren devised a plan for updating the group's intake process that consisted of a rigorous practice of screening prospective members. Incoming membership candidates had to complete the BNF's Membership Orientation Program, which consisted of a questionnaire including essay questions designed to "stimulate" their "intellectual senses and to encourage critical thinking," as well as a two-part interview. Prospective members were also required to attend three consecutive meetings, to learn the Black Pledge of Allegiance written by Kevin Powell, and to read Zak Kondo's *The Black Student's Guide to Positive Education.* After new members were screened, they were put to the task of what Warren later described as "building capacity" by having their skills matched with the organization's needs.[33] Over the next few months, the group endeavored to develop a framework for a sustainable movement.

Although BNF remained unchartered, Warren and Executive Minister April Silver decided that it needed to develop an organizational structure. So they sat down over the summer and created what would become "The Guidelines and Policies of Black Nia F.O.R.C.E." With the aid of Carlisle Sealy, this work began initially as an effort to develop "bylaws."[34] The eventual document indeed has the tenor of a constitution, featuring an extensive preamble that establishes the aims and methods of the group as grounded in the "intellectual, psychological, and spiritual re-education" of the Black community. The resultant "force" created by such a reeducation was the goal.[35] The document essentially put on paper what BNF had already practiced and believed. But "Guidelines" also detailed the duties of the leadership and the "masses" of the organization, mandated the order of the meetings, and conceived of a judiciary process to handle organizational issues. While "Guidelines" is an otherwise traditional governing document, its framers also created unique forms of governance in later versions, such as the "democratic veto," in which the masses could overrule the executive board.[36] The document, completed by the beginning of the next school year, was ready for implementation as BNF faced the prospect of gaining new energy amid the fallout from the successful protest.

By September, there was a noticeable "disciplining" of the organization under Silver's leadership that sought to instill a sense of structure and commitment that the guidelines had stipulated. While there was a pretense of rigor installed at the organization's birth, this moment saw those foundations strengthened and new dictates enforced. Dues were collected. Fines for lateness to meetings were incurred. And plans to develop and train leaders were afoot.[37] No doubt, as part of this organizational intiative, Kondo was invited to address the group directly in October.[38] But none of these changes came without their associated challenges. The question here, of course, was whether too much discipline would lead to the sorts of problems that could plague the organization with perceptions that it was too tightly wound. While it was clear that there was too little discipline before, there was also a concern that there was a possibility that in screening members and mandating a more discernible structure, the organization was going too far for many people. Despite these concerns, BNF pushed forward with this restructuring as it sought to fulfill its agenda.[39]

Other forms of organizational health were also of major importance. In the fall, the men of BNF event went on a fast. This was as much about spiritual wellness as it was about physical fitness.[40] The organization had also recently become plagued with interpersonal issues that needed to be resolved. On many occasions, romantic relationships between BNF members had begun to lead to various levels of disquiet. As a consequence, the group instituted men's and women's meetings to help deal with questions of character and personal development. It was likely at these sessions that solutions to issues involving interpersonal relationships were discussed and that spiritual matters like the idea of the fast were conceived.[41]

As the internal dimensions of the organization were strengthened, BNF continued to participate and develop programs for the outside world. That November, BNF created and planned a Cultural Festival that celebrated African traditions, which undoubtedly helped spur an Afrocentric consciousness on campus.[42] But perhaps the biggest external project had to do with police violence. All semester, BNF members worked with student leaders in planning a response to the Greekfest police brutality incidents that occurred over Labor Day weekend in Virginia Beach, which resulted in arrests, criminal charges, and a lawsuit by the National Association for the Advancement of Colored People (NAACP).[43] With regard to the incident, HUSA president Daniel Goodwin appointed William Simms to create a new vehicle called the Concerned Black Awareness Council, which, combined with another umbrella organization, Peace Productions, became the avenue through which BNF members allied with other student groups to address the Virginia Beach issue. The Greekfest response was a long-term issue that took the entire school year to evolve. There were implications, of course, for BNF's ideological development as it involved many of the issues that concerned them and other Black student activists, such as the nature of public space, economic empowerment, hip hop, and electoral politics, as the incident occurred amid Douglas Wilder's campaign for governor of Virginia.[44]

Black Nia F.O.R.C.E was also involved in providing support for Florida judge Alcee Hastings and his infamous "double jeopardy" impeachment proceedings. And when Washington, DC, Mayor Marion Barry was arrested for drug possession as a result of a federal sting operation in January 1990, BNF was out front providing support for him. On January 31, BNF mounted a rally of over eighty students at the District Building. More than just returning the favor of Barry's intervention that previous March, the group saw the Barry case, as much as it did the Hastings incident, as evidence of an assault on Black leadership. Concerning Barry, Silver stated, "There is a game in the political arena to arouse criticism against black politicians."[45]

As the involvement in all of these issues and the organizational restructuring was taking place, the strategy to participate in another takeover soon emerged. It would be of a different sort, but no less dramatic. This one would involve taking over the student government. All of the disciplining appeared to be preparatory to advancing the organization to this next stage of engagement.

A New Leadership

Largely inspired by the efforts of previous movements broadly and on campus, April Silver and Ras Baraka's decision to run for HUSA president and vice-president, respectively, was not made out of any sense of personal ambition. It was not to be a stepping-stone for their eventual career choices, as it has been for others. Rather, what they sought was the ability to capture the capital—both monetary and social—necessary to advance the aims of BNF. Their campaign slogan, "Leadership for the Masses," was meant to signify as much. The wording was intentional—with "for," not "of"—as they sought to be truly representative of the student body and its interests as part and parcel of a larger thrust to be representative of the interests of the masses of people of African ancestry. The longer version of the slogan included another clause that signified again the source of their leadership. It read, "Leadership for the Masses, from the Masses."[46]

The initiative was much broader than just the Howard University Student Association, which is run much like the executive function of the U.S. government. Howard also has student councils—akin to state governments—that represent students in each of its schools and colleges. In addition to seeking executive office, BNF decided to run slates in the student council contests as well. Garfield Bright, who was asked to run for office in the College of Liberal Arts, remembers the strategy as a "bright idea" to consolidate the budgets of the entire student body under one ideological umbrella: "These student organizations had like fifty thousand dollar budgets, so they were like we could win all these and consolidate those budgets, and HUSA's budget, with the like-mindedness, we could put on some serious programming, that the campus had never seen before."[47] With successful campaigns, the sharp changes in Howard's student life that the protest introduced could be institutionalized.

It was something that was largely out of the ordinary, for both BNF members and for the school at large. Howard student government is largely a microcosm of Black American politics writ large and its well-worn methodologies of elite "talented tenth" representative politics against divergent attempts to break free from this model (with the largely exceptional campaigns represented by Haqq Islam and others discussed in chapter 4, in this volume, as exemplary of this tendency). The former is more common with the figure of the mainstream Howard student politician, usually someone groomed for such a position with internships on Capitol Hill, mentorships with the campus's upper ad-

LEADERSHIP FOR THE MASSES

APRIL SILVER, HUSA PRESIDENT

RAS BARAKA, HUSA VICE PRESIDENT

VOTE FEBRUARY 28, 1990

Figure 7.1. "Leadership for the Masses," campaign flyer. April Silver Collection, private collection.

ministration, and a sense of duty and purpose that is often more in line with the costume of political power than its actual instantiation. Silver recalls that this costuming was also literal, revealing that she had to be told to wear the business suits and pearl necklaces befitting the position, something she would come to resent. Given who Silver and Baraka were and their association with BNF, those who normally occupied such positions in the Howard hierarchy saw their campaign and its attempts to do something unique as a threat to their domains.[48]

Very quickly into the election season, many begin to exhibit fear and mistrust of the "radical" nature of Silver and Baraka's politics. While BNF had been able to transcend much of the student body's fear or antipathy of them during the protest, the space of student elections was another challenge. Baraka, in particular, was saddled with questions about his qualifications. Despite having worked in previous HUSA administrations and his leadership of youth organizations locally and nationally, it was thought that mainstream, normal Howard politics were above his abilities.[49]

Then there were real flaws that Baraka had exhibited that made the campaign vulnerable. These included his vices and predilections for extracurricular activities that stemmed back to his time with the crews from his freshman year. Black Nia F.O.R.C.E knew that this would be a weak point in the campaign, and they worked hard to mitigate it—with the men's and women's sessions again becoming a vehicle that essentially tried to channel them away from youthful indiscretions.[50]

The contentious speakouts that mark election season at Howard became during this campaign the occasions in which Baraka's personal and ideological issues were raised constantly. At one such event, Baraka finally broke the formalities and spoke from the heart about the meaning of his politics and what BNF represented and, in particular, the sacrifices that they had all made in fighting for a new Howard. Shawn Houston remembers this as one of "the most inspirational speeches anyone had ever heard." He recalled that "it was unbelievable. It gave you chills. And that was the end of the race."[51]

With regard to the issues, "Leadership for the Masses" had three main principles: information, education, and unity. With information, Silver and Baraka wanted to make sure that the university became more transparent as to its governance decisions and their impact on the students.

As HUSA president and vice president, Silver and Baraka vowed to share all that they could access concerning how the university operated and what decisions came down in real time. Education was, of course, part of the larger BNF mission to approach the question of human knowledge with unique philosophical and methodological approaches that addressed themselves to the white supremacist underpinnings of formal knowledge and to the creation of new vehicles for knowing. A major feature of this campaign plank was the continued work on ensuring that Howard created a graduate program in African American Studies. Finally, unity was about restoring relationships to the campus and the wider alumni and DC community. Representing another of the ambitions of the protest, they believed that Howard could not become some insular ebony tower that was aloof from the community or saw the community only through an adversarial lens. Further, unity also signified developing a network of Black students at other colleges, akin to the earlier efforts of the National Organization of Black University and College Students and the Student Nonviolent Coordinating Committee.[52]

On election day, February 28, with the combination of the campaign's message and the support it engendered among those who might not have normally participated in campus politics, the Silver-Baraka campaign captured 50.7 percent of the vote, outdueling three opponents. Falling five votes short of the 51 percent majority requirement, they were forced to participate in a runoff to take place a week later.[53]

It was poetic that the runoff election was to occur in the midst of the one-year commemorations of the protest. In that week's edition of *The Hilltop*, editor in chief Alonza Robertson provided space for Baraka to address his critics. In an editorial titled, "No Apologies: Just Truth," he responded to the idea that BNF is too radical by asserting, "I am not going to apologize for what I am. I am not going to apologize for being in Black Nia F.O.R.C.E." He proclaimed that it was BNF that nurtured his leadership capabilities, arguing that "we came together to effect change" and "we have done that." Regarding his personal issues, he stated, "I want Howard students to know that I am Ras Baraka because of you. I stood up because of you." Asking students not to "believe the hype," he closed by inviting them to check out a BNF meeting for themselves and literally opened his dormitory doors—much as he did in the fall of 1986—to anyone who wanted to meet to discuss these questions further.[54]

The piece was part of an entire edition that took stock of the university a year after the protest. Interviewed by *The Hilltop*, Silver and Webb both felt that the protest had opened some doors, but they implored everyone to realize that the power of students had not fully resulted in the change that they sought. It was time to continue to press and hold the administration accountable.[55] This is not to say that there had been no changes: The university had begun to address the financial aid system failures, tuition had not increased significantly, and there was lip service given to plans to renovate the dormitories. Perhaps most significant for the university was that it had selected a new president, Franklyn Jenifer, who was poised to take the helm at the end of March.[56] It was a historic moment in the university, rife with great potential.

After a record number of students voted in the runoff, Houston's prediction that the race was over came true. Silver and Baraka claimed victory. Riding their coattails, if you will, were a number of school and college wins, including Bright's victory.[57] *The Hilltop* editorialized that "the ties between last year's student protest and their victory is unmistakable." Addressing the critiques, the editorial continued, "Silver and Baraka demonstrated to all that they are willing and able to mobilize large numbers of students on this campus to take a strong stand for what is right and in their interest."[58] The win would give them a year to begin to enact a vision that they had scarified so much for. As Silver wrote that March, they would have "a unique opportunity to reshape the character and direction of the university" toward "traditional African values and customs suited to meet contemporary needs," a direction she labeled "Afrocentric."[59]

A New African

The period of the late eighties and the early nineties saw educational circles awash in debates about multiculturalism. The emergence of the "culture wars" brought more attention to the effort to think differently about the historical and social realities of the United States. The philosophical analogue was postmodernism and its assault on the grand narrative, and politically, the emergence of the post-1989 world rendered everything as if it were in flux. The conservative response to late capitalism was to reassert authority and control of the West's cultural and political apparatus. The university was a battleground for much of this work.[60] For many the question was how to infuse other cultures into preexisting university and public school curricula, so as to become more representative of the tapestry of the United States. For conservatives, this meant the loss of American (*read*: white American) identity, and for liberals and progressives it meant broadening the meaning of America, to be more inclusive and welcoming.[61] But for Black students and faculty across the nation, the varying responses to this context congealed largely around what came to be known as Afrocentricity.

Although its roots are in a longer history, the conceptual thrust of Afrocentricity is linked to the work of Molefi Kete Asante, a scholar of rhetoric and communications. The idea appeared in the conceptual arc of his and his then-partner Kariamu Welsh Asante's work while at the State University of New York at Buffalo, where he served as chair of the Department of African American Studies and Communications. The result was the first written iteration of the idea in his 1980 work, *Afrocentricity: The Theory of Social Change*.[62] Moving to Temple University in the middle of the decade, Asante argued for the creation of a graduate program in African American Studies by largely asserting a methodological distinction grounded in Afrocentricity that would mark disciplinary work in the new formation as unique and necessary. Building upon these arguments, Asante would show that African American Studies was in fact "disciplinary" insofar as it was premised on approaches that centered the unique histories and agency of Africana peoples. As Greg Carr characterizes it, this project sought "an alternative epistemology" designed "to generate the theories, methods, and reliability-standards necessary to establish academic legitimacy for their study of African people."[63] Asante's later works, *The Afrocentric Idea* (1987) and *Kemet, Afrocentricity, and Knowledge* (1990) sought the creation of a "metatheory" by bringing these ideas directly into the construction of a disciplinary formation. Asante's Temple project was viewed as a major front in the culture wars, even though many of its participants were largely unconcerned with who got to define the terms of American belonging.[64]

Afrocentricity was also deeper and wider than its academic evolution. It was the basis of a popular culture retrieval of African identity. And of the major battles of the culture wars, hip hop represented a crucial space to debate and discuss African history and culture and its relationship to diasporic identity. It is likely out of these connections that BNF members were introduced to the term, as it traveled from the scholars to the streets and back, inspiring changes in dress and hairstyles, as much as it inspired distinct approaches to scholarship and political movements.[65] As a *Hilltop* article noted at the time, "Howard students have replaced the chains, earrings, and jheri curls to sport a more Afrocentric look. Wooden beads, nose rings, and natural haircuts—hi-top fades and ramps—resembling crowns worn by ancient African kings and queens, are worn now by many students." And these were not superficial connections, as Darnell Dinkins asserted, "It was a way of life."[66] In more ways than one. Recall that the language of Afrocentricity had earlier made its appearance in the demands made to the administration during the protest, marking the first time that members of the administration were forced to respond to the concept. What events two years later would show is that it would not be the last.

Many attempts to understand BNF affixed the label "Afrocentric" to the organization.[67] They were not far off base. The organization's logo featured Kemetic (Egyptian) iconography. It supported and hosted scholars like Anthony Browder and Yosef Ben-Jochannan. And the Cultural Festival, mentioned above, featured members and guests donning African attire. What drove their Afrocentric position was something that was much larger than a trend, however. As Silver wrote, "Trends die."[68] Theirs was an acknowledgment of the ongoing injustice that has defined the meaning of being of African ancestry in the modern world, as well as the desire to secure relief by accessing and deploying systems of thought that were untainted by those conceptual and epistemological locations. This was, in fact, what ultimately grounded the idea of Afrocentricity. It was not solely or even primarily about infusing curricula with facts about peoples of African ancestry. It was about the ultimate transformation of knowledge from an African center, a transformation that BNF believed educational approaches at historically Black colleges and universities (HBCUs) should be premised upon.

Featured along with the *Harvard Law Review* editor Barack Obama in an August 1990 *Ebony Magazine* story on new student leadership, Silver emphasized the sincerity of those committed to having a "positive impact on the school and the Black community."[69] In a *Hilltop* story she declared to the campus community that "it's going to be a productive

Figure 7.2. Black Nia F.O.R.C.E logo. Akanke Washington Collection, private collection. Photograph by the author.

year."[70] At the outset, their objectives were to bring to the university and surrounding DC area an approach that refocused the meaning of education around nationalist ideals. True student empowerment would only come with unity and a greater knowledge of self. With that in mind, President Silver, with the emphatic support of Vice President Baraka, continued the process of fulfilling one of the protest's demands in her participation on the Howard University Task Force on Graduate African American Studies.

Convened shortly after the takeover, in the summer months of 1989, the task force's work began in earnest a year later as Silver took leadership of the student body. Chaired by the anthropologist Michael Blakey, it encompassed a faculty team that worked to imagine what an African American Studies graduate program would look like with the unique intellectual resources that Howard possessed. These resources included those faculty who had participated in and helped structure many of the debates on Afrocentricity, as well as others like the Moorland-Spingarn Research Center, one of the largest archival spaces on the modern African experience in the world. Of those interlocutors, it was Afro-American

Studies Department Chair Russell Adams who had thought and written the most about the specific question of African American Studies and the epistemological questions raised by Afrocentric thought.[71] While Silver was the only nonfaculty member on the task force, the student viewpoint was in her capable hands. And Afrocentricity was on the agenda from the outset. Representing how many students saw things, D. Malcolm Carson had earlier written in *The Hilltop* that, historically speaking, Afrocentricity was never intended to permeate the university but that the struggle to establish those ideas represent the "century-long struggle to make Howard" the fount of this philosophical tradition.[72]

In an extensive memorandum to the group, Blakey broadened the understanding of what he called "Afrocentrism" beyond the work of the Afrocentric school of Asante. His major argument was grounded on the assertion that the critiques emanating from this school too often mirrored the logic of those it sought to challenge and that Afrocentrism was a "condition of knowledge" that called for us to examine its greater complexities.[73] Also shaping the work of the task force was the chair of the English department, Eleanor Traylor. Recapitulating her oft-quoted citation of W. E. B. Du Bois's notion of "broad sympathy," her imprint was clear in the draft report of the task force, which asserted that "recurring themes structure our consideration of those continuing values transmitted through African inspired social, intellectual, and aesthetic traditions, continentally and diasporically."[74] Prodded by her influence, the task force asserted that these values were

> syncretism (the blending of ways of being, ways of thinking, and ways of doing and making in the world), memory (an emphasis upon history and heritage or the presence of the ancestral even in the yet unborn); ritual (the practice of customs, beliefs, and shared traditions revealing the distinctiveness of a people in themselves, for themselves, and of themselves); and critique (the constant examination of memory and ritual through syncretic and improvisational methods which retain the useful, expunge the anachronistic or tainted, and re-member or reclaim or invent useful contemporary structures of thought and practice and things).[75]

Buoyed by these new structures of thought and practice, they argued that we can no longer "privilege the *other* while failing to exalt the *differences of the self* which, as well as any *other* defines the world." Howard must be the something other and cease to "betray the strength of institutional memory and ritual in the process of what might be called imitation."[76]

Many of these comments reappeared verbatim in the final report of the task force, which was released in February and called for the creation of an MA and PhD program in the discipline as well as the creation of the Africana Studies Research Center (to go along with the already existing Afro-American Studies Resource Center) and a commitment to strengthening other resources and infrastructure affecting the department.[77]

As Silver worked with this task force, there was another working group that was seeking to reevaluate the university's academic programs. It was the brainchild of President Jenifer and was known colloquially as the "Commission." Funded by a grant from the Andrew Mellon Foundation, the Commission was a return on the promise that Jenifer had made as he took the helm of the university that it would be necessary for Howard to "prune the tree."[78] This euphemism for academic downsizing was rationalized as the need for Howard to modernize by addressing the demographic and industrial labor changes that were a feature of late capitalism. But this initiative was also, in part, an attempt to demonstrate Howard's relevance in the American struggle to restore its leadership from international threats from the East.[79] The so-called Japanese Miracle—the recovery of the Japanese economy at the end of the World War II to the end of the Cold War—had been based on technological advancements and caused U.S. nationalists to lament that their country was losing ground.[80] This basic argument was repeated in the language of the Commission as they sought to place Howard and the Black community in service to American national interests. Heavily skewed toward the professional and the business world with faculty from those schools and colleges and nonfaculty members like Frank Savage, Vernon Jordan, and Dennis Hightower, the report emphasized the need for Howard to be aware of, and participate in, these changes in order to "restore America to world leadership."[81]

Noticeably missing from their language was "Afrocentricity." The Commission, led by the physician LaSalle Leffall, never once gestured to the existence of this term and conceptual movement. It was not quite ironic but was nevertheless a demonstration of the "two Howards" that would prove consequential for both traditions. While there was a single member that overlapped both working groups—the civil engineer Taft H. Broome—it was obvious that the groups saw Howard differently. It might have even been the reason that Jenifer was chosen in the first place.

It was hardly a secret that the students, and partisans of an Afrocentric education, preferred H. Patrick Swygert, the other contending finalist for the presidency. Swygert, along with Jenifer, was a Howard alumnus but, unlike him, had contributed to the Afrocentric project, helping to create Temple University's graduate program in African American Studies with Asante when he served as vice president of that institution. Unimpressed with Jenifer's performance at his meeting with students during the decision phase, *The Hilltop* had enthusiastically supported Swygert to become the new president. To add further controversy, students felt that they had no real representation in the decision, one they felt was too secretive, which represented a complete disregard for the principles underlying that previous spring's protest.[82]

So when Jenifer's Commission released the preliminary version of its report, the doubts about him resurfaced. Making the report widely available, HUSA began to mobilize once again. Late that fall, Silver, along with two other student representatives, Toni Blackman and George Daniels, helped to put together a response to the Commission's recommendations, which, while ignoring the debate around Afrocentricity, had called for the creation of a Human Civilizations Program, which sought to address multiculturalism while also "strengthening the continuation of the present Eurocentric liberal arts education."[83] These may have well been fighting words. At a board meeting Daniels, Blackman, and Silver each gave presentations emphasizing the importance of Afrocentricity. Although the students' critique never received a formal response, the final version of the Commission's report eliminated any further mention of a Human Civilizations component.[84]

This final version, entitled *Howard 2000*, included eighty-two recommendations, which were endorsed by Jenifer and the Board on April 27, 1991. It called for the elimination of the entire School of Human Ecology, as well as other programs across campus, and the merger of many others, while asserting the need to offer broader support for the professional schools and—in the parlance of today's academy—the STEM programs.[85] In line with this, it situated the future of Howard University in the realm of research, exhibiting a trend of that period to frame university productivity as the end product of scientific innovation, what has been labeled "academic capitalism."[86] This would require, Jenifer argued, an increase in faculty research support as well as a tightening of admissions standards.[87] In a belated gesture, Jenifer implored the university to remember its "continuing commitment to Afrocentricity"—it was his second attempt to publicly respond to the students' concerns, but the only mention of Afrocentricity in *Howard 2000*.[88]

In the weeks before the release of the preliminary report, President Jenifer had offered his first take on Afrocentricity. Published in *The Hilltop*, the essay showed a surface-level understanding of the concept, attempting to satiate its partisans by asserting his support of the idea of the importance of Black history. He, however, signified his misunderstanding of the concept repeatedly, arguing that a soft notion of service to the race should be the "philosophical base of Afrocentricity." Addressing its intellectual thrust, Jenifer made the claim that the goal should be adding an "Afrocentric flavor" to Howard's current course offerings, wary of the potential that it might have to devolve into to "sloganeering and posturing" or—sounding like an ardent cultural warrior—"an excuse for a kind of strident anti-intellectualism." As a scientist, Jenifer posited that Afrocentricity belonged only to the world of humanities, since there was "no such thing as black physics or black electrical engineering or black microbiology." In this way, he sought to segregate the concept into the world of only one of C. P. Snow's "two cultures"—obscuring perhaps that there were not two, but one Western intellectual culture that had overdetermined what it meant to "reason" in the modern world.[89] Jenifer was right to assert that many of the seeds of Afrocentric thought lie in the soil of Howard University. Unlike the task force's report, however, the basis for continuing their germination were left unexamined, the complexities that generated the thought of Alain Locke and William Leo Hansberry were left unnamed.[90]

It was therefore no surprise that the Commission's final report and the Howard University Task Force on Graduate African American Studies could not come to represent the same view of the future of the university. Despite the fact that both groups considered themselves to be working on the academic mission of the university at the time, the official efforts of the Commission did not so much as mention, let alone support, efforts to create a graduate program in African American Studies. Afrocentricity and the lines it drew around the question of knowledge was essentially an ideological question, but for those aligned with the upper administration, it was often reduced to a question of inclusion and exclusion.[91] While the Commission's view of the University eventually won out, even outliving Jenifer's presidency—which, ironically, was followed by Swygert—the broad rubric of Afrocentric and African-centered knowledge production continues to represent great and untapped potential. Much of Traylor's notion of broad sympathy and the faculty prowess it cited have struggled to remain afloat, but the vision inherent in her formulation of knowledge production characterizes African American Studies work at the university and in other cognate areas today, despite the fact that the proposal for a graduate program submitted to the board in 1991 never resulted in its creation.[92]

As the battles over the Commission went forward, the Silver and Baraka administration managed to keep the energy on campus alive by hosting events like the Back to Black Weekend (a boycott of, and alternative to, Greekfest at Virginia Beach), the Awake lecture series, and Community Unity Day, which featured Eraka Rouzorondu and Jawanza Kunjufu, respectively.[93] But perhaps their biggest programming victory was HUSA's collaboration with TransAtlantic Crossing Management and the convening of the first hip hop conference.

A New Initiative

After graduating, the organizer and activist Haqq Islam continued to work in and around Howard University as well as at other institutions as a budding music executive. Meeting the legendary founder of Philadelphia's International Records, Kenny Gamble, at a Saviour's Day convention, Islam was inspired to take his organizing talents to the music world, later founding his own University Records and management company, TransAtlantic Crossing. This relationship had also provided dividends for BNF. With Silver and Baraka in need of financial support for their campaign, Islam phoned Gamble, who offered a crucial donation.[94] Islam subsequently returned to campus in the fall months of 1990 with a proposal that eventuated in the collective effort to put together what is generally believed to be the first hip hop conference.[95]

Along with Howard graduate Hakim Quest, Islam had founded the conference to demonstrate the necessity of Black ownership and the economic power that lay untapped in the music industry. It was the logical extension of classes he had taught on campus called "The Business of Music." There, he had exposed students to the then small cadre of label owners and executives like Russell Simmons and Kevin Liles, who visited campus echoing the message of the importance of ownership. Entrepreneurship was also a major plank of Silver and Baraka's HUSA administration. Under the leadership of HUSA staff member Timothy Jones, they generated initiatives to create and support businesses that would then redistribute their wealth to support on-campus needs. This was what also defined the mission of Peace Productions, the vehicle that had organized the Back to Black Weekend in Virginia Beach over the Labor Day holiday. The conference was the perfect alignment of Islam's work and HUSA's project.[96]

The organizers included an array of figures who were connected to Islam's long genealogy of youth leadership both on Howard's campus and beyond, as well as an all-hands-on-deck cadre of forces from BNF. Together they put together the conference, held on the weekend of February 21–23, 1991, titled, "Hip-Hop at its Crossroads . . . Seizing the Cultural Initiative." Just as they had seized the Administration Building, another front in the war for self-determination became the control of the very music that they created and that had served as their political inspiration.

That weekend featured a staggering amount of cultural (and eventual star) power, perhaps as much as had existed in hip hop up to that point. Speaking on various topics—ranging from how to start a record label to depictions of women in the music—were such figures as Gamble, James Mtume, Doug E. Fresh, Lisa "Sister Souljah" Williamson, Paris, Kool Moe Dee, Daddy-O, Chubb Rock, MC Lyte, Harmony, Melle Mel, Harry Allen, Chuck D, and a young Sean "Puff" Combs, the Rooftop Posse member who had recently left Howard for Uptown Records. They were joined by BNF members on panels, including Silver; Baraka; and Deric "D.O.P" Angelettie and Ron "Amen-Ra" Lawrence's group, Two Kings in a Cipher; as well as others. Howard artists like Paris Lewis's The Defiant Giants were also featured.[97]

Central to the event was the participation of established rappers offering advice on the proper way to seize control of an industry that was now—in the estimation of the "media assassin" Harry Allen—being diluted in much the same way rock and roll had been. They called for more Black entertainment lawyers, accountants, managers, and publicists and an awareness of the industry's predator nature, a set of arrangements that made artists vulnerable, especially absent a unified team in place to protect their interests.[98] There were also spirited conversations about misogyny, with some rappers vowing to remove the word "bitch" from their rhymes. (Unfortunately, the invited guests for this panel, titled "Hoes and Skeezers," Hoes With Attitudes and Bytches With Problems, did not show up.) Participating in both discussions, Souljah—now working with Public Enemy—implored the audience "to seize hip hop from the white people who stole it from us." Addressing the "bitch" question, she asserted that the use of this epithet was the outcome of the fact that "we reject African thinking and the idea that we are African people," gesturing to the inferiority complex resulting from trying to massage Blackness into an American identity.[99]

And then there was the presence of some elder statesmen, who along with Gamble and Mtume included Afrika Bambaataa, who did not participate in any panels but was present to offer advice and direction to up-and-coming artists. The confab ended, of course, with parties and performances, including a major party thrown by Don C and Ron DeBerry that featured performances from The Leaders of the New School and X Clan.[100] But it appears that the major event was the concert at the Citadel in Adams Morgan, a four-hour, seventeen-act affair that was described by Gil Griffin of the *Washington Post* as a "politically significant event—the reclaiming and preservation of the art form by its black creators, seizing hip-hop from corporate America and giving it to smaller-scale black promoters and returning the music to its inner city environs."[101] It was a decidedly Afrocentric concert featuring the latest in "message rap," dominated by groups like X Clan as well as other Nation of Islam–inspired rappers, whose values deeply resonated with BNF.[102]

In the year to follow, an organization called The Cultural Initiative was born. This group organized the conference five more times, becoming a critical annual event in BNF's repertoire on campus. Later gatherings featured young artists like Shock G of Digital Underground, Speech of Arrested Development, Organized Konfusion, Common Sense, Tupac Shakur, and Busta Rhymes, along with the staple group of more established artists like Heavy D. Executives like Chris Lighty and journalists like dream hampton also showed the other sides to being part of the industry. After she graduated, April Silver became the president of the nonprofit organization, declaring after the third conference that "we wanted to galvanize that power and transform people's mind-set from an irresponsible 'I'm just out to make money' type of mind-set to using their talent and their art form and that which they created to empower their people."[103] This statement became Silver's professional philosophy, as she used this work as a launching pad to a long career as a publicist. Timothy Jones followed Silver's tenure and similarly shaped his professional identity as an education scholar. Working in The Cultural Initiative also placed many other BNF members and friends of BNF on paths to the music industry itself, helping to generate the transformation it sought by inspiring many members to go out and start their record labels and then hire their staff from their group of comrades. Others became hip hop journalists, entertainment lawyers, and publicists. While Combs's ascent is well known, joining him and Haqq Islam into the upper reaches of the industry were Lawrence, Angelettie, Matt Middleton, Anthony Hubbard, V. Jimale Ridgeway, Ron DeBerry, and many others, where they remain to the present. Garfield Bright went from BNF to the Nation of Islam and then became the lead singer of the R&B group Shai, never losing sight of the cultural and political consciousness that working in The Cultural Initiative helped to foster. Baraka's memorable appearance as the teacher on perhaps the most important hip hop record of the 1990s, *The Miseducation of Lauryn Hill*, stands out as an exemplar of this group's contributions to the shaping of the music of their generation.[104]

These students asserted that without ownership of Black cultural productions the ability to shape the message of unity would be compromised. And for the most part, this has tragically proven to be true. While the Howard hip hop conferences have yet to feature in the histories of hip hop, let alone in the histories of the business of hip hop, they must be counted as one of the clear legacies of student consciousness of the late

1980s and 1990s—of which the Afrocentric movement and the energies of the 1989 protest were a part.[105] Fighting the power was the thing to do, and as other events of the spring of 1991 showed, it was not to be a fight over the spoils of American imperialism.

A New Flag

If the Commission sought to ensure that Howard participated in the restoration of American global leadership, a further rejection of such aims by the students resulted in perhaps the most dramatic repudiation of the United States by Howard students since the disruption of draft board head General Lewis Hershey's visit at the height of Vietnam antiwar activity and the subsequent effigy burnings of him and then President James Nabrit and Dean Frank Snowden.[106] As students returned from winter break, they were forced to respond to the war drums of the Bush administration as it geared up for conflict in the Persian Gulf region. President George H. W. Bush called for UN and congressional support for an air-and-ground assault to prevent the incursion of an erstwhile ally, Saddam Hussein, into nearby Kuwait, where 9 percent of the world's oil reserves were located—a clear U.S. economic interest. The air assault, Operation Desert Shield, was broadcast live on Cable News Network (CNN), giving the world a front-row seat to the devastation caused by American military might. Drawing upon the war doctrine of Colin Powell, February's Operation Desert Storm placed American and other U.S.-led Coalition troops on the ground, pushing the Iraqi invasion back.[107]

Aware of the inequalities in defense spending versus domestic issues, the overrepresentation of poor Black soldiers who would be sent to fight, and arrayed against the imperial ambitions of the war, Howard students like Talib Karim helped organize yet another coalition, Student Call Against War, that resulted in a major antiwar rally on Martin Luther King Day outside the White House. Silver and Baraka were joined by Jesse Jackson, Sister Souljah, and other national leaders.[108] Again lines were drawn. Riding a wave of widespread student concern, BNF allied with other student groups in DC and across the country to condemn America as the ultimate aggressor, rather than Hussein. In the wake of rumblings of an eminent ground assault, students angered about the war took symbolic action. Two years earlier, students at Howard had replaced the American flag with the Black liberation flag. This time, they torched the Stars and Stripes and left it smoldering on the main Yard.[109] Although flag burning was protected speech, it could make for an awkward conversation for a university administration that had to testify to Congress every year to receive and rationalize its budget. No one took formal responsibility for the flag burning, but an anonymous student wrote in *The Hilltop* that "this symbol of oppression" was not more honorable or more important than their vision of New Howard.[110]

* * *

Commenting on their administration's effectiveness, Silver and Baraka believed that, although they achieved much, there was much else that they could have done.[111] The institutional changes they sought were incomplete, yet much of their vision had been (re)deposited in the soil—if not yet the soul—of the university. Issues that had been the basis of the demands of 1989—like financial aid, housing, and security—were being addressed. Student opinion, if not elicited, was sometimes acknowledged, even if it was subsequently ignored. Finally, Howard could no longer profitably ignore the Afrocentric cultural assertion and its corollary in hip hop.

But, as BNF members graduated, beginning with Silver and Baraka and many others in May 1991, it would be difficult to continue to organize for the kinds of institutional changes that these movements sought. Further, as the political scientist Alvin Thornton believes, the election of a Democrat to the presidency in 1992 was seen as somewhat of a relief to the persistent white supremacist reaction in American politics—a sigh of relief that he felt was misguided.[112] Bill Clinton's infamous "Sister Souljah moment" should have signaled as much, and it was perhaps more evidence of a gulf between the politics of Black youth vis-à-vis the liberal establishment.[113] Nevertheless, in the waning years of BNF's influence, Howard settled somewhat awkwardly into the Third Way national political trajectory, finding comfort in the concessions of the neoliberal age, but all the while struggling financially and experiencing drops in enrollment during these years.[114] Reaching its breaking point, Jenifer's presidency had ended by 1993 amid controversy surrounding the "culture war" and charges of harboring anti-Semitism on campus by allowing Khalid Muhammad to speak. The Black sociologist Joyce Ladner, editor of *The Death of White Sociology*,[115] assumed the presidency of the university in an interim capacity as it welcomed Nelson Mandela for a special convocation in 1994. But she was not retained permanently. H. Patrick Swygert, who was passed over for the presidency in 1989, was chosen to lead the university into the twenty-first century. As a sign of shifting times, perhaps it was Swygert's ties to the Jewish lobby, as opposed to his ties to Afrocentricity, that played the most significant role in the decision.[116] Needless to say, the tensions that had traditionally produced protest, dissent, and a battle for the soul of Howard continued to linger. In reality, there was nothing truly new.

8

Nia

I wanna be Them, They, Us, We, I, I and I
blackness, not as in down or decadence but as
in life, livelihood, as in things unseen
—Ras Baraka[1]

Directly preceding and following the 1989 protest at Howard was something greater than merely a smattering of student upheavals. What can only be described as a wave of activity took the nation and world by storm in the late 1980s and early 1990s—a wave that was akin to the student uprisings at historically Black colleges and universities in the 1920s, "the Black campus movement" of the late 1960s, and the recent protests of 2015.[2] Africa medallions and "X" hats were a ubiquitous presence among Black college students who expressed a pride in Blackness that updated their parents' "Black is beautiful" with "It's a Black thang, you wouldn't understand." On the campuses of historically Black colleges and universities (HBCUs) and historically white colleges and universities (HWCUs), the emergence of protest movements garnered attention. The former were under assault, once again by the assumption that they were losing relevance, and the latter housed both the right-wing, "fraternity hi-jinks" variant of racism and the softer liberal racisms cloaked in the robes of "Western civilization," making Black consciousness an untenable presence on those campuses. More than simply the folly of youth, as it is often rendered, the Black student activists of this era produced an important and lasting addition to the long history of Black resistance in both the cultural and political realms. They continued the transformation of colleges and universities undertaken by previous generations, one that has had both positive and unintended consequences. And as they matured, they helped to cultivate what has come to be known as "hip hop activism"—a vision of social change grounded in these collective experiences that is still struggling to realize the substantive desires of an ideal world that inspired the activism of the nineties.

Black Nia F.O.R.C.E (BNF) both stimulated and participated in this national efflorescence. In the immediate aftermath and in the long term, BNF members—many of who had cut their teeth organizing and planning the 1989 protest and by working in the BNF-controlled Howard University Student Association (HUSA) and in The Cultural Initiative—engaged Black student activists on other campuses and contributed to the development of broader national organizations and other efforts to make good on what the movement represented. That work would eventuate in a short-lived effort to make BNF a national organization, with the purpose being, as it had always been, to create a force.

A Black Thang

The relationships that BNF cultivated with activists on other campuses began in 1989 while they were still in the Administration Building. As word got out about the takeover, students from "as far away as Morehouse College in Atlanta and as close as the University of Maryland" showed up in DC to lend their support as well as to trade notes on their particular struggles.[3] Others took indirect inspiration. Before that semester transitioned into summer at least three similar takeovers took place.

At Morris Brown College, a private HBCU in the Atlanta University Center (AUC, a consortium of HBCUs in the Atlanta area), students, triggered by a dormitory fire, called for the creation of an African American Studies program, improved housing, and more time to settle delinquent fees. Though they only numbered twenty, they were able to mount a two-day takeover on April 4, buoyed by the support of 150–200 picketing AUC students outside. After commandeering an office to demand accountability, Faith Tuckenberry and other protest leaders were jailed and then expelled from their schools. Dubbed the "AUC 20," they were subsequently readmitted after a lawsuit, but their activism took a toll, with a few of the students unable to continue their studies. Nevertheless, they felt that they had changed Morris Brown for the better with the approval of their proposed African American Studies program constituting a huge lift.[4] Today, however, Morris Brown is struggling after losing its accreditation in 2002 in the wake of an embezzlement scandal.

The debate and lamentation over Georgia's first independently Black founded institution's plight rages on.[5]

The year also saw protests at several HWCUs. A week after the Morris Brown takeover, Black students at Detroit's Wayne State University, led in part by Cherine Shaaban and future political scientist Errol Henderson, engineered a takeover of that institution's student services building that lasted eleven days. Numbering over one hundred at the height of the occupation, these students, participating in what they dubbed a "study-in," demanded an Africana Studies program, more scholarships for Black students, and more Black faculty.[6] Unlike the HBCU protests, there were fewer "quality of life" concerns, and although this protest occurred in the eighties, it was also seemingly more reminiscent of protests at HWCUs in the sixties.

There were more recent precedents, too. At Pennsylvania State University, the previous year had seen protests by Black students who demanded an increased effort to recruit Black students to the university and the hiring of a vice president of Pan-African affairs. The fifteen-hour takeover of the school's telecommunications building resulted in the arrests of all eighty-nine participants. This too, was an echo of the protest movements of years past. However, one of its leaders, the future state senator Kevin Parker, was close to members of BNF and thus shared many of the same "eighties" ideological influences.[7]

Black Nia F.O.R.C.E directly supported a student protest at another HWCU. Traveling home to New York, many BNF members participated in the late April protests in the City University of New York (CUNY) system against the gargantuan 80 percent tuition hike widely seen as a way to force poorer students out.[8] Traditionally the bastion of working-class upward mobility, the CUNY colleges had free tuition up until 1976. City College, the most famous of the schools, had been the home of many important Black Studies figures like Toni Cade Bambara and the poet June Jordan, whose essay "Black Studies: Bringing Back the Person" was a memorable foray into the power of declaring space in and under the Western academy. The year she penned that work, students at City College and elsewhere in the system had valiantly fought for open admissions, which was one of the victories that seemed to be under direct assault by the proposed increases of 1989.[9] Able to stop operations of multiple campuses in the system, the students achieved a temporary victory. In the years following, however, the austerity politics of the 1990s assured that the downward pressure of budget cuts would be felt by poorer students. Another protest followed in 1991, and a more recent demonstration over the closing of the Morales-Shakur Center at the City College of New York in 2013—a community and student center that was part of the victory of the students in 1989—reveals the ongoing struggles for public higher education in New York.[10]

There were similar pressures exerted on publicly funded HBCUs. As the neoliberal economic model was imposed, public funds became more and more unavailable to support higher education.[11] Black institutions were hit the hardest. In some cases, public HWCUs were given more state funding than HBCUs, even as the former had more sources of private support. The result was that those burdens were passed along to students in the form of tuition increases. In an attempt to solve the problems caused after this naturally resulted in lower enrollment, some state governments suggested mergers with other state institutions. The idea to merge colleges and universities was a standard solution for conservative lawmakers in their attempts to save state funds by denying the continued necessity of these HBCUs. Amid the decisions in the *Adams* and *Fordice* cases, HBCU advocates fought for the very survival of these institutions.[12]

This assault on the legacies of land-grant institutions was resisted at places like Tennessee State University in Nashville. By 1990, matters had come to a head, leading to a protest lasting upward of three weeks. Led by student government president, jeff carr, the student body planned an elaborate takeover of the school's administration building after the administration's nonresponsiveness to demands that it address issues around the maintenance of the university. Students were plagued with "bad plumbing, rats and vermin, poor lighting and crumbling conditions in and around dorms and classrooms on campus."[13] In a document titled, "The 1990 Manifesto," the students demanded extra attention to improvements in the library and computer laboratory, security on campus, and an emphasis on Black history month.[14] When the university did not respond, over five hundred students shut down the building on February 21. By that afternoon, a one-hundred-fifty-member SWAT team showed up, threatening to forcibly remove the students. Faced with an important decision about safety, the remaining seventy-five students decided to leave the building shortly before midnight. But the protest continued.[15]

Relocating to the downtown campus later in the week, the direct action transitioned to an extended sit-in, as student activists demanded the resignation of key administration officials and amnesty. Around this time, the national news began to cover the events in Nashville.[16] At Howard, BNF was working to elect Silver and Baraka and preparing to note the anniversary of their own protest. But in the midst of those concerns, members decided to travel to Nashville on the second weekend of the protest to show support and solidarity with the Tennessee State students. Packing two fifteen-passenger vans, a crew of BNF members and associates including Aarian Pope, Jam Shakwi, and Ras Baraka made their way to the downtown campus to meet with carr and others. Expecting a scene much like theirs the previous year (and the previous week at Tennessee State), they came with lessons learned about security and other tactical measures. But the situation was slightly different. By the time they arrived, the Tennessee State students were in the midst of a hunger strike designed to dramatize their issues and concerns. The BNF delegation stayed for a few hours before wishing them well and beginning the long drive back to DC, conceding that there was not much else that they could do.[17]

In the end, the importance of the trip turned out to be the connections it fostered, particularly as Silver and Baraka's HUSA campaign sought to build a network of Black student activists across the country.[18] It was clear that, just as the March protest at Howard had done, events at Tennessee State were shaping up to be significant to the future of student struggle and higher education. However the protest at Tennessee State ended, it would result in the expansion of the reach of BNF.

The Tennessee State situation was resolved on March 9, about a week after BNF left.[19] But protests at public HBCUs were hardly over. At two Maryland institutions the issue was rising fees—the austerity budgets of that state had recommended increases in student fees, even as spending per pupil and/or dedicated resources remained stagnant and unequal across the state's Black institutions. In Morgan State University's case, these resources were not enough to overcome historic shortfalls in funding, which led to an aging infrastructure.[20]

As students were ending their ordeal in Tennessee, two hundred Morgan State students shut down Truth Hall on March 6. Led by Travis Mitchell, the students organized a weeklong strike. The general neglect of the institution's physical plant, coupled with the plan to increase tuition, led student activists to focus their attention on Annapolis and the policies of Governor William Donald Schaefer.[21] During the week, busloads of students marched to his office and demanded an audience. While the state did not shift on its planned budget, it conceded on issues surrounding security and updated plans for renovations, while the students vowed to keep pressure on the governor. A year later, an appearance by Governor Schaefer to dedicate the new buildings erupted in violence, when students, angered by the rumors that they would be merged with crosstown Coppin State, were forcibly removed by the police.[22]

Later that March, students occupied the administration building of nearby Bowie State University, in Princes Georges County, Maryland, for thirty hours, "irate" at the increased fees for room, board, and other related charges. After a negotiation with the administration, they were able to force the university to lower the planned increases.[23]

That summer did not quell things. Much like the previous summer with Public Enemy's "Fight the Power" as the soundtrack, youth discontent only intensified as new conscious albums from Ice Cube, X Clan, and A Tribe Called Quest narrated the mood. A month after students returned to classes, yet another demonstration at a public HBCU was taking place. On Wednesday, September 26, students at the University of the District Columbia (UDC) took over Building 38, the institution's nerve center, and demanded the removal of members of its board of trustees.

The protest was led by Mark Thompson, head of the Pan-African Student Association and student government president Lisa Shaw.[24] Thompson had worked with BNF members earlier that month at the Back to Black Virginia Beach boycott and was close to many of the leaders of Howard's 1989 protest. By afternoon, Howard students were there to help secure an additional building, the neighboring Building 39.[25] A *Washington Times* photographer depicted April Silver and Sheri Warren storming the structure, perhaps unaware that they were Howard students. By Thursday, UDC was effectively shut down, and the protest leaders and administration were debating some forty-two demands. The major issue that students had with the board was the belief that it was frivolously spending money on initiatives that had very little to do with their education while neglecting the primary needs of many members of its student body. The large number of demands reflected the inadequate attention given to even basic questions, like the availability of textbooks by the first day of classes. The students were supported by both the faculty and the city council and other community leaders aided in the negotiations. Howard students on the scene aided by giving UDC students advice from their own experiences of the struggles, which led them to create an area in the occupied building that was designated for study. Fortunately, the police were not called in, and by October 6, the protest—dubbed "Kiamsha," Swahili for "that which wakes you up"— ended in a victory for the students.[26]

The question of public funding of state institutions has been a critical one in recent years, with the #FeesMustFall movement in South Africa and the attempts to imagine and create a tuition-free system in the United States.[27] The foresight of these protests then represents another vantage point for understanding the nature of higher education policy amid the erosion of the welfare state. As many of these institutions continue to struggle today, the options for solving problems of unequal funding are being increasingly remanded to philanthropic organizations and public-private partnerships at best. But equal funding, as the students in Tennessee and Maryland have shown, is a moral issue at its heart. Their parents paid taxes, too, after all. And, broadly speaking, one could also conceive of higher education as a form of reparative justice.

Protests would continue for at least two years and beyond at HBCUs and urban HWCUs with substantial Black populations like Temple and Rutgers. Unlike other upheavals, such as the anti-apartheid protests of a few years earlier, activists who convened in the summer of 1990 for a march around these issues were "overwhelmingly Black." What held these various direct actions together was an emphasis on the strength of Black institutions, whether they were as large as HBCUs or as small as the Black Studies departments and Black Student Unions on HWCU campuses. Black students exhibiting this "cultural awareness" believed that their people required their own institutions.[28] They also saw the changing world around them, not as evidence of the decline of a self-determined identity, but as a signal that that identity needed to be strengthened now more than ever. What Michael Dawson calls "community nationalism," the idea of Black communal identity, ensued from this generation's beliefs in the basic idea of Black institutional development.[29] In their hands, Blackness remained a way of being in the world, despite the momentous challenges that peoples of African ancestry faced. That consciousness would need to follow students to the so-called real world, a world they faced with less naïveté, with the experience of participating in resistance and a greater commitment to realizing a more ideal world.

Beyond Howard

Black Nia F.O.R.C.E members spent Spring Break 1991 in upstate New York at a leadership retreat, fostering an environment where many of the graduating members discussed the next steps of the organization.[30] In order to realize and enact the worlds that they imagined at Howard, BNF members created two chapters beyond the campus and an overarching national structure. As many of the original members graduated and moved back home, these chapters were located in New York City and eventually in Newark, New Jersey. They essentially continued much of what had taken place at Howard, holding regular meetings and training sessions as well as participating in marches and rallies. April Silver was named national executive minister, Ras Baraka was named executive minister of the New York chapter, and Lisa "Sister Souljah" Williamson joined the organization as the minister of external affairs for the New York chapter. Chuck Webb and Carlisle Sealy would also serve on the National Executive Board during this phase. As the new chapters got off the ground in 1991, there was some difficulty in understanding the new direction of the organization, particularly as it related to the campus chapter, which was rebranded as the DC chapter. The next few executive ministers of the organization in DC were Sevie Zawdie, Jelani Makalani (Cobb), and Shawn Houston, each with different styles and skills brought to bear on the organization's mission. During the year and a half after the new chapters and executive leadership positions were established, some felt that the relationship between the local chapters and the national board needed to be clarified and that the new structure was difficult to follow.[31]

In December 1992, the governing document of the organization was revised to clarify the role of the National Executive Board's relationship with the regional chapters and the responsibilities of each. The national leadership also mandated committee work as a way to alleviate the pressures upon the central leadership and to instill a sense of discipline and ownership among the masses. Although these were important changes, the rigor of constructing a national organization was more complicated than anything the group had faced while being domiciled at Howard. Many of the tactics that they had employed were unique to the Howard experience and could not be easily replicated in New York and New Jersey.[32] Although these challenges were ongoing, the group continued with plans to expand the organization to include Illinois (Chicago) and Georgia (Atlanta) chapters.

As they were updating their internal governance documents, the national executive board members of BNF worked to develop a comprehensive national strategy by creating a platform akin to the Nation of Islam's ten-point platform and the Black Panther Party's Ten Point Program.[33] Like its predecessors, the platform exhibited a mixture of nationalist, socialist, and liberal ideas calling for (1) self-determination: an "independent mass revolutionary political party"; (2) education: equal funding and history "taught based upon the truth"; (3) economic and social empowerment: "collective ownership and control of the economic institutions in our communities," an "end to exploitation," full employment, free health care, and decent and affordable housing; (4) democracy: "an end to private investment in campaigns," the abolition of the electoral college and lifetime appointments to the Supreme Court; (5) the end of state violence: "an end to the state and police occupations of our community" and "an end to police brutality, harassment, and infiltration," (6) an end to the drug trade: "We want the government to stop sending drugs and guns into our community"; (7) an exemption from military service: "We refuse to help the USA dominate and oppress other Nations of World"; and (8) justice: "juries that are truly representative of our community," "affordable bail," "a more human penal system," reparations, and "an immediate release of all political prisoners and prisoners of war!!!"[34] Under "What We Believe," they asserted their ideological alignments with

> 1) Nationalism: we have a common history, culture, language, origin and enemy. We must come together to define, develop, and defend our own institutions; 2) Pan Africanism: Afrikan people throughout the world share a common rich culture and a history of slavery, colonialism, culture oppression, and economic exploitation [and] if Afrika is not free then Black people through the world will not be free; 3) Internationalism: all oppressed people, national and internationally, must unite and organize against their common oppressor [and] coalitions should be established on the basis of equality and independence; 4) Socialism: capitalism is based on individualism, exploitation, and oppression [and the] only just society is one in which the masses of people own and control the wealth for their collective benefit; 5) Reformism is Futile: the Amerikkkan society has proven to be incapable of producing true freedom, justice, and equality, [and as such] we must organize and mobilize a mass revolutionary movement; 6) Self Defense: Afrikan people, as all people have the right to defend themselves *by any means necessary!!!!*[35]

These principles would be applied in numerous ways. Continuing to frame this work as revolution, The Cultural Initiative's Hip-Hop Conference remained the premier event at Howard. In addition to the hip hop conferences, the DC chapter of BNF continued to work closely with the Howard student leadership, develop community programs with local children, and edit a newspaper entitled *The FORCE*. On campus, BNF members managed to mount an impressive array of public programming, focusing on issues as varied as electoral politics and bridging religious divides on campus. And there was always a rally to attend and support. Internally, the chapter maintained a comradely love, fostering deep and abiding connections with their retreats, men's and women's meetings, and other tributes they paid to one another as they worked toward the revolution.[36]

The New York BNF chapter met at the historic Minisink Townhouse in Harlem, training every Saturday in Red Hook, Brooklyn. In addition to holding a major series entitled "The State of Black Youth" at Friendship Baptist Church in Brooklyn, the chapter participated and helped organize the high school student walkouts to protest the Rodney King verdict and other direct actions around the issue of police brutality. Black Nia F.O.R.C.E was there as organizations like the Malcolm X Grassroots Movement and the December 12th Movement demonstrated against the rampant use of force by the New York Police Department, making it perhaps the most significant domestic social justice issue of that period.[37]

In Newark, the BNF chapter under the leadership of Baraka actively sought to create the city's first civilian complaint review board in 1992. There were at least three major police-involved killings of Black youth, leading to a November rally led by BNF at City Hall calling for more oversight. It was Baraka's first foray into the thick of Newark's municipal politics. With Mayor Sharpe James and other city councilpersons opposing the creation of the board, the fight over the board would become an important preface to the emergence of the hip hop generation's more formal participation in politics.[38]

While BNF's national presence was an example of a prominent youth organization working for social and political change, theirs was not the only hip hop inspired movements taking place across the country and world. A cadre of hip hop activists had emerged by the early 1990s, including veteran organizers like Sister Souljah, Kevin Powell, Conrad (Tillard) Muhammad, Lisa Sullivan, Steven Wilson, Matthew Countryman, Mark Thompson, and Malik Zulu Shabazz, along with activists like Van Jones and Rosa Clemente.[39] As Bakari Kitwana's *The Hip Hop Generation* shows, Black youth were organizing across various issues and ideological hues. But just as it would be for the generation that has begun to organize under the broad umbrella of Black Lives Matter in the mid 2010s, police brutality was an issue that unified Black youth in the early to mid-1990s. Kitwana writes that "the collapse of trust in law enforcement" that has ensued from police violence had played "a role in the view Black youth share about legislation, law enforcement, and criminal justice."[40] Representing the sharp disagreements regarding solutions to police brutality between younger Black activists against the old guard, a twenty-four-year-old Ras Baraka threw his hat into the Newark mayoral race in 1994.

Reflecting a strategy that was utilized by his father and the Committee for a Unified Newark—and most recently BNF's attempt to take over

HUSA—Baraka's decision to work from the inside of a city government did not immediately achieve consensus among all BNF members. It was thought that working on the inside meant becoming the establishment, as opposed to raging against it, which had become a key facet of BNF's identity. Could the platform created in 1992 be fulfilled from the mayor's office?[41]

To make matters worse, BNF again struggled internally around other issues as Baraka's decision to run for office was floated. Questions of leadership, direction, contradictions in interpersonal relationships, and what Aaron Lloyd characterizes as "real-life" problems began to challenge the sustainability of BNF as it had been constructed. Along with some fractured relationships, the latter concern would become one of the factors that would lead to the demise of BNF as an organization. According to Lloyd, those real-life issues produced a critical distinction between the kinds of organizational challenges they faced as young adults and those they faced as students. Consequently, the group never achieved the kind of membership they had hoped for and envisioned, resulting in the core of the organization being burdened with a workload that made it difficult to maintain. After less than five years, the beginning of the end for the national organization's imprint in New York was imminent.[42]

Nevertheless, the group maintained the bonds that were forged in this struggle. The connections that Silver made in her work in BNF and The Cultural Initiative influenced the development of her public relations firm. She told Angela Ards that "one of its missions" was to "'deglamorize' hip-hop for school-age kids." On the role of the artist, she argued that "you can't just wake up and be an artist. We come from a greater legacy of excellency than that. Artists don't have the luxury to not be political."[43] Joining many others in the music and arts communities, Silver's *nia* has remained consistent.

The vast majority of BNF organizers ended up working in education. They found their vocations in both independent African-centered institutions as well as public and higher educational school systems. This reflected the commitments that had begun at the outset of the organization's creation and was shown in both the governing documents and platform, as well as the organizational injunction to study and the consistent dissemination of reading lists.[44] Black Nia F.O.R.C.E veterans include school principals like Sheri Warren and teacher-training professionals like Akanke Washington, among a coterie of teachers that also includes Carlisle Sealy and Jam Shakwi. Regarding the prevalence of educators among former BNF members, Akanke Washington believes it to be a consequence of "the experience that people have when they come to Howard. . . . They realize there was all this stuff left out of their history, and [then they] learn to explain phenomena in their communities and . . . and start to want children to not experience that."[45]

In the closing years of BNF's existence, they all pitched in to ensure that what began as an assault against apathy would transform into something resembling a permanent transformation in the world of politics. Still together in 1994, BNF would, of course, eventually endorse Baraka's run. Killa Patterson remembers going to Newark in the frigid weather to campaign for Baraka, demonstrating that, although there were now newer chapters, there was still a sense of "togetherness. We were all together."[46] Perhaps it was *nia* that had brought them warmth.

Under the slogan "The People's Platform," Baraka's campaign called for a total restructuring of city government to center the self-determination of Newark's residents. Baraka worked as an eighth-grade teacher at the time, but this mayoral run ultimately became the new beginning of a lifelong vocation. It was the opening salvo of an extensive attempt to remake municipal politics in a moment where Black mayors were increasingly representing the status quo. Although he came in third in that election, receiving only 8 percent of the vote, this was only the beginning, and everyone seemed to realize that.[47]

At the end of the 1990s, while BNF was no more, Baraka was busy helping to organize the Hip Hop Convention of 2004, a formation that was modeled on the Gary National Black Political Convention of 1972, which his father Amiri had helped convene.[48] After a stint as deputy mayor, Baraka was again ready to run for mayor in 2014. Cory Booker, who had represented politics as usual, much more than even Sharpe James, had been mayor the previous seven years, often bumping heads with Baraka.[49] In 2013, Booker was appointed to the U.S. Senate, leaving the mayoral seat vacant. After a campaign during which his father made his transition, former BNF comrades mobilized to help Baraka get elected on May 13, 2014. His words to the city on the night of his victory echoed his campaign slogan: "We are the mayor."[50] The "people's platform" had been rearticulated, and in many ways the *nia* of Black Nia F.O.R.C.E now informed the collective head of the New Ark. Despite major structural difficulties, Baraka was elected to a second term. The final scenes of that story are still unfolding.

Coda

None but those who feel it know.
—Kelly Miller[1]

The conditions that necessitated the protests of 1968 persisted into 1989. And they continued to persist in 2018. Months into the presidency of Donald J. Trump—a harrowing replay of the New Right's ascendancy—students at Howard again mounted a demonstration, leading to the first major takeover in almost thirty years. Coupled with the outrage of the university's welcome to members of Trump's administration and the continued "quality of life" problems on campus, a group bearing the name HUResist began to organize. Inspired by the words of Sonia Sanchez, they also reflected the unique questions raised by a generation of students shaped by the so-called identitarian movements of the 2010s that have been so roundly rejected by both the Left and the Right.[2]

While the issues stemmed from the same conditions, we might, like Michael Blakey, think of the challenges of Howard as more representative of certain "conditions of knowledge," rather than conceiving them as simply conditions of student life and university maintenance, although the two are intimately related. Reflecting a deeper understanding of what is at work, we might ask: Under what conditions would Black thought and thinking traditions determine the nature of what it means to fulfill the goals of our institutions?[3]

A year of organizing led to a breaking point on March 29, 2018. While the news media, activated by the distortions of the social media world, located the cause of the protest to a financial aid scandal, many of the larger issues that moved the Howard students were the same as they had always been. Rehashing and updating the energy from the sixties, the student leadership again called for a "Black university." Demanding that the administration be more responsive to issues facing the surrounding campus community, the students also looked inward and found the university's policies surrounding campus rape culture and mental health, as well as the formal grievance process, to be wanting. Their nine demands also spoke to concerns that were much the same as for the earlier takeover, such as housing and tuition increases. Feeling that these issues could not be resolved under the current leadership, they demanded the resignations of the executive committee of the board and the president of the university.[4]

The students remained in the building for nine days, receiving widespread community, faculty, and alumni support. And as always, there were those who dissented, particularly on the demand that called for new leadership. The paradox, as true as it had been in 1989, is that all involved desired a university that was responsible and responsive to the various communities it represented.[5] But what made the students in 1968, 1989, and again in 2018 move to drastic action was a struggle over meaning. It was not over Howard's mission, for that has been settled. The struggle is one of why, as much as it informs the method of how. And this "why" as much as the "how" was and continues to be a question of ideology.

Howard is both blessed and cursed to contain the multitude of ideological variations that exist under the broad rubric of the Black community. The perception of particular political challenges then produces not only debate but also grave and enduring disagreements that resonate strongly along whatever ideological terrain one finds oneself. Everyone believes that they are right. And it is often true that, much of the time, if we are not clear about how we frame the questions, we hollow out the very real contradictions that define HBCUs generally and Howard in particular.[6] To stake a position is less about Howard's motto of "truth and service" than it is a question of teleology—what sort of purposes our actions serve. The tension that produced the moments of upheaval in 2018 was resolved without resolution to those larger, more exacting concerns.[7] We have not answered W. E. B. Du Bois's 1960 question of "Whither now and why?"—of how we might organize and orient Black life and our cultural messages to address human problems.[8] Thinking with Du Bois's question—and the larger intellectual tradition that produced him—will help us address the twenty-first-century challenges of late capitalism, neoliberalism, climate change, and a resurgent globalized white nationalism that make *this* world increasingly unlivable.[9]

The oft-quoted dictum of Frantz Fanon concerning the discovery of each generation's mission is always prescient, but it is often deployed to suggest that that mission is self-evident without a deep reckoning with the traditions that constitute communities of meaning and the activation of resistance.[10] If, as the Zulu believe, a person is a person because of people, a generation is a generation because of generations. And a student movement is a student movement because of student movements. A discovery of a mission cannot truly occur absent a deep recovery of genealogy.

In these moments of discovery, we might reflect on the story of the 1989 protest, for it reminds us that the complex motivations structuring student action were grounded in a tradition of a particular kind of struggle. The various labels we affix to the energy present on the ground often do not suffice. At Howard, Black thought is decidedly shaped by the contradictions of the Black elite, who often contain a strand that is defined by Cedric Robinson as the Black Radical intelligentsia—a variant of the Black Radical tradition—that exists for a different purpose than those structuring the elite from which it has diverged.[11] As Greg Carr asserts, it is often love that causes these "often-discordant strains" to "cohere," a love that emanates from a conception of the world that understands that our only hope is "to act collectively to contain the dissonances and search for harmonic resolution."[12] This is an act and a vocation that is guided by a set of "ideals."[13] The vast and capacious notion of a Black Radical tradition renders Blackness not merely as a racialized category but also as a cultural identity, as a way of being and acting upon this world. It is this tradition that guided students in Black Nia F.O.R.C.E in their belief that their cultural traditions made their identity something that had to be preserved as a first-order premise in order for them to be truly educated and truly human. It was the very thing that concerned Du Bois in 1960.

The story of the 1989 protest reminds us that ultimately the struggles for and with universities are not about any formulaic notion of democracy or access to a decision-making apparatus. Black radicalism is not merely the idea of speaking truth to power or disrupting the status quo. Black radicalism is not merely responding to the ways of white supremacy, the forms it takes, the structures it rationalizes. Protest is not simply the pursuit of a set of demands. It is about making certain that our ways of being remain with us, for they provide answers to the question of how and why "we be." They are our answers to the question of what it is to be human.

What the media has not been able to fully capture is that Black student protest was and is this categorical rejection of *this* world, this way of being in it. The desire to struggle and create carries with it the literal memories of a world where Black people are more than this world has rendered them, where they are *other* than this world. This otherworldliness, this sacred and spiritual energy that resolves, rather than distorts, is what makes Black radicalism what it has been and must be. April Silver reminds us that "the sacrifice of what we were fighting for, the preservation, there's a spiritual connection there that can't be quantified. The connection to our ancestors, physically, for the students there and the alumni. And then the broader African [world] . . . that is for me, in terms of my lens, probably the biggest [and most] important factor of what we did."[14]

It is the unseen but felt that moves and inspires. The student protest of 1989 was, above all, a feeling. And none but those who felt it will ever know. It is available if we are open to feeling, to imagining. We can all connect to that knowing and to that movement so that we can feel for ourselves what we must do in the name of liberation. And if we feel it, we, too, can envision a future where Blackness, Black being—a backward-gazing improvisation of a rhythm for our present situation—structures and orients our imagination of what the future world can be.

It is a dream, but it is in imagination where we find what makes the struggle beautiful, where we find what is worth fighting for.

ACKNOWLEDGMENTS

I never set out to write a history. But this work is a testament to an energy and force that we must draw upon again and again, for it is eternal. I am thankful first and foremost to Akanke Washington, Jam Shakwi, and April Silver for trusting me with the responsibility to put it into words. Each of them has in their own way made every single element of this book possible. From the initial outline to their indispensable advice, the connections that they helped to make and the private archives that they made available, their contributions are the warp and woof of this history. It is really their book. Along those lines, I am grateful to all of the members and friends of Black Nia F.O.R.C.E who agreed to be interviewed for this history. Time is a sacred possession, and each of you did all that you could to make space for the necessary conversations that made this text. May your memories be the inspiration for the continued struggle for the ideals for which you sacrificed. I should point out especially Haqq Islam, who committed time above and beyond his interview to helping me understand the culture of Black nationalism in the 1980s and in providing leads to important archival sources—there are still stories to be told concerning your life and work. I also want to thank the many others who agreed to be interviewed for other portions of the text.

No book is possible without libraries. We would do well to remember and honor the work of individuals who too often go nameless. Any writer that seeks to tell the story of Africans in the diaspora will likely encounter the wonderful staff of Howard University's Moorland-Spingarn Research Center. And of course, any book on Howard University will benefit greatly from their work. I would like to thank Kenvi Phillips, JoEllen ElBashir, Sonja Woods, Lopez Matthews, Alhaji Conteh, Richard Jenkins, Ishmael Childs, and Amber Junipher for their help in extraordinary and quotidian ways. The same is true of the staff in other branches of the Howard University Libraries who helped me to track down various resources.

This work also benefited greatly from commentaries and critiques of other scholars. My own colleagues Shauna Morgan, Robert Edgar, and David Green read portions of the earlier drafts. It was also enhanced from conversations with Jocelyn Imani, the author of a forthcoming work on an earlier Howard protest. I must also thank others for random words of encouragement, inquiries about my progress, and other forms of support: my colleagues in the Department of Afro-American Studies at Howard—Greg Carr, Valethia Watkins, Mario Beatty, Amy Yeboah, Andrew Billingsley, and Donald'A Gaddy—as well as others at Howard and in the broader academy who did so in big and small ways— Yolonda Wilson, Dana Williams, Justin Dunnavant, Gerald Horne, Ashon Crawley, Robin D. G. Kelley, Corey D. B. Walker, James Pope, Charisse Burden-Stelly, Harold McDougall, and Ida Jones. In the later stages, Joseph McCormick and Alvin Thornton provided an important perspective to the events of 1989. I am thankful for Professor McCormick's donation of a private collection of clippings on the protest. The section on apartheid was enhanced by the connections made through conversations with Sylvia Hill, who was always willing to listen. Thanks also to Bill Stephney and Jeff Chang for clearing up the details regarding the 1987 conference at Howard University, where Public Enemy made an appearance.

My students at Howard University are a reflection of the brilliance articulated in these pages. In these pages you will find some of what animates the approach taken in our courses together.

Nina Burkett, Chauncey Dennie, James Pope, DeVona Mitchell, Jocelyn Imani, Greg Carr, Courtney Javois, and Jahaan Shaheed helped improve earlier drafts of this work—all at a moment's notice. One thing I will remember from that experience is both the power and impotence of the indefinite pronoun. Thank you for dropping what you were doing to ensure that this work sang.

A special thanks and shout-out to Marc Lamont Hill, who allowed us to conduct a group interview at his beautiful space in the Germantown neighborhood of Philadelphia. I am thankful as well to the three anonymous reviewers solicited by New York University Press. Their comments forced me to reckon with the nature of American historiography and the question of Black self-determination anew. The philosophical thrust of this work is largely the result of that introspection.

New York University Press has been a joy to work with. I am thankful to Clara Platter, Amy Klopfenstein, and their team for their work in making this process a smooth one.

Finally, to my family, friends, as well as co-members of a number of organizations, especially to those who felt that this work took me away from them. Please know that this work was and is about more than a job or career, that it is larger than that. I want to thank each and every one of you for understanding that even when it was not immediately clear. I must name specifically Ava Wilson, Nicole Triplett, Chigozie Onyema, Jahaan Shaheed, Malik Washington, Christina Brantley, O. Christopher Buckner, Mario Antwine, Ray Baker, Kioni Kai Jaminnia Rosalind Wells States, Sawdayah Brownlee, and Makina Table. Alexsandra Mitchell has been there from the beginning to end, listening to little tidbits of history, laughing at the wild stories that will never make it into print, and, most important, encouraging the completion of this work. Thanks for being in the tradition of Jean Blackwell Hutson. I am thankful for the eldership of A. Peter Bailey, Dorie Ladner, Ron McCoy, Moriba Kelsey, Ife Carruthers, Acklyn Lynch, and Karen Spellman, who offered encouragement and perspective, specific to this work, but more often about matters much larger.

To my immediate and extended family—my parents James and Joyce, brother Chris and sister Jennifer and my uncle Alton—thanks for your questions, concerns, and encouragement. I hope the final product is something that you can learn from.

And then there are the ancestors, who are always in front.

NOTES

INTRODUCTION

1 A version of this story can be found in Joyce A. Joyce, "Interviews with Amiri Baraka, Askia Touré, and Sonia Sanchez," in her *Black Studies as Human Studies* (Albany: State University of New York Press, 2005), 156–157.

2 See W. E. B. Du Bois, *Autobiography of W.E.B. Du Bois: A Soliloquy on Viewing My Life from the Last Decade of Its First Century* (New York: International Publishers, 1968); Paul Robeson, *Here I Stand* (Boston: Beacon Press, 1958); Gerald Horne, *Black and Red: W.E.B. Du Bois and the Afro-American Response to the Cold War, 1944–1963* (Albany: State University of New York Press, 1986); Paul Goodman, *Paul Robeson: A Watched Man* (London: Verso, 2013); and Tony Martin, *Race First: The Ideological and Organizational Struggles of Marcus Garvey and the Universal Negro Improvement Association* (Westport, CT: Greenwood Press, 1976).

3 Annie Finch, "Form and Spirit: A Conversation with Sonia Sanchez," in *Conversations with Sonia Sanchez*, ed. Joyce A. Joyce (Jackson: University Press of Mississippi, 2007), 28–29. On Hutson, see Glendora Johnson-Cooper, "African-American Historical Continuity: Jean Blackwell Hutson and the Schomburg Center for Research in Black Culture," in *Reclaiming the American Library Past: Writing the Women in*, ed. Suzanne Hildenbrand (Norwood, NJ: Ablex, 1996), 27–51.

4 April Silver, "Howard U Student Protest of 1989: The Takeover, 25 Years Later," *Liberator Magazine* (July 2014), posted at the *Live from Planet Earth* website, www.live-fromplanetearth.org.

5 Gil Troy, *Morning in America: How Ronald Reagan Invented the 1980s* (Princeton, NJ: Princeton University Press, 2005); and James Patterson, *Restless Giant: The United States from Watergate to Bush v. Gore* (New York: Oxford University Press, 2005).

6 See Michael Dawson, *Black Visions: The Roots of Contemporary African American Political Ideologies* (Chicago: University of Chicago Press, 2001), 85–134, on the history of nationalism and its resurgence in the 1990s. On the idea of the "Mecca," see Sohail Daulatzai, *Black Star, Crescent Moon: The Muslim International and Black Freedom beyond America* (Minneapolis: University of Minnesota Press, 2012), 89–136.

7 Doug Rossinow, *The Reagan Era: A History of the 1980s* (New York: Columbia University Press, 2015), 119–138.

8 See Michael Flamm, *Law and Order: Street Crime, Civil Unrest, and the Crisis of Liberalism in the 1960s* (New York: Columbia University Press, 2005); and Keeanga-Yamahtta Taylor, *From #BlackLivesMatter to Black Liberation* (Chicago: Haymarket Books, 2016).

9 The literature on the Civil Rights movement/Black Power and the New Right is vast and might usefully be gleaned from the following: Sundiata Keita Cha-Jua and Clar-

ence Lang, "The 'Long Movement' as Vampire: Temporal and Spatial Fallacies in Recent Black Freedom Studies," *Journal of African America History* 92, no. 2 (Spring 2007): 265–288; Peniel Joseph, "The Black Power Movement: A State of the Field," *Journal of American History* 96, no. 3 (December 2009): 751–776; and Kim Phillips-Fein, "Conservatism: A State of the Field," *Journal of American History* 98, no. 3 (December 2011): 723–743.

10 An exception to this general tendency is Sekou Franklin, *After the Rebellion: Black Youth, Social Movement Activism, and the Post-Civil Rights Generation* (New York: New York University Press, 2014). See also Richard Iton, *In Search of the Black Fantastic: Politics and Popular Culture in the Post Civil Rights Era* (New York: Oxford University Press, 2009).

11 Ngugi wa Thiong'o, *Something Torn and New: An African Renaissance* (New York: Basic, 2009).

12 See Greg Carr, "'You Don't Call the Kittens Biscuits': Disciplinary Africana Studies and the Study of Malcolm X," in *Malcolm X: A Historical Reader*, ed. James L. Conyers, Jr., and Andrew P. Smallwood (Durham, NC: Carolina Academic Press, 2008), 353–375, and "Towards an Intellectual History of Africana Studies: Genealogy and Normative Theory," in *The African American Studies Reader*, ed. Nathaniel Norment, Jr. (Durham, NC: Carolina Academic Press, 2007), 438–452. I am inspired here also by the work of Cedric Robinson, *Black Marxism: The Making of the Black Radical Tradition* (Chapel Hill: University of North Carolina Press, 2000); and Vincent Harding, *There Is a River: The Black Struggle for Freedom in America* (Orlando, FL: Harcourt Brace Jovanovich, 1981).

13 The Howard University historian Rayford W. Logan uses this term in his centennial history of the university, *Howard University: The First Hundred Years* (New York: New York University Press, 1968), 562.

14 This "civic mythology" is, of course, "(Martin Luther) King-centric" with other important touchstones such as *Brown v. Board of Education* (1954) and the Civil Rights Act (1964) and the Voting Rights Act (1965). The juxtaposition of a triumph with the rendering of Black anger as "excessive" works to imagine an America that sees itself as no longer needing race-based remedies. See Nikhil Pal Singh, *Black Is a Country: Race and the Unfinished Struggle for Democracy* (Cambridge, MA: Harvard University Press, 2005), 5. In terms of the official strategies of the movement, many theorists point to Bayard Rustin's seminal "From Protest to Politics: The Future of the Civil Rights Movement," *Commentary* 39 (February 1965): 25–31, in establishing the origin of this notion of a "post–Civil Rights era."

15 On the uses (or abuses) of this consensus view, see Houston Baker, Jr., *Betrayal: How Black Intellectuals Have Abandoned the Ideas of the Civil Rights Era* (New York: Columbia University Press, 2008), 71–80.

16 On each of these, see Jacquelyn Dowd Hall, "The Long Civil Rights Movement and the Political Uses of the Past," *Journal of American History* 91 (March 2005): 1233–1263; Cha-Jua and Lang, "The 'Long Movement' as Vampire"; Peniel Joseph, "The Black Power Movement," and "Introduction: Toward a Historiography of the Black Power Movement," in *The Black Power Movement: Rethinking the Civil Rights–Black Power Era*, ed. Peniel Joseph (New York: Routledge, 2006), 1–27; and Jonathan B. Fenderson, "'When the Revolution Comes': New Perspectives on Black Student Activism and the Black Studies Movement," *Journal of African American History* 98 (Fall 2013): 607–622. Peniel Joseph's *Dark Days, Bright Nights: From Black Power to Barack Obama* (New

York: Basic Books, 2010) is an example of the extension of the consensus historiography of the Civil Rights era to the field of Black Power studies.

17 On the ways in which African American identity has been and can be rendered more fruitfully with transnational approaches to history, see Singh, *Black Is a Country*; and Gerald Horne, "Toward a Transnational Research Agenda for African American History in the 21st Century," *Journal of African American Studies* 91 (Summer 2006): 288–303, as well as his transnational approach to understanding African American experiences at the moment of the founding of the United States, *The Counterrevolution of 1776: Slave Resistance and the Origins of the United States* (New York: New York University Press, 2014). For Black skepticism toward the founding documents of the United States and the ways in which it dovetailed with the period that saw the emergence of African-centered historiographies, see John Ernest, *Liberation Historiography: African American: African American Writers and the Challenge of History, 1794–1861* (Chapel Hill: University of North Carolina Press, 2004), esp. chap. 4. On the class element, see Cedric Robinson, *Black Movements in America* (New York: Routledge, 1997), 96–97.

18 See Martha Biondi, *The Black Revolution on Campus* (Berkeley: University of California Press, 2012); and Ibram Rogers, *The Black Campus Movement: Blacks and the Racial Reconstitution of Higher Education, 1965–1972* (New York: Palgrave Macmillan, 2012).

19 W. E. B. Du Bois, "The Field and Function of the American Negro College," in *The Education of Black People: Ten Critiques*, ed. Herbert Aptheker (New York: Monthly Review Press, 2001), 131.

CHAPTER 1. A SPACE FOR BLACK IDEAS

1 UJAMAA, "What We Want," *Spear and Shield* 1 (March 1968): 1.

2 Adherence to either tendency has been by no means stable. The fluidity between these poles is tied to shifts in external political contexts. But it is important to remember that although different eras produced heightened exposure to each, both have *always* been present in some form. Neither is this limited to the United States. See Harold Cruse, *The Crisis of the Negro Intellectual* (New York: Morrow, 1967); August Meier, *Negro Thought in America, 1880–1915* (Ann Arbor: University of Michigan Press, 1963); Wilson Jeremiah Moses, *The Golden Age of Black Nationalism* (New York: Oxford University Press, 1978); Cedric Robinson, *Black Movements in America* (New York: Routledge, 1997); Roderick Bush, *We Are Not What We Seem: Black Nationalism and Class Struggle in the American Century* (New York: New York University Press, 1999); Michael Dawson, *Black Visions: The Roots of Contemporary Black Political Ideologies* (Chicago: University of Chicago Press, 2001); Robin D. G. Kelley, *Freedom Dreams: The Black Radical Imagination* (Boston: Beacon Press, 2002); and Martin Kilson, *Transformation of the African-American Intelligentsia, 1880–2012* (Cambridge, MA: Harvard University Press, 2014).

3 I am thankful to Professor Harold McDougall for clarifying the distinction between institutional Howard and communal Howard (personal conversation, May 2014). On the social location of the founders of Howard University and their place in the American landscape, see Rayford W. Logan, *Howard University: The First Hundred Years* (New York: New York University Press, 1968), 12–20. In tune with the Western model of higher education, Howard's founders—mostly white Congregationalist men—were largely concerned with the question of a developing a leadership class for Africans who were

coming out of slavery, as well as for other marginalized groups. On the idea of bureau-cratization of university spaces, particularly those that emulate the German ideal, see William Clark, *Academic Charisma and the Origins of the Research University* (Chicago: University of Chicago Press, 2006). See also Bill Readings, *The University in Ruins* (Cambridge, MA: Harvard University Press, 1996), for an assessment of the university's place in the national imagining and its relationship to the corporate environment. The idea of the undercommons stems from Stefano Harney and Fred Moten, "The University and the Undercommons: Seven Theses," *Social Text* 79 (Summer 2004): 101–115.

4 The term is from Derrick A. Bell, Jr., "*Brown v. Board of Education* and the Interest-Convergence Dilemma," *Harvard Law Review* 93 (January 1980): 518–533.

5 E. Franklin Frazier, "The Failure of the Negro Intellectual," in *The Death of White Sociology: Essays on Race and Culture*, ed. Joyce A. Ladner (Baltimore: Black Classic Press, 1998), 52–66.

6 Cedric Robinson, *Black Marxism: The Making of the Black Radical Tradition* (Chapel Hill: University of North Carolina Press, 2000), xxx.

7 In another context, Greg Carr labels this approach the "sui generis," where certain periods can become "points of departure for theorizing large-scale African identity." See his "What Black Studies Is Not: Moving from Crisis to Liberation in Africana Intellectual Work," *Socialism and Democracy* 25 (March 2011): 181.

8 See ibid., 170–171.

9 W. E. B. Du Bois, *Black Reconstruction: An Essay toward a History of the Part Which Black Folk Played in the Attempt to Reconstruct Democracy in America, 1860–1880* (New York: Harcourt, Brace, & Co., 1935).

10 Michael Winston, "The Story behind Howard's Seal," *The Hilltop*, December 3, 1976.

11 On some of these conflicts, many of which involve the Howard sociologist, mathematician, and dean Kelly Miller, see Logan, *Howard University*, 231–242; Raymond Wolters, *The New Negro on Campus: Black College Rebellions of the 1920s* (Princeton, NJ: Princeton University Press, 1975), 70–136; and Zachery Williams, *In Search of the Talented Tenth: Howard University Public Intellectuals and the Dilemma of Race, 1926–1970* (Columbia: University of Missouri Press, 2009), 23–34. A later example involves the Black Studies pioneer Nathan Hare. See his "Final Reflections on a 'Negro' College: A Case Study," *Negro Digest*, March 1968, 40–46, 70–76.

12 Williams, *In Search of the Talented Tenth*, 11–17. On "racial uplift" and its variants in the New Negro movement, see Wilson Jeremiah Moses, *The Golden Age of Black Nationalism*, and "The Lost World of the Negro, 1895–1919: Black Literary and Intellectual Life before the Renaissance," *Black American Literature Forum* 21 (1987): 61–84.

13 This is the title of chap. 6 of Robinson, *Black Marxism*, 121–166. For Du Bois's trajectory, see ibid., 194; as well as Wolters, *The New Negro on Campus*, 29–69, for his contribution to the Fisk protests. Du Bois would use *The Crisis* to articulate his and other actors' viewpoints on the ultimate source of Black resistance and the ideal resolution to questions of Negro education. For a sampling of these ideas, see W. E. B. Du Bois, *The Education of Black People: Ten Critiques, 1906–1960*, ed. Herbert Aptheker (New York: Monthly Review Press, 2001). For a vantage point different from Cedric Robinson's on Du Bois and the terms under which the Black intelligentsia oriented their critique of society, see Kilson, *Transformation of the African-American Intelligentsia*.

14 Jonathan Scott Holloway, *Confronting the Veil: Abram Harris Jr., E. Franklin Frazier, and Ralph Bunche, 1919–1941* (Chapel Hill: University of North Carolina Press, 2002).

15 See Sterling Stuckey, *Slave Culture: Nationalist Theory and the Foundations of Black America* (New York: Oxford University Press, 1987), 8–9, 168–172.

16 On Johnson's background and impact, see Williams, *In Search of the Talented Tenth*, 40–69; and Richard I. McKinney, *Mordecai, the Man, and His Message: The Story of Mordecai Wyatt Johnson* (Washington, DC: Howard University Press, 1997).

17 On the ring shout, see Stuckey, *Slave Culture*, 10–17. On spirituals, theology, and Black college musical scholarship and performance, see Jon Michael Spencer, *The Rhythms of Black Folk: Race, Religion, and Pan-Africanism* (Trenton, NJ: Africa World Press, 1995), 1–22. On Black Greek letter organizations and Africa, see Gloria Harper Dickinson, "Pledged to Remember: Africa in the Life and Lore of Black Greek-Letter Organizations," in *African American Fraternities and Sororities*, ed. Tamara L. Brown, Gregory S. Parks, and Clarenda M. Phillips (Lexington: University Press of Kentucky, 2005), 11–36.

18 What Lindon Barrett calls the "conceptual impossibility" of Blackness is the theoretical inability for the African to constitute a fully human subject—possessive of culture—in the eyes of the theorists of modernity. See Lindon Barrett, *Racial Blackness and the Discontinuity of Western Modernity* (Urbana: University of Illinois Press, 2014), 1–43. On the notion of "impossibility" and Black radical transformation, see also Vincent Harding, "Black Students and the Impossible Revolution," *Journal of Black Studies* 1 (September 1970): 75–100.

19 See William H. Watkins, *The White Architects of Black Education: Ideology and Power in America, 1865–1924* (New York: Teachers College Press, 2001); and Christi M. Smith, *Reparation and Reconciliation: The Rise and Fall of Integrated Higher Education* (Chapel Hill: University of North Carolina Press, 2016), 188–205.

20 "Howard Participates in the Suffragette and Inaugural Parades," *Howard University Journal* (March 14, 1913); and Anthony Platt, *E. Franklin Frazier Reconsidered* (New Brunswick, NJ: Rutgers University Press, 1990), 22–30.

21 Logan, *Howard University*, 220–222; "Howard Strikers Go back to College," *Afro-American*, May 23, 1925; "Why We Struck!!" Student Protests folder, Howard University Archives, Moorland-Spingarn Research Center. In summary of these historical events, Wolters has the following to say: "Going beyond their brothers and sisters at Fisk, who demanded only that they be given a larger role in the management of their university, Negroes at Howard insisted on control of their school." See Wolters, *The New Negro on Campus*, 136. See ibid., 3–28, for his view of the wider context of external control of Black education, issues also discussed by Watkins, *The White Architects*.

22 See Alain Locke, "The New Negro," in *The New Negro: Voices of the Harlem Renaissance*, ed. Alain Locke (New York: Touchstone, 1992), 3–16.

23 See Nikhil Pal Singh, *Black Is a Country: Race and the Unfinished Struggle for Democracy* (Cambridge, MA: Harvard University Press, 2005), 109–119, among many other sources.

24 See Holloway, *Confronting the Veil*, 1–16.

25 In ibid., 82–83 and 211–113, Holloway argues that, even as scholars argued for a class-based analysis, the raw facts of segregation made them articulate these ideas from Black organizations and institutions. Holloway, however, assumes that these were not the preferred spaces from which to articulate such positions. For W. E. B. Du Bois, at least, this was not the assumption. He emphasizes the importance of race organizations in his "Conservation of Races" (reprinted in *African American Social and Political*

Thought, 1850–1920, ed. Howard Brotz [New Brunswick, NJ: Transaction Publishers, 2008], 489). Historically Black colleges and universities were often the spaces to interrogate questions of the nexus between race and class. Whether these spaces were the ideal locations for such an interrogation has spawned debate among intellectual historians of African America. Williams, *In Search of the Talented Tenth*; Kilson, *Transformation of the African-American Intelligentsia*; and Holloway, *Confronting the Veil*, among others, consider this issue.

26 Lyonel Florant, "Youth Exhibits a New Spirit," *Crisis* (August 1936): 237–238, 253. See also Erik Gellman, *Death Blow to Jim Crow: The National Negro Congress and the Rise of Militant Rights* (Chapel Hill: University of North Carolina Press, 2013), 113–115; and Holloway, *Confronting the Veil*, 59–80.

27 In addition to Gellman, *Death Blow to Jim Crow*, see Sekou Franklin, *After the Rebellion: Black Youth, Social Movement Activism, and the Post–Civil Rights Generation* (New York: New York University Press, 2014), 47–70; and Lopez Matthews, "The Southern Negro Youth Congress: Its Legacy and Impact" (PhD diss., Howard University, 2009).

28 See Ras Makonnen, *Pan-Africanism from Within* (New York: Diasporic Africa Press, 2016), 101–102; Minkah Makalani, *In the Cause of Freedom: Radical Black Internationalism from Harlem to London, 1917–1939* (Chapel Hill: University of North Carolina Press, 2011), 150; and Leslie James, *George Padmore and Decolonization from Below: Pan-Africanism, the Cold War, and the End of Empire* (London: Palgrave, 2015), 23–24.

29 "Howard Football Strike Goes into Deadlock," *New York Amsterdam News*, November 28, 1936. This was the second protest. The first occurred in 1927.

30 On this transition, see Gerald Horne, *Black and Red: W.E.B. Du Bois and the Afro-American Response to the Cold War, 1944–1963* (Albany: State University of New York Press, 1986); and Singh, *Black Is a Country*, 159–173.

31 See Howard Zinn, *SNCC: The New Abolitionists* (Boston: Beacon Press, 1964).

32 Stokely Carmichael with Ekwueme Michael Thelwell, *Ready for Revolution: The Life and Struggles of Stokely Carmichael [Kwame Ture]* (New York: Scribner & Sons, 2003), 147, 250–276.

33 Ibid., 145–146, 163–165. See also Peniel Joseph, *Stokely: A Life* (New York: Basic Civitas, 2014), 23–30.

34 See Sam Pollard and Sheila Bernard, directors, *Eyes on the Prize* (1990; DVD, Alexandria, VA: PBS Video, 2006); and Robin Gregory, "Howard University, 1967–1968: You Saw the Silhouette of Her Afro," in *Voices of Freedom: An Oral History of the Civil Rights Movement from the 1950s through the 1980s*, by Henry Hampton and Steve Fayer, with Sarah Flynn (New York: Bantam Books, 1990), 427–429, 433–436.

35 See Jonathan B. Fenderson, "'When the Revolution Comes': New Perspectives on Black Student Activism and the Black Studies Movement," *Journal of African American History* 98 (Fall 2013): 607–622.

36 In addition to contemporary newspaper accounts, oral histories of the protest can be found at the Moorland-Spingarn Research Center on the campus of Howard University. See also Lawrence B. de Graaf, "Howard: The Evolution of a Black Student Revolt," in *Protest! Student Activism in America*, ed. Julian Foster and Durward Long (New York: William Morrow & Co., 1968), 319–344; Otis Bryant, "The Howard University Student Protest Movement: A Quest for Student Empowerment, 1965–1970" (MA thesis, Howard University, 1992); and Jerrold Wimbish Roy, "Student Activism and the Historically Black University: Hampton Institute and Howard University, 1960–1972"

(EdD diss., Hampton University, 2000). See also Martha Biondi, *The Black Revolution on Campus* (Berkeley: University of California Press, 2012), 142–150.

37　These were the demands, issued on March 14, 1968, as reported by Bryant: (1) for curriculum expansion in Afro-American history, with specifics related to slavery, Reconstruction, turn-of-the-century and contemporary movements, and an Afro-American history course without the American history prerequisite; (2) to add jazz courses to Fine Arts; (3) for the expansion of African Studies with more emphasis on ancient, modern, and contemporary political movements in Africa; (4) to ensure that the economics, social science, and government departments deal with the specific problems of African/Afro-American peoples and the study of communal systems and governments in the non-Western world, with emphasis on how Afro-Americans fit into the American economic political system; (5) for Afro-American literature to be taught every semester on the undergraduate level with specific emphasis on folklore, poetry, and novels; (6) for all Afro-American and African published newspapers to be made available on campus; (7) for the establishment of an Afro-American research institute; (8) for the implementation of a credited work-study program in the Black community; (9) for the establishment of fair criteria for faculty tenure and promotion; (10) to invest academic legislative power in the faculty and not in trustees; (11) to reinstate professors dismissed for political activism; (12) for the freeing of student government and student newspaper from administrative control; (13) to abolish the women's dormitory curfews; (14) for the administration to make a clear list of rules governing student conduct and fair trials for all students subject to disciplinary action; and (15) for the resignation of all administrators not in favor of a democratic Black university. See Bryant, "The Howard University Student Protest Movement," 63–64.

38　Howard students occupied the Mordecai Wyatt Johnson Administration Building on March 19, 1968, and stayed until March 23. After a negotiation with the board of trustees—who with the foresight of Kenneth Clark refused to bring in the police—the students felt that continuing the takeover would bear no fruit and collectively exited the building. But as Otis Bryant shows, their acceptance of the terms of the negotiation was not an "end in itself." See ibid., 68.

39　See de Graaf, "Howard: The Evolution of a Black Student Revolt," 322–324; and Bryant, "The Howard University Student Protest Movement," 1.

40　There was however, a key difference. The students, activists, and intellectuals were not going to wait for Howard to become that Black university, as the concept itself transcended the internal politics of the university. For many at this conference, Howard was necessarily forced to choose whether it would become relevant. If it did not, the concept of a Black university *still* had to be one that must be actualized. See the conference organizer and then Howard professor Acklyn Lynch's comments along these lines in George P. Davis, "A Step Forward? The Howard University Conference," *Negro Digest*, May 1969, 44–48. For a broader vision of the Black university concept, see Vincent Harding's seminal article, "Toward the Black University," *Ebony*, August 1970, 156–159. On Miller's notion of the National Negro University, see Williams, *In Search of the Talented Tenth*, 35. On Kelly Miller, generally, see Ida Jones, *The Heart of the Race Problem: The Life of Kelly Miller* (Washington, DC: Tapestry Press, 2011).

41　Wole Soyinka, *Of Africa* (New Haven, CT: Yale University Press, 2012), xiii.

42　William C. McFeely, *Yankee Stepfather: General O.O. Howard and the Freemen* (New Haven, CT: Yale University Press, 1968).

43 After being dismissed from Howard, Nathan Hare, a sociologist, would become the director of the first full-fledged Department of Black Studies at San Francisco State University. See his "Questions and Answers about Black Studies," *Massachusetts Review* 10 (Autumn 1969): 727–736, and "The Challenge of the Black Scholar," in Ladner, ed., *The Death of White Sociology*, 67–80. Also see Dick McCutchen, narrator, *Color Us Black* (film, New York: National Educational Television and Radio Center, 1968); as well as Bryant, "The Howard University Student Protest Movement"; and Roy, "Student Activism and the Historically Black University."

44 This three-dimensional orientation toward resistance and culture is drawn from Vincent Harding, "The Vocation of the Black Scholar and the Struggles of the Black Community," in *Education and Black Struggle: Notes from the Colonized World*, ed. Institute of the Black World (Cambridge, MA: Harvard Education Review, 1974), 8–9.

45 Harding, "Toward the Black University," 157.

46 W. E. B. Du Bois, "The Field and Function of the American Negro College," in Du Bois, *The Education of Black People*, ed. Aptheker, 125.

47 Social scientists studying the movement showed that the inclusion of these "career-oriented" individuals indicates how much the "militant black nucleus" had spread its ideals. See Sophia F. McDowell, Gilbert A. Lowe, Jr., and Doris A. Dockett, "Howard University's Student Protest Movement," *Public Opinion Quarterly* 34 (Autumn 1974): 388.

48 For an account of the Spring 1969 protests, see Biondi, *The Black Revolution on Campus*, 149–153.

49 About 48 percent of students surveyed agreed (about half "strongly") with the statement that "Howard should not pattern its academic program after white or European-oriented universities." See McDowell et al., "Howard University's Student Protest Movement," 386.

50 See "60 Students Continue Sit-in," February 18, 1983, and Ed Bruske and Lawrence Feinberg, "Ousted Editor Reinstated at Howard," February 26, 1983, both in the *Washington Post*.

51 Vincent Harding, *There Is a River: The Black Struggle for Freedom in America* (Orlando, FL: Harcourt Brace Jovanovich, 1981).

52 From Malcolm X's speech at the Oxford Union, December 3, 1964. For a complete transcript, see the *Live from Planet Earth* website, www.livefromplanetearth.org. For a look at the importance of this speech, see Saladin Ambar, *Malcolm X at Oxford Union: Racial Politics in a Global Era* (New York: Oxford University Press, 2014).

53 James Emanuel, "Blackness Can: A Quest for Aesthetics," in *The Black Aesthetic* (New York: Doubleday, 1971), 192–223.

54 June Jordan, "Black Studies: Bringing Back the Person," *Evergreen Review* 17 (October 1969): 71.

55 On the fight for the spirit of the Negro college, W. E. B. Du Bois stated that "Fisk University has failed on evil days; it has gotten money and lost the Spirit. . . . This great institution must be rescued or it will die." Quoted in Wolters, *The New Negro on Campus*, 40.

56 Du Bois, "The Field and Function of the American Negro College," 131.

CHAPTER 2. RACIST ETIQUETTE

1 William Simms, quoted on the *CBS Evening News with Dan Rather*, CBS, March 7, 1989.

2 For the wider context, see Sheila Slaughter and Larry L. Leslie, *Academic Capitalism: Politics, Policies, and the Entrepreneurial University* (Baltimore: Johns Hopkins University Press, 1997), 7–8.

3 See, generally, Henry Giroux, *Neoliberalism's War on Higher Education* (Chicago: Haymarket Books, 2014); and Wendy Brown, *Undoing the Demos: Neoliberalism's Stealth Revolution* (New York: Zone Books, 2015), 175–200. On the ways that this environment affected how universities dealt with questions of race and difference, see Roderick Ferguson, *The Reorder of Things: The University and Its Pedagogies of Minority Difference* (Minneapolis: University of Minnesota Press, 2012).

4 This phrase is from Ronald W. Walters, *White Nationalism, Black Interests: Conservative Public Policy and the Black Community* (Detroit: Wayne State University Press, 2003).

5 Hanes Walton, Jr., and Robert C. Smith, *American Politics and the African American Quest for Universal Freedom* (Boston: Longman, 2012), 147–148; and Nancy Weiss, *Farewell to the Party of Lincoln: Black Politics in the Age of FDR* (Princeton, NJ: Princeton University Press, 1983).

6 Weiss, *Farewell to the Party of Lincoln*. For the racial politics of the New Deal and Truman's civil rights platform, see Thomas J. Sugrue, *Sweet Land of Liberty: The Forgotten Struggle for Civil Rights in the North* (New York: Random House, 2008), 49–58, 96–102.

7 Mary Brennan, *Turning Right in the Sixties: The Conservative Capture of the GOP* (Chapel Hill: University of North Carolina Press, 1995), 27–28.

8 Ibid., 29–34; and Walton and Smith, *American Politics*, 147.

9 Ira Katznelson argues that a pluralist orientation toward liberal democracy worked to compromise the more salient restructuring of American society, a goal he ties to the project of social democracy. See his "Was the Great Society a Lost Opportunity?" in *The Rise and Fall of New Deal Order, 1930–1980*, ed. Steve Fraser and Gary Gerstle (Princeton, NJ: Princeton University Press, 1989), 185–211. On the business bona fides of Kennedy's New Frontier, see Thomas Ferguson and Joel Rogers, *Right Turn: The Decline of the Democrats and the Future of American Politics* (New York: Hill & Wang, 1986), 46–57.

10 Malcolm X, quoted in Michael Dawson, *Black Visions: The Roots of Contemporary African American Ideologies* (Chicago: University of Chicago Press, 2001), 240. Dawson argues that Black liberalism in its radical egalitarian permutation argues against the elevation of the individual and affirms a communal orientation rooted in group solidarity and equality and favors a central state rather than the market to ensure "positive" freedoms. In many ways, this liberal vision meant a "revolutionary restructuring of the American state" (268).

11 Charles E. Cobb, Jr., *This Nonviolent Stuff'll Get You Killed: How Guns Made the Civil Rights Movement Possible* (New York: Basic Books, 2014), 2–3.

12 Katznelson, "Was the Great Society a Lost Opportunity?" 185.

13 On the link between the War on Poverty and the draft, see ibid. On the origins of the War on Poverty and its strategic purview, see Hugh Heclo, "The Political Roots of Antipoverty Policy," in *Fighting Poverty: What Works and What Doesn't*, ed. Sheldon H. Danzinger and Daniel H. Weinberg (Cambridge, MA: Harvard University Press, 1986), 312–340; and Allen J. Matusow, *The Unraveling of America* (New York: Harper & Row, 1984), 97–127.

14 Johnson's vehicle for affirmative action was Executive Order 11246, issued in September 1965, which enacted a range of efforts to ensure that firms positively sought to eliminate discrimination within their hiring practices. On the background of Executive Order 11246, see Nicholas Lemann, "Taking Affirmative Action Apart," in *Affirmative Action: Social Justice or Reverse Discrimination?* ed. Francis J. Beckwith and Todd E. Jones (Amherst, NY: Prometheus Books, 1997), 34–55. For Johnson's well-known June 4, 1965, Howard University commencement address that enumerates his view of positive liberalism and civil rights, see Lyndon B. Johnson, "To Fulfill These Rights," in ibid., 56–63. The speech is also posted at the *American Presidency Project* website at the University of California, Santa Barbara, www.ucsb.edu.

15 Martin Luther King, Jr., was one of many Black freedom fighters who raised this contradiction, stating:

> There is at the outset a very obvious and almost facile connection between the war in Vietnam and the struggle I, and others, have been waging in America. A few years ago there was a shining moment in that struggle. It seemed as if there was a real promise of hope for the poor—both black and white—through the Poverty Program. There were experiments, hopes, new beginnings. Then came the build-up in Vietnam, and I watched the program broken and eviscerated as if it were some idle political plaything of a society gone mad on war, and I knew that America would never invest the necessary funds or energies in rehabilitation of its poor so long as adventures like Vietnam continued to draw men and skills and money like some demoniacal destructive suction tube. So, I was increasingly compelled to see the war as an enemy of the poor and to attack it as such. [Martin Luther King, Jr., "Beyond Vietnam: A Time to Break Silence," in *The Radical King*, ed. Cornel West (Boston: Beacon Press, 2015), 203]

> On the guns and butter dilemma, see Jeffrey W. Helsing, *Johnson's War/Johnson's Great Society: The Guns and Butter Trap* (Westport, CT: Praeger, 2000); and on its contribution to austerity policies, see Julian E. Zelizer, *The Fierce Urgency of Now: Lyndon Johnson, Congress, and the Battle for the Great Society* (New York: Penguin Press, 2015), 263–302.

16 See Heclo, "The Political Roots of Antipoverty Policy," 323; and Matusow, *The Unraveling of America*, 119–120.

17 Given that the radical visions of Black activists have been routinely pilloried as naïve and/or fantastical, it remains necessary to assert that the liberal ideologies that are often foisted upon the freedom fighters during the heroic era were neither fully accurate nor hegemonic in that era or in the periods that directly preceded them. Cedric Robinson asserts that,

> by the second half of the nineteenth century, two alternative black political cultures had arisen, each nurtured by a particular Black experience. Akin to the social divergences that appeared throughout slave societies in the New World, communities of free Blacks gravitated toward the privileged social and political identities jealously reserved for non-Blacks. At the same time, on the plantations and in slave quarters, slaves tended to form a historical identity that presumed a higher moral standard than that which seemed to bind their masters.
> Among the two formations in the United States, the better publicized was the assimilationist Black political culture that appropriated the values and objectives of the dominant American Creed. Especially among the urban free Blacks

of the colonial and antebellum periods, a liberal, bourgeois consciousness was nourished, packed with capitalist ambitions and individualist intuitions. A constant before and after the Civil War and into the new century, this consciousness manifested itself in a tendency toward an American optimism about integration/assimilation. When assimilation seem ill-conceived, the quiescent Black middle stratum of wage labors and professionals hunkered down, and a minority and renegade species of Black nationalist desires was enjoined. But within this galaxy of liberalism, regardless of variant, a special affection for republican value predominated, grounded on a presumption that leadership was reserved for an elite defined by nature and excellence. It was, to other Americans, the more easily understood of the two political cultures, because it flowed from the political and social intercourse between this free Black "elite" and American society in general. Moreover, since bourgeois Black culture mirrored dominant political beliefs, it had the advantage of an economy of expression. Taking American material values and national ambitions for granted, liberal Black political culture could resonate with the ongoing public articulation of the American majority. Given this license, it was possible to frequently create the illusion and self-serving conceit that such values and interest represented Blacks *en masse*.

To the contrary, the Black mass movements of the late nineteenth and twentieth centuries proved both the existence and vitality of an alternative Black political culture, emergent from the brutal rural regimes of slavery, and later peonage. Inventive rather than imitative, communitarian rather than individualistic, democratic rather than republican, Afro-Christian rather than secular and materialist, the social values of these largely agrarian people generated a political culture that distinguished between the inferior world of the political and transcendent universe of moral goods. Separatism was the principal impulse of this culture and over the next century or more this separatism would assume several forms already familiar: marronage, emigration, migration, domestic and external colonization. Although it foreclosed the possibility of integration or assimilation, separatism in its most sanguine manifestations accommodated the possibility of social coexistence, avoiding the moral squalor of Black racism. But in times of acute oppression, the impulse could assume the forms of xenophobia, including the most virulent forms of race-hatred rising from both real and imagined experiences." [Cedric Robinson, *Black Movements in America* (New York: Routledge, 1997), 96–97]

See also the following works on Black political ideologies, which are not rooted in the limited assumption that Black people simply affirmed American liberal principles: Dawson, *Black Visions*; Vincent Harding, *There Is a River: The Black Struggle for Freedom in America* (Orlando, FL: Harcourt Brace Jovanovich, 1981); Roderick Bush, *We Are Not What We Seem: Black Nationalism and Class Struggle in the American Century* (New York: New York University Press, 1999); Robin D. G. Kelley, *Freedom Dreams: The Black Radical Imagination* (Boston: Beacon Press, 2002); and Nikhil Pal Singh, *Black Is a Country: Race and the Unfinished Struggle for Democracy* (Cambridge, MA: Harvard University Press, 2004).

18 For these contexts, see Gerald Horne, *Fire This Time: The Watts Uprising and the 1960s* (Charlottesville: University Press of Virginia, 1995), 3–42; and Joshua Bloom and Waldo E. Martin, Jr., *Black against Empire: The History and Politics of the Black Panther Party* (Berkeley: University of California Press, 2013), 82–98.

19 According to Michael W. Flamm, "At a popular level, law and order resonated both as a social ideal and political slogan because it combined an understandable concern over the rising number of traditional crimes—robberies and rapes, muggings and murders—with implicit and explicit unease about civil rights, civil liberties, urban riots, antiwar protests, moral values, and drug use. Of course, street crime differed in important ways from the other causes of civil unrest, but politicians, pundits, and propagandists across the political spectrum hastened to blur this distinction. In the process, they loaded law and order with layers of meaning virtually impossible to disentangle and turned it into a Rorschach test of public anxiety." See Michael W. Flamm, *Law and Order: Street Crime, Civil Unrest, and the Crisis of Liberalism in the 1960s* (New York: Columbia University Press, 2005), 4.

20 Ibid., 118–119.

21 Dan T. Carter, *The Politics of Rage: George Wallace, the Origins of the New Conservatism, and the Transformation of American Politics* (New York: Simon & Schuster, 1995), 324–370.

22 Ibid., 328–330; and Flamm, *Law and Order*, 167–178.

23 See Matusow, *The Unraveling of America*, 395–439; Ronald Radosh, *Divided They Fell: The Demise of the Democratic Party, 1964–1996* (New York: Free Press, 1996); Robert O. Self, *All in the Family: The Realignment of American Democracy since the 1960s* (New York: Hill & Wang, 2012), 248–275; and Bruce Miroff, *The Liberals' Moment: The McGovern Insurgency and the Identity Crisis of the Democratic Party* (Lawrence: University Press of Kansas, 2007).

24 Jerome Himmelstein, *To the Right: The Transformation of American Conservatism* (Berkeley: University of California Press, 1990), 77. On the "new class," see Daniel T. Rodgers, *Age of Fracture* (Cambridge, MA: Belknap Press of Harvard University Press, 2011), 81–85; and B. Bruce-Briggs, "An Introduction to the Idea of the New Class," in *The New Class?* ed. B. Bruce-Briggs (New York: McGraw-Hill, 1981), 1–18.

25 The standard account responsible for establishing this tripartite division is George H. Nash, *The Conservative Intellectual Movement in America since 1945* (New York: Basic Books, 1976), 154–185. For a discussion of this "fusionism," see Himmelstein, *To the Right*, 13–15, 28–62.

26 It should go without saying that the Black freedom movement on both the domestic and global fronts was implicated in the Red Scare, therefore the notion of conservative (or liberal) anticommunism cannot be decoupled from race—particularly as Southerners pointed to Communists as directing the Southern theater of the freedom struggle, just as Northern liberals had earlier led the persecution of radicals like W. E. B. Du Bois and Paul Robeson. Most accounts of the conservative movement fail to consider this connection. On these connections, see Kelley, *Freedom Dreams*, 51–59; Singh, *Black Is a Country*; Gerald Horne, *Black and Red: W.E.B. Du Bois and the Afro-American Response to the Cold War, 1944–1963* (Albany: State University of New York Press, 1985); and Richard Iton, *In Search of the Black Fantastic: Politics and Popular Culture in the Post–Civil Rights Era* (New York: Oxford University Press, 2009), 30–80. Similarly, moral traditionalism and its preoccupation with permissiveness had more than racial overtones, when one considers the ways that entrance of racial justice into the conversation of "American values" disrupted notions of traditional American rights and identity. Traditionalism represented a return to the values disrupted by the progressivism of the early twentieth century that morphed into the values movements

toward the end of the century. On this general point, see Elaine Tyler May, "Cold War—Warm Hearth: Politics and Family in Postwar America," and Maurice Isserman and Michael Kazin, "The Failure and Success of the New Radicalism," both in Fraser and Gerstle, eds., *The Rise and Fall of the New Deal Order*, 153–181 and 212–242, respectively. A clear example can be seen in the racist implications of the reproductive rights movement, which was ostensibly also driven by "values." See Self, *All in the Family*, 148–153; and Dorothy Roberts, *Killing the Black Body: Race, Reproduction, and the Meaning of Liberty* (New York: Pantheon, 1997).

27 The book was ghostwritten by William F. Buckley, Jr.'s brother-in-law, L. Brent Bozell, Jr. See Barry Goldwater, *The Conscience of a Conservative* (Shepherdsville, KY: Victor Publishing Co. [Publishers Printing Co.], 1960).

28 On the "Draft Goldwater" movement and the subsequent electoral performance, see Brennan, *Turning Right in the Sixties*, 60–103.

29 Ibid., 104–119; and Lisa McGirr, *Suburban Warriors: The Origins of the New American Right* (Princeton, NJ: Princeton University Press, 2001), 122–146.

30 Steven F. Hayward, *The Age of Reagan: The Fall of the Old Liberal Order, 1964–1980* (Roseville, CA: Forum, 2001), 227–257; Rick Perlstein, *Nixonland: The Rise of a President and the Fracturing of America* (New York: Scribner, 2008), 393–396; and Robert Mason, *Richard Nixon and the Quest for a New Majority* (Chapel Hill: University of North Carolina Press, 2004).

31 As opposed to the realism of previous administrations. The idealism of human rights, however, should not be conflated with the UN conventions and the ways that they approach this concept. Nevertheless, Carter's appreciation for human rights rendered him "weak" in the minds of realists and hawks, who were concerned with extending American dominance. See Sean Wilentz, *The Age of Reagan: A History, 1974–2008* (New York: Harper, 2008), 100–110; and Mary E. Stuckey, *Jimmy Carter, Human Rights, and the National Agenda* (College Station: Texas A&M University Press, 2009). For a broader overview of the concept of human rights, see Samuel Moyn, *Human Rights and the Uses of History* (London: Verso, 2014).

32 For an overview, see Robin D. G. Kelley, "Into the Fire: The 1970s to the Present," in *To Make Our World Anew: A History of African Americans*, vol. 2, ed. Robin D. G. Kelley and Earl Lewis (New York: Oxford University Press, 2008), 265–280; and David Chappell, *Waking from the Dream: The Struggle for Civil Rights in the Shadow of Martin Luther King, Jr.* (New York: Random House, 2014). On the work of the National Black Political Convention, the Congress of Afrikan People, the African Liberation Support Committee, and the Combahee River Collective, see Kelley, *Freedom Dreams*; and Ronald W. Walters, *Pan Africanism and the African Diaspora: An Analysis of Modern Afrocentric Political Movements* (Detroit: Wayne State University Press, 1993), 54–88.

33 King did not believe that the 1964 Civil Rights Act was the culmination of his work. For King's "revolution of values" statement, see Martin Luther King, Jr., "The World House," in West, ed., *The Radical King*, 91–96. Cornel West's introduction to the volume (ibid., ix–xvi) provides a contextualization of King's revolutionary vision and the response to this vision by the apparatus of the state. As is well known, the Federal Bureau of Investigation's Counterintelligence Program (COINTELPRO) actively undermined King's organization and other Black revolutionary groups. See Kenneth O'Reilly, *Racial Matters: The FBI's Secret File on Black America, 1960–1972* (New York: Free Press, 1989); and Bloom and Martin, *Black against Empire*, 199–246.

34 The political strategy of reaching to the silent majority is often attributed to Kevin Phillips and his idea of a Southern strategy to attract white voters to the Republican Party. See Kevin Phillips, *The Emerging Republican Majority* (New Rochelle, NY: Arlington House, 1969). However, disaffected Democrats were not only Southerners; they also included the ethnic working class of the urban North. On the work of Howard Phillips, Richard Viguerie, and Paul Weyrich, see Himmelstein, *To the Right*, 80–89; and Sara Diamond, *Roads to Dominion: Right-Wing Movements and Political Power in the United States* (New York: Guilford Press, 1995), 170–176. There have been a spate of new studies on the grassroots movements of the New Right in the South. Some of the most widely cited are McGirr, *Suburban Warriors*; Kevin Kruse, *White Flight: Atlanta and the Making of Modern Conservatism* (Princeton, NJ: Princeton University Press, 2005); Matthew Lassiter, *Silent Majority: Suburban Politics in the Sunbelt South* (Princeton, NJ: Princeton University Press, 2006); and Joseph Crespino, *In Search of Another Country: Mississippi and the Conservative Counterrevolution* (Princeton, NJ: Princeton University Press, 2007). Lily Geismer shows that this was not merely a Southern/Sunbelt or strictly conservative phenomenon. Her case study of suburban Boston shows that liberalism also housed the mobilization of backlash politics. See Lily Geismer, *Don't Blame Us: Suburban Liberals and the Transformation of the Democratic Party* (Princeton, NJ: Princeton University Press, 2015). For a review of this conversation and the much broader field of conservative history, see Kim Phillips-Fein, "Conservatism: A State of the Field," *Journal of American History* (December 2011): 723–743.

35 John C. Whitehead, "Racial Economic Inequality and Discrimination: Conservative and Liberal Paradigms Revisited," in *African Americans in the U.S. Economy*, ed. Cecilia Conrad et al. (Lanham, MD: Rowman & Littlefield, 2006), 83–93. Conservatives also argue that greater emphasis should be placed on individual behavior and culture, which reduce the amount of "human capital" in Black communities. On "taste for discrimination," see Gary Becker, *The Economics of Discrimination* (Chicago: University of Chicago Press, 1957).

36 See Jean Hardisty, *Mobilizing Resentment: Conservative Resurgence from the John Birch Society to the Promise Keepers* (Boston: Beacon Press, 1999), 9–68.

37 Self, *All in the Family*, 11–12.

38 Diamond, *Roads to Dominion*, 228–256. On the emergence of the Christian Right, see McGirr, *Suburban Warriors*, 102–109, 235–261; Hardisty, *Mobilizing Resentment*, 53–57; Kim Phillips-Fein, *Invisible Hands: The Making of the Conservative Movement from the New Deal to Reagan* (New York: Norton & Co., 2009); Darren Dochuk, *From Bible Belt to Sunbelt* (New York: Oxford University Press, 2011); Daniel Williams, *God's Own Party: The Making of the Christian Right* (New York: Oxford University Press, 2010); and Bethany Moreton, *To Serve God and Wal-Mart: The Making of Chrsitian Free Enterprise* (Cambridge, MA: Harvard University Press, 2009).

39 For an overview of the origins of neoconservatism, see Gary Dorrien, *The Neoconservative Mind: Politics, Culture, and the War of Ideology* (Philadelphia: Temple University Press, 1993), 19–67; Peter Steinfels, *The Neoconservatives: The Men Who Are Changing America's Politics* (New York: Simon & Schuster, 1979), 25–32; and Sidney Blumenthal, *The Rise of the Counter-establishment: The Conservative Ascent to Political Power* (New York: Times Books, 1976), 122–165.

40 Diamond, *Roads to Dominion*, 109–202.

41 Dorrien, *The Neoconservative Mind*, 174–176; Diamond, *Roads to Dominion*, 216–217; and Blumenthal, *The Rise of the Counter-establishment*, 145.

42 Burton I. Kaufman and Scott Kaufman, *The Presidency of James Earl Carter* (Lawrence: University Press of Kansas, 1993), 37–50; and Wilentz, *The Age of Reagan*, 95–98.

43 Doug Rossinow, *The Reagan Era: A History of the 1980s* (New York: Columbia University Press, 2015), 29; and Andrew E. Busch, *Reagan's Victory: The Presidential Election of 1980 and the Rise of the Right* (Lawrence: University Press of Kansas, 2005), 15–28.

44 Lou Cannon, *President Reagan: The Role of a Lifetime* (New York: Touchstone, 1991), 32–100; Hayward, *The Age of Reagan: The Fall of the Old Liberal Order, 1964–1980*, 677–711; and Busch, *Reagan's Victory*, 48–54.

45 Rossinow, *The Reagan Era*, 1–10.

46 Charles Mills, *The Racial Contract* (Ithaca, NY: Cornell University Press, 1997). On American exceptionalism or universalism and the question of racial inclusion, see Singh, *Black Is a Country*, 15–57.

47 This is not to award "liberalism" a clean bill of health on these matters. See Charles Mills, "Racial Liberalism," *PMLA* 123 (October 2008): 1380–1397.

48 The political scientist Paul Frymer has argued that the American two-party system is essentially built on privileging and conserving white citizenship as a primary function: "Even when race is not 'present' in the party system, its underlying presence has great consequences for both party leaders and the way black interests are represented. Party leaders work actively and almost constantly to deny the salience of black interests. The failure to address seriously the consequences of white racism on party behavior has led, in turn, to a relative ignorance of how electoral institutions have legitimated, empowered, and ultimately perpetuated ideologies and polices of racial inequality. Instead of giving rise to a truly nonracial politics and nonracist ideologies, the two-party system legitimates an agenda reflecting the preferences of white voters, and it structures black interests outside party competition." See Paul Frymer, *Uneasy Alliances: Race and Party Competition in America* (Princeton, NJ: Princeton University Press, 1999), 28.

The preservation of whiteness is often "colorblind," that is, it is perpetuated more by the normal functioning of the cultural, legal, and economic systems in place, rather than by individual attitudes. See Mills, *The Racial Contract*; Eduardo Bonilla-Silva, *Racism without Racists: Color-Blind Racism and the Persistence of Racial Inequality in America*, 4th ed. (Lanham, MD: Rowman & Littlefield, 2014); David Roediger, *The Wages of Whiteness: Race and the Making of the Working Class* (London: Verso, 1991); George Lipsitz, *The Possessive Investment in Whiteness: How White People Benefit from Identity Politics* (Philadelphia: Temple University Press, 1998); Winthrop Jordan, *White over Black: American Attitudes toward the Negro, 1550–1812* (Chapel Hill: University of North Carolina Press, 1968); A. Leon Higginbotham, *In the Matter of Color: Race and the American Legal Process: The Colonial Period* (New York: Oxford University Press, 1978); Derrick Bell, *Faces at the Bottom of the Well: The Permanence of Racism* (New York: Basic Books, 1992); Daria Roithmayr, *Reproducing Racism: How Everyday Choices Lock in White Advantage* (New York: New York University Press, 2014); and Cedric Robinson, *Forgeries of Memory and Meaning: Blacks and the Regimes of Race in American Theater and Film before World War II* (Chapel Hill: University of North Carolina Press, 2007).

49 Hayward, *The Age of Reagan: The Fall of the Liberal Order, 1964–1980*, 695.

50 Amy Ansell, *New Right, New Racism* (New York: New York University Press, 1997).

51 Walters, *White Nationalism, Black Interests*, 38–66.

52 David Theo Goldberg, *The Racial State* (Malden, MA: Wiley-Blackwell, 2002).

53 See Steven F. Hayward, *The Age of Reagan: The Conservative Counterrevolution, 1980–1989* (New York: Three Rivers Press, 2009), 57–95. On the economics of the supply siders, see Rodgers, *Age of Fracture*, 68–73; Robert Collins, *More: The Politics of Economic Growth in Postwar America* (New York: Oxford University Press, 2000), 179–191; and Paul Krugman, *Peddling Prosperity: Economic Sense and Nonsense in the Age of Diminished Expectations* (New York: Norton & Co., 1994), 82–95.

54 Thomas Byrne Edsall and Mary D. Edsall, *Chain Reaction: The Impact of Race, Rights, and Taxes on American Politics* (New York: Norton & Co., 1991), 59–166. See also Collins, *More*, 191–213; and Center on Budget and Policy Priorities, *Falling Behind: A Report on How Blacks Have Fared under Reagan* (Washington, DC: Center on Budget and Policy Priorities, 1984).

55 See Peter Custers, "Military Keynesianism Today: An Innovative Discourse," *Race and Class* 51 (April 2010): 79–94.

56 See Edsall and Edsall, *Chain Reaction*, 21, for "top-down coalition," and 142–148, for "conservative egalitarianism."

57 Walters, *White Nationalism, Black Interests*, 67–77.

58 Ansell, *New Right, New Racism*, 103–141.

59 See Steven A. Shull, *A Kinder, Gentler Racism? The Reagan-Bush Civil Rights Legacy* (Armonk, NY: M. E. Sharpe, 1993).

60 For a Black critique of, and mobilization against, the Reagan administration and its foreign policy, see Manning Marable, *Black American Politics: From the Washington Marches to Jesse Jackson* (London: Verso, 1985), 108–124; and Hayward, *The Age of Reagan: The Conservative Counterrevolution, 1980–1989*, 320, 370–371. On Black communities in America's support for the anti-apartheid movement, as well as the Grenadian and Sandinista revolutions, see Walters, *Pan Africanism in the African Diaspora*, 262–268, 311–314; and Karin Stanford, *Beyond the Boundaries: Reverend Jesse Jackson in International Affairs* (Albany: State University of New York Press, 1997).

61 Ferguson and Rogers, *Right Turn*, 3–39; and Himmlestein, *To the Right*, 167–181.

62 Ansell, *New Right, New Racism*, 260.

63 Ferguson and Rogers, *Right Turn*, 78–113.

64 Himmelstein, *To the Right*, 129–164.

65 Ibid., 80–94.

66 On the fairness doctrine and its abolition, see Robert M. Entman, *Democracy without Citizens: Media and the Decay of American Politics* (New York: Oxford University Press, 1989), 102–106. Its impact on the "conservative media establishment" is explored in Kathleen Hall Jamieson and Joseph N. Cappella, *Echo Chamber: Rush Limbaugh and the Conservative Media Establishment* (New York: Oxford University Press, 2008), 45.

67 Edsall and Edsall, *Chain Reaction*, 167, 210–211.

68 Frymer, *Uneasy Alliances*, 21–22; Kathleen Hall Jamieson, *Dirty Politics: Deception, Distraction, and Democracy* (New York: Oxford University Press, 1992).

69 Tali Mendelberg, *The Race Card: Campaign Strategy, Implicit Messages, and the Norm of Equality* (Princeton, NJ: Princeton University Press, 2001), 3–27.

70 Pat Schroeder, quoted in John Brady, *Bad Boy: The Life and Politics of Lee Atwater* (Reading, MA: Addison-Wesley, 1997), 195.

71 On Atwater's life and career, see ibid.; and Stefan Forbes, director, *Boogie Man: The Lee Atwater Story* (DVD, New York: InterPositive Media, 2009).

72 Lee Atwater, quoted in Bob Herbert, "Impossible, Ridiculous, Repugnant," *New York Times*, October 8, 2005.

73 David C. Anderson, *Crime and the Politics of Hysteria: How the Willie Horton Story Changed American Justice* (New York: Times Books, 1995), 129. Anderson's account is the most extensive treatment of this history, and it is the basis for this paragraph.

74 Lee Atwater, quoted in Brady, *Bad Boy*, 218. This account is based on ibid., 170–194; Edsall and Edsall, *Chain Reaction*, 221–225; and Jack Germond and Jules Witcover, *Whose Broad Stripes and Bright Stars? The Trivial Pursuit of the Presidency, 1988* (New York: Warner Books, 1989), 157–165.

75 Robert James Bidinotto, "Getting Away with Murder," *Reader's Digest*, July 1988, 57–63.

76 Mendelberg, *The Race Card*, 142; and Edsall and Edsall, *Chain Reaction*, 223–224.

77 Jamieson, *Dirty Politics*, 9–10.

78 On the creation of the ads, see Brady, *Bad Boy*, 204–208. In the DVD *Boogie Man* (Forbes, director), Roger Stone recounts that during a strategy session he tried to convince Atwater not to utilize the NSPAC ad (they had "officially" claimed that the campaign was not involved) because it was racist. According to Stone, Atwater turned to his team and bemoaned them, saying "Y'all pussy!"

79 On the content of the ads and the ways that they manipulated viewers, see Jamieson, *Dirty Politics*, 15–42.

80 On the idea that Jackson's comments shifted the conversation into an explicitly racial one, see Mendelberg, *The Race Card*, 152–154.

81 Ibid., 4.

82 Brady, *Bad Boy*, 200–204. See also Susan Estrich, "Willie Horton and Me," *Washington Post Magazine*, April 23, 1989.

83 Mendelbeg, *The Race Card*, 138–144.

84 On Dukakis as neoliberal, see Geismer, *Don't Blame Us*, 270–278. On Bill Clinton and other Democrats' appropriation of the tough-on-crime posture and policies in the wake of Dukakis's failure, see Walters, *White Nationalism, Black Interests*, 183–195. Naomi Murakawa's research has revealed that liberals were in fact responsible for much of the crime-control mechanisms put in place by the federal government during the twentieth century. Thus it should come as no surprise that Democrats would employ the tough-on-crime language assumed to be the preserve of conservatives, given that it was the former who developed this discursive terrain. See Naomi Murakawa, *The First Civil Right: How Liberals Built Prison America* (New York: Oxford University Press, 2014).

85 "Tar baby": the term is from Brady, *Bad Boy*, 195–218.

86 Leah Wright-Rigueur, *The Loneliness of the Black Republican: Pragmatic Politics and the Pursuit of Power* (Princeton, NJ: Princeton University Press, 2015).

87 Rayford Logan, *Howard University: The First Hundred Years* (New York: New York University Press, 1968), 18.

88 Ibid., 558–569. See Zachery Williams, *In Search of the Talented Tenth: Howard University Public Intellectuals and the Dilemmas of Race, 1926-1970* (Columbia: University of Missouri Press, 2009); and Jonathan Holloway, *Confronting the Veil: Abram Harris Jr., E. Franklin Frazier, and Ralph Bunche, 1919-1941* (Chapel Hill: University of North Carolina Press, 2002).

89 There is a connection between the ways that the students envisioned "the Black university" as discussed in chapter 1, in this volume, and Cheek's initial vision. In his inaugural address, Cheek stated: "We shall begin the development of the New Knowledge and fashioning the new social technology that will raise up new kinds of social engineers, technically competent and morally committed to the special needs of Black Americans." See James E. Cheek, "To Seek a New Direction: Howard in the Decade of the Seventies," speech, Howard University, Washington, DC, August 25, 1969, transcript in author's possession. See also, "Dr. James E. Cheek to Be Inaugurated: 'To Seek a New Direction: Howard in the Decade of the Seventies,'" *Afro-American*, April 25, 1970.

90 This formulation drives the thesis of Bill Readings, *The University in Ruins* (Cambridge, MA: Harvard University Press, 1996). See also Roderick Ferguson, *The Reorder of Things: The University and Its Pedagogies of Minority Difference* (Minneapolis: University of Minnesota Press, 2012), which reads these changes through the lens of confronting "minority difference"; Henry Giroux, *The University in Chains: Confronting the Military-Industrial-Academic Complex* (Boulder, CO: Paradigm Press, 2007), and *Neoliberalism's War on Higher Education*; and Slaughter and Leslie, *Academic Capitalism*.

91 Brown, *Undoing the Demos*, 192–193; and Christopher Newfield, *Unmaking the Public University: The Forty-Year Assault on the Middle Class* (Baltimore: Johns Hopkins University Press, 2008).

92 Nick Aaron Ford, *Black Studies: Threat or Challenge?* (Port Washington, NY: Kennikat Press, 1993), 161–175; and Martha Biondi, *The Black Revolution on Campus* (Berkeley: University of California Press, 2012), 142–143.

93 Lawrence Feinberg, "Howard Polishing Its Lucky Charm in U.S. Fund Bid," *Washington Post*, June 18, 1981. Cheek's staff prepared an internal document that compared Howard's research allocation to its "aspirational peers." Here Cheek was concerned less with remaking Howard University into a "Black university" and more concerned with creating a modern research university on par with these institutions. Along with Yale, Johns Hopkins, and Stanford, the report studied Case Western Reserve, the University of Chicago, Duke, Emory, Georgetown, the University of Rochester, Tulane, and Vanderbilt. See "The Lingering Legacy of Neglect and Deprivation," paper (Washington, DC: Howard University, June 1970), Andrew Billingsley Papers, private collection.

94 Howard intellectuals—both faculty and staff—were at the heart of the fight for intellectual independence in this era, which manifested itself as a fight to emancipate knowledge about the world from Eurocentric foundations. Many of them understood this objective as a precursor to the kinds of social justice concerns that animated Cheek's inaugural address ("To Seek a New Direction"). A greater sense of this sort of work can be gleaned from Joyce Ladner, ed., *The Death of White Sociology* (New York: Random House, 1973), a collection that includes many scholars who would call Howard home in the 1970s and whose intellectual and political philosophies and concerns were much broader than even this provocative title would indicate. In many ways the authors included in Ladner's volume were calling for the death of "white" knowledges or "white" ways of understanding reality.

95 On the history of Howard's federal appropriation and Mordecai Wyatt Johnson's role, see Holloway, *Confronting the Veil*, 47–48; and Logan, *Howard University*, 203–204.

96 Ronald D. White, "Howard U. Seeks to Cut Costs to Reverse Its Large Deficit," *Washington Post*, August 13, 1983.

97 Dorothy Gilliam, "Streets and Suites Meet on the Righthand Side," *Washington Post*, February 9, 1981.

98 South Carolina State and Jackson State were two such sites of state violence against protesting HBCU students. See "Black College Presidents Tell Nixon of Repression Fears," *Jet*, June 4, 1970. On the violent repression at Black colleges, see Biondi, *The Black Revolution on Campus*, 142–173.

99 James Cheek, "Black Institutions and Black Students," *Integrated Education* 8 (November–December 1970): 16–20. See also Biondi, *The Black Revolution on Campus*, 161–163; and Wright-Rigueur, *The Loneliness of the Black Republican*, 161–162, for a discussion of Nixon and HBCU policy.

100 Gilliam, "Streets and Suites."

101 Dorothy Gilliam, "Presidents," *Washington Post*, May 22, 1982. See also Department of Education, "Howard University," in its *Biennial Evaluation Report, 1995–1996* (Washington, DC: Government Printing Office, 1997), 536-1 to 536-4, posted at the U.S. Department of Education website, www.ed.gov.

102 See Gilliam, "Presidents." Also see Gilliam, "Streets and Suites"; White, "Howard U. Seeks to Cut Costs"; and Keith B. Richburg, "Bush Speaks at Howard," *Washington Post*, May 10, 1981.

103 Manning Marable, *How Capitalism Underdeveloped Black America: Problems in Race, Political Economy, and Society* (Boston: South End Press, 1983), 172–180; Gayle T. Tate and Lewis A. Randolph, "Introduction," in *Dimensions of Black Conservatism in the United States: Made in America*, ed. Gayle T. Tate and Lewis A. Randolph (New York: Palgrave, 2002), 1–10; and Michael L. Ondaatje, *Black Conservative Intellectuals in Modern America* (Philadelphia: University of Pennsylvania Press, 2010).

104 Brady, *Bad Boy*, 235–236.

105 Nothing that Atwater proposed was antiracist or without precedent. Attempts to get out the Black vote were not only common in Republican politics, they were also less risky, given what we know about electoral capture. Moreover, Atwater's concerns were most likely geared toward winning elections, as opposed to generating progressive policy that targeted problems in Black communities. On Republican campaigning in Black communities during this era, see Wright-Rigueur, *The Loneliness of the Black Republican*, 261–279. For a discussion of the concept of electoral capture, see Frymer, *Uneasy Alliances*, 7–10.

106 Matt Schudel, "Howard President's Tenure Marked by Turmoil," *Washington Post*, January 10, 2010.

CHAPTER 3. THE MESSAGE

1 Eric B. & Rakim, performers, "Move the Crowd," single composed by Eric Barrier and William Griffin, on the album *Paid in Full* (New York: 4th and B'way Records, 1987).

2 See Martin Luther King, Jr., "A Christmas Sermon," quoted in James Cone, *Martin and Malcolm and America: Dream or Nightmare?* (Maryknoll, NY: Orbis Publishers, 1992), 213. Despite their best efforts to prevent the nightmare scenario from fully playing out, those successors to King's legacy ultimately were only able to produce a symbolic "dream"—the larger fight they waged for economic justice would be a dream that was deferred. See David Chappell, *Waking from the Dream: The Struggle for Civil Rights in the Shadow of Martin Luther King, Jr.* (New York: Random House, 2014).

3 "Decade of nightmares" is from Philip Jenkins, *Decade of Nightmares: The End of the Sixties and the Making of Eighties America* (New York: Oxford University Press, 2006). On readings of the film *The Big Chill* (directed by Lawrence Kasdan [Culver City, CA: Columbia Pictures, 1983]) as a metaphor for eighties sensibilities toward the upheavals of the sixties, see Gil Troy, *Morning in America: How Ronald Reagan Invented the 1980s* (Princeton, NJ: Princeton University Press, 2005), 115–146. Most histories of the decade treat Reagan's presidency as not only consequential but as positively consequential. Their treatments of racial inequality either rely on Black middle-class success as a barometer for the new possibilities of America or as a problem too big for any one administration to solve—both treat race as subordinate to political economy and the cultural politics that shifted during the decade. For the former, see Troy, *Morning in America*, 175–189; and John Ehrman, *The Eighties: America in the Age of Reagan* (New Haven, CT: Yale University Press, 2005), 181–193. For the latter, see Robert M. Collins, *Transforming America: Politics and Culture during the Reagan Years* (New York: Columbia University Press, 2007), 124–133, 239–241. Doug Rossinow's more recent history is an attempt to go beyond what he calls the "hagiography" of Reagan and the eighties. See his *The Reagan Era: A History of the 1980s* (New York: Columbia University Press, 2015), 10; as well as the earlier history of the journalist Haynes Johnson, *Sleepwalking through History: America in the Reagan Years* (New York: Anchor Books, 1991), although it, unlike Rossinow's book, ignores the administration's legacy on racial issues. For a broader reading of the failure of the Right to achieve a stable social conservatism during the decade, see David T. Courtwright, *No Right Turn: Conservative Politics in Liberal America* (Cambridge, MA: Harvard University Press, 2010); and Robert O. Self, *All in the Family: The Realignment of American Democracy since the 1960s* (New York: Hill & Wang, 2012). Although these issues were not unconnected to questions of race and the welfare state, it became clear that right-wing strategists placed a higher policy priority on the latter, rather than risk losing face with moderates to fulfill the dreams of the "captured" evangelicals who had voted for them en masse. Although they may have lost many public battles, the Religious Right would come to play an increasingly critical role in Republican Party politics, as seen in the makeup of the party today. Clearly, the party's positions on civil rights policies could be used to both reduce the size of government as well as continue to court Sunbelt voters galvanized by family- values issues. On the idea of a captured electorate and its possible application to evangelicals, see Paul Frymer, *Uneasy Alliances: Race and Party Competition in America* (Princeton, NJ: Princeton University Press, 1999), 193–199.

4 "Internal enemy" is from Alan Taylor, *The Internal Enemy: Slavery and War in Virginia, 1772–1832* (New York: Norton & Co., 2013), 1–10. For the argument that inequality made American economic growth possible during the period, see Godfrey Hodgson, *More Equal than Others: America from Nixon to the New Century* (Princeton, NJ: Princeton University Press, 2004), 12–25.

5 See Denys Vaughn-Cooke, "The Economic State of Black America—Is There a Recovery?" in *The State of Black America, 1984*, ed. James D. Williams (New York: National Urban League, 1984), 1–23. The reports for the years of the 1980s chronicle many of the other issues cited above. See also Center on Budget and Policy Priorities, *Falling Behind: A Report on How Blacks Have Fared under Reagan* (Washington, DC: Center on Budget and Policy Priorities, 1984); Manning Marable, *How Capitalism Underdeveloped Black America: Problems in Race, Political Economy, and Society* (Boston: South

End Press, 2000), xviii–xix, 231–253, and *Race, Reform, and Rebellion: The Second Reconstruction and Beyond in Black America, 1945–1990* (Jackson: University Press of Mississippi, 1991), 206–213; Bradford Martin, *The Other Eighties: A Secret History of America in the Age of Reagan* (New York: Hill & Wang, 2011), 119–123; and Doug Rossinow, *The Reagan Era*, 149–158.

6   The phrase "economy of expression" is from Cedric Robinson, *Black Movements in America* (New York: Routledge, 1997), 97. On the logic of Black conservatism, see esp. Houston Baker, *Betrayal: How Intellectuals Abandoned the Ideals of the Civil Rights Era* (New York: Columbia University Press, 2008), 127–196; Marable, *How Capitalism Underdeveloped Black America*, 172–180; and Michael Dawson, *Black Visions: The Roots of Contemporary African American Political Ideologies* (Chicago: University of Chicago Press, 2001), 281–302.

7   On the issue of civil rights, see Ronald W. Walters, *White Nationalism, Black Interests: Conservative Public Policy and the Black Community* (Detroit: Wayne State University Press, 2003), 116–144; and Marable, *Race, Reform, and Rebellion*, 191–206. On the Reagan administration's response to AIDS, see Doug Rossinow, *The Reagan Era*, 212–215; Hodgson, *More Equal than Others*, 186–191; and Martin, *The Other Eighties*, 171–187.

8   Collins, *Transforming America*, 193–234.

9   Rossinow, *The Reagan Era*, 261–279; Martin, *The Other Eighties*, 3–66; Piero Gleijeses, *Visions of Freedom: Havana, Washington, Pretoria and the Struggle for Southern Africa, 1976–1991* (Chapel Hill: University of North Carolina Press, 2013); Francis Njubi Nesbitt, *Race for Sanctions: African Americans against Apartheid, 1946–1994* (Bloomington: Indiana University Press, 2004), 111–122; Ronald W. Walters, *Pan Africanism and the African Diaspora: An Analysis of Modern Afrocentric Political Movements* (Detroit: Wayne State University Press, 1993), 263–268; Karin Stanford, *Beyond the Boundaries: Reverend Jesse Jackson in International Affairs* (Albany: State University of New York Press, 1997), 56–61; Gerald Horne, *Black and Red: W.E.B. Du Bois and the Afro-American Response to the Cold War, 1944–1963* (Albany: State University of New York Press, 1986); and Mary Dudziak, *Cold War Civil Rights: Race and the Image of American Democracy* (Princeton, NJ: Princeton University Press, 1994).

10   Mark D. Alleyne, "U.S. Motives Are against Grenada," *The Hilltop*, November 4, 1983; Caribbean Student Association, "CSA Gives Their Views on Grenada Invasion," *The Hilltop*, November 18, 1983; Naomi Travers, "HUSA [Howard University Student Association] Answers Inquiry into Officials' Lybian [sic] Trip," *The Hilltop*, October 10, 1986; and Ellen L. Armstrong, "HUSA Speaks on Libyan Trip," *The Hilltop*, October 24, 1986.

11   R. K. Byers, *The Real HU* (New York: Banned Books, 2012).

12   Christina Sharpe, *In the Wake: On Blackness and Being* (Durham, NC: Duke University Press, 2016).

13   Richard Iton, *In Search of the Black Fantastic: Politics and Popular Culture in the Post–Civil Rights Era* (New York: Oxford University Press, 2009).

14   Tricia Rose, *Black Noise: Rap Music and Black Culture in Contemporary America* (Hanover, NH: Wesleyan University Press, 1994), 21–27. See also Iton, *In Search of the Black Fantastic*, 250–255.

15   For Flash's comment, see Jeff Chang, *Can't Stop Won't Stop: A History of the Hip-Hop Generation* (New York: Picador, 2005), 129.

16   On the contradictions and limitations of hip hop as political movement and hip hop as industry, particularly one in a neoliberal capitalist order, see Charise Cheney, *Brothers*

Gonna Work It Out: Sexual Politics in the Golden Age of Rap Nationalism (New York: New York University Press, 2005); Lester Spence, *Stare in the Darkness: The Limits of Hip-Hop and Black Politics* (Minneapolis: University of Minnesota Press, 2011); Todd Boyd, "Check Yo Self, before You Wreck Yo Self: Variations on a Political Theme in Rap Music and Popular Culture," in *The Black Public Sphere: A Public Culture Book*, ed. Black Public Sphere Collective (Chicago: University of Chicago Press, 1998), 293–316; and S. Craig Watkins, *Hip Hop Matters: Politics, Pop Culture, and the Struggle for the Soul of a Movement* (Boston: Beacon Press, 2005). On the need to build a political movement, see Bakari Kitwana, *The Hip Hop Generation: Young Blacks and the Crisis in African-American Culture* (New York: Basic Books, 2002).

17 This is what Lester Spence calls "consumption." See his *Stare in the Darkness*, 5–6. For a discussion of the debate among nationalist rappers and activists on the question of political responsibility, see Cheney, *Brothers Gonna Work It Out*, 149–171; and Chang, *Can't Stop* Won't Stop, 273–276.

18 Public Enemy, *Yo! Bum Rush the Show* (New York: Def Jam Recordings/Columbia Records, 1987).

19 Chang, *Can't Stop Won't Stop*, 231–297; and Clarence Lusane, "Rap, Race, and Politics," *Race and Class* 35 (1993): 41–56. On "attitude," see Ernest Allen, Jr., "Making the Strong Survive: The Contours and Contradictions of Message Rap," in *Droppin' Science: Critical Essays on Rap Music and Hip Hop Culture*, ed. William Eric Perkins (Philadelphia: Temple University Press, 1996), 160. For an understanding of how rappers imagined their work and its relevance, see particularly the primary source collection of Joseph D. Eure and James G. Spady, eds., *Nation Conscious Rap* (Brooklyn, NY: PC International Publishers, 1991).

20 Spike Lee, director, *Do the Right Thing* (Universal City, CA: Universal Pictures, 1989).

21 Public Enemy, "Fight the Power" (single; Detroit, MI: Motown Records, 1989); Chang, *Can't Stop Won't Stop*, 220–229, 276–280; and Marcus Reeves, *Somebody Scream! Rap Music's Rise to Prominence in the Aftershock of Black Power* (New York: Faber & Faber, 2008), 63–91.

22 Chang, *Can't Stop Won't Stop*, 231–261.

23 Boogie Down Productions, "My Philosophy," on *By All Means Necessary* (Beverly Hills, CA: Jive/RCA Records, 1988).

24 The description is from the contemporaneous William Julius Wilson, *The Truly Disadvantaged: The Inner City, The Underclass, and Public Policy* (1987; reprint, Chicago: University of Chicago Press, 2012).

25 Watkins, *Hip Hop Matters*, 239–244; Rose, *Black Noise*, 142–144; and Iton, *In Search of the Black Fantastic*, 166.

26 Imani Perry, *Prophets of the Hood: Politics and Poetics in Hip Hop* (Durham, NC: Duke University Press, 2004), 33–37; and Iton, *In Search of the Black Fantastic*, 8–19.

27 Allen, "Making the Strong Survive," 179–185. Echoing this sensibility, Cheney argues that this bravado exhibited a particularly sexist and conservative cant, arguing that visions of an (often violent) overthrow of the oppressive order exhibited a politics of substitution, rather than one of liberation. See Cheney, *Brothers Gonna Work It Out*, 63–96.

28 On the calls for a movement, see Kitwana, *The Hip Hop Generation*; and Hashim Shodari, *From the Underground: Hip Hop Culture as an Agent of Change* (Fanwood, NJ: X-Factor Publications, 1995). On the successes, challenges, and contradictions of hip-hop political formations, see Spence, *Stare in the Darkness*, 95–129.

29 Perry, *Prophets of the Hood*, 86–101. On gangsta rap, see Robin D. G. Kelley's seminal treatment in *Race Rebels: Culture, Politics, and the Black Working Class* (New York: Free Press, 1994), 183–227.

30 Allen, "Making the Strong Survive."

31 Chang, *Can't Stop Won't Stop*, 275.

32 Queen Latifah, "Ladies First," single on *All Hail the Queen* (New York: Tommy Boy Records, 1989).

33 For a discussion of "Ladies First" and the larger question of women and rap, see Tricia Rose, *Black Noise*, 146–182, and her "Never Trust a Big Butt and a Smile," *Camera Obscura* 8 (1990): 108–131. For a critique of the gender politics of message and/or "nationalist" rap, see Cheney, *Brothers Gonna Work It Out*, 97–118.

34 Martin, *The Other Eighties*, 45–66; and Sekou Franklin, *After the Rebellion: Black Youth, Social Movement Activism, and the Post–Civil Rights Generation* (New York: New York University Press, 2014), 88–94.

35 On the importance of South Africa to the hip-hop generation, see Chang, *Can't Stop Won't Stop*, 215–220. For Williamson's background, see Eure and Spady, *Nation Conscious Rap*, 233–245.

36 On the District of Columbia, see the characterization of the scholar-activist scene in Anthony Bogues, "C.L.R. James, Pan-Africanism and the Black Radical Tradition," *Critical Arts* 25 (2011): 484–499.

37 Of these, the most well publicized was SASP's Southern Africa Week, which included a radiothon organized by Howard University's radio station, WHUR, where Kathy Flewellen was employed. See "Interview with Sylvia Hill," August 12, 2004, *African Activist Archive Project*, Michigan State University, www.msu.edu; Adwoa Dunn-Mouton, interview by the author, March 26, 2017; and Joseph Jordan, interview by the author, March 30, 2017.

38 Sylvia Hill, email communication with the author, March 13, 2017. See also Program, National Conference: "Building Forces against United States Support for South Africa," June 8, 1981, Southern Africa Support Project Papers, box 1, folder 44, Moorland-Spingarn Research Center, Howard University.

39 Nesbitt, *Race for Sanctions*, 4.

40 Robert Edgar, ed., *Sanctioning Apartheid* (Trenton, NJ: Africa World Press, 1990); Robert Kinloch Massie, *Loosing the Bonds: The United States and South Africa in the Apartheid Years* (New York: Nan A. Talese, 1997); Alvin Tillery, Jr., *Between Homeland and Motherland: Africa, U.S. Foreign Policy, and Black Leadership in America* (Ithaca, NY: Cornell University Press, 2011); and Nesbitt, *Race for Sanctions*.

41 Tony Vellela, *New Voices: Student Political Activism in the '80s and '90s* (Boston, MA: South End Press, 1988), 19–38.

42 Robert Edgar, interview by the author, March 14, 2017.

43 Kuae Noel Kelch, "Free South Africa Movement: Berry Blasts Apartheid," *The Hilltop*, February 1, 1985; Nesbitt, *Race for Sanctions*, 123–127; and Massie, *Loosing the Bonds*, 558–560.

44 Kuae Noel Kelch, "Howard Protests Apartheid," *The Hilltop*, March 8, 1985.

45 In a forum, the activist—and Howard graduate student at the time—Joseph Jordan, struck by students' absence, encouraged them to join the protests. In an interview years later, Joseph asserted that, in his conversations with Howard students at the embassy, they were put off by the multiracial character of the protests, and many left.

Jordan notes the perennial problem of Black student organizations and the question of continuity, given the sense that a college student's tenure is "terminal." This may have contributed to the hesitation, as earlier moments of Southern Africa activity (i.e., Robert Mugabe's visit to campus) were, by all accounts, explosive. That said, Howard students were involved in the multiracial DC Student Coalition Against Apartheid and Racism and with an American Committee on Africa–sponsored action on the anniversary of Martin Luther King, Jr.'s assassination. See Joseph Jordan, interview by the author, March 30, 2017; Ghana O. Wilson, "Where Are the Students?" *The Hilltop*, February 22, 1985; and Karlyn Barker, "Apartheid Protests to Mark King Anniversary," *Washington Post*, April 3, 1985.

46 The September 6, 1985, edition of *The Hilltop* ran a special series entitled "Focus on South Africa," which encompassed many of the debates taking place around the country. For a sampling of these ideas and the activity that occurred across this high point of the movement, see "We Must Protest," *The Hilltop*, September 6, 1985; Cassandra Ward, "Sigmas Arrested at Embassy," *The Hilltop*, October 4, 1985; Benjamin James, "Greeks Arrested," *The Hilltop*, October 18, 1985; advertisement, "Howard University against Apartheid," *The Hilltop*, October 18, 1985; and Paul S. Burley, "Student-Organized Protest Ends with 2 Arrests," *The Hilltop*, January 20, 1986.

47 Robert Edgar, interview by the author, March 14, 2017; Adwoa Dunn-Mouton, interview by the author, March 26, 2017; and Alonza Robertson, "Biko Rally Focuses on Activism," *The Hilltop*, September 19, 1986.

48 Benjamin James, "HUSA Sponsors 'Azania Update,'" *The Hilltop*, August 19, 1985. On the Tutu visit, see Henry Boyd Hall and Ghana O. Wilson, "Tutu Speaks on Apartheid," *The Hilltop*, November 9, 1984. For Maki Mandela's visit, see Suzanne Alexander, "Mandela Seeks Support for Struggle in South Africa," *The Hilltop*, September 12, 1986; and Rachel Swarns, "Mandela Challenges Apartheid," *The Hilltop*, September 12, 1986.

49 Kelly Mitchell-Clark, "Forum Denounces Racist South Africa," *The Hilltop*, April 13, 1984; Imani Countess, interview by the author, March 24, 2017.

50 Nelson Mandela and Thabo Mbeki were awarded honorary doctorates in 1994 and 2000, respectively. After the pivotal 1994 election, in which Howard professors participated as observers, Howard launched a formal exchange project with the new government.

51 Stetsasonic, Featuring the Reverend Jesse Jackson with Olatunji and the Drums of Passion, "A.F.R.I.C.A." (single, vinyl LP; New York: Tommy Boy, 1987), TB 899.

52 Lusane, "Rap, Race, and Politics," 47.

53 See Stetsasonic, "A.F.R.I.C.A." Stetsasonic's work was part of a campaign that included a research guide and the album featuring Jesse Jackson and the Nigerian drummer Babatunde Olatunji. The proceeds from the project raised funds for the Frontline states. See "Newsmakers," *Billboard*, December 26, 1987.

54 Chang, *Can't Stop Won't Stop*, 215–229.

55 On the makeup of the campaign organization, see Manning Marable, *Black American Politics: From the Washington Marches to Jesse Jackson* (London: Verso Press, 1985), 269–271; Paulette Pierce, "Neglected Legacy: The Black Power Movement and Jesse Jackson's Presidential Campaigns," *Humanity and Society* 16 (February 1992): 21–39; Ronald W. Walters, "The Issue Politics of the Jesse Jackson Campaign for President in 1984," in *The Social and Political Implications of the 1984 Jesse Jackson Presidential Campaign*, ed. Lorenzo Morris (Westport, CT: Praeger, 1990), 20–23; Charles Henry, *Jesse*

Jackson: The Search for Common Ground (Oakland, CA: Black Scholar Press, 1991), 54–63; and Sheila Collins, *The Rainbow Challenge* (New York: Monthly Review Press, 1986), 120–140.

56 Amiri Baraka, "Black People and Jesse Jackson II," in *The LeRoi Jones/Amiri Baraka Reader*, ed. William J. Harris (Chicago: Lawrence Hill Books, 1999), 463.

57 As a veteran of the mobilizations of the 1970s, Baraka's characterization of this moment is prescient:

> But our push for Jesse is part of our push for ourselves. We do not just want another famous Negro famous for being with white folks. We want democracy in America, we want equality. Jesse represented our desire for Self-Determination, the shaping of our own lives with the same opportunity possessed by any other American. But Jesse's great run ended with the ignominious confirmation of our continued slavery. The convention finally, I could understand, was just the big house during a holiday season. And now the house negroes did sing and dance and clap their hands. And were it not for the fact that there was an outside to the house, and the night real and moving away in all directions, in which real people lived and desired, all of those goings on would seem like utter foolishness. But there is, and they did. [Ibid., 480].

58 James Early, "An Interview: Jack O'Dell," *Black Scholar* 15 (September/October 1984): 54–55; Collins, *The Rainbow Challenge*, 302–332; and Franklin, *After the Rebellion*, 104.

59 Robert C. Smith, "From Insurgency toward Inclusion: The Jackson Campaigns of 1984 and 1988," in Morris, ed., *The Social and Political Implications of the 1984 Jesse Jackson Presidential Campaign*, 215–230, and *We Have No Leaders: African Americans in the Post–Civil Rights Era* (Albany: State University of New York Press, 1996), 237–238. For Smith, the major differences were the composition of the campaign staff, the concession on rules challenges, and the focus on valence issues such as drug abuse. On the 1988 campaign, generally, see also Amiri Baraka, "Black People and Jesse Jackson II"; Marshall Frady, *Jesse: The Life and Pilgrimage of Jesse Jackson* (New York: Simon & Schuster, 2006), 378–401; Elizabeth Colton, *The Jackson Phenomenon: The Man, The Power, The Message* (New York: Doubleday, 1989); and Penn Kimball, *"Keep Hope Alive!" Super Tuesday and Jesse Jackson's 1988 Campaign for the Presidency* (Washington, DC: Joint Center for Political and Economic Studies Press, 1992).

60 Amiri Baraka, "Black People and Jesse Jackson II," 466–467; Colton, *The Jackson Phenomenon*, 241–278; and Smith, *We Have No Leaders*, 239.

61 See Ellen Hume, "Politics '84—Big Man on Campus: Hart Revives Student Activism," *Wall Street Journal*, March 12, 1984; Gerald M. Pomper, "The Nominations," in *The Election of 1984: Reports and Interpretations*, ed. Marlene Michels Pomper (Chatham, NJ: Chatham House Publishers, 1985), 21–23; Jack Germond and Jules Witcover, *Wake Us When It's Over: Presidential Politics of 1984* (New York: Macmillan, 1985), 142; and Sean Wilentz, *The Age of Reagan: A History, 1974–2008* (New York: Harper, 2008), 171–173.

62 Michael Preston, relying on National Black Election Study data, argues that this support did not necessarily translate into expected turnout figures. Nonetheless, the preference for those Black youth who *did* vote was Jesse Jackson. Other polls showed that this was not necessarily the case for Black voters over the age of fifty, particularly in the South. See Michael B. Preston, "The 1984 Presidential Primary Campaign: Who Voted for Jesse Jackson and Why?" in *Jesse Jackson's 1984 Presidential Campaign*, ed. Lucius

Barker and Ronald Walters (Champaign: University of Illinois Press), 136–138. See Thomas Cavanagh and Lorn Foster, *Jesse Jackson's Campaign Primaries and Caucuses* (Washington, DC: Joint Center for Political and Economic Studies, 1984), 25.

63 Lorenzo Morris, "The Range and Limits of Campaign Politics," in Morris, ed., *The Social and Political Implications of the 1984 Jesse Jackson Presidential Campaign*, 3–4.

64 On Howard scholars and earlier organizing around presidential politics, see Cedric Johnson, *Revolutionaries to Race Leaders: Black Power and the Making of African American Politics* (Minneapolis: University of Minnesota Press, 2007), 108.

65 Walters, "The Issue Politics of the Jesse Jackson Campaign," 23. In addition to Morris, ed., *The Social and Political Implications of the 1984 Jesse Jackson Presidential Campaign*, and Barker and Walters, eds., *Jesse Jackson's 1984 Presidential Campaign*, see Ralph C. Gomes and Linda Faye Williams, eds., *From Exclusion to Inclusion: The Long Struggle for African American Political Power* (Westport, CT: Praeger, 1992).

66 D. Orlando Ledbetter and Henry Boyd Hall, "300,000 March on Capital," *The Hilltop*, September 2, 1983; Christopher Brown, "Campus Politically Apathetic?" *The Hilltop*, September 2, 1983.

67 "Don't Run Jesse," *The Hilltop*, September 2, 1983. Others showed concern about Jackson's past, questions of political viability, and the possibilities of violence. See also "Sound Off," *The Hilltop*, October 7, 1983.

68 Dexter Chestnut, "LASC Brings Black Mayors to Howard," *The Hilltop*, November 18, 1983; and "Black Mayors Rally behind Jesse Jackson Campaign," *The Hilltop*, November 18, 1983.

69 Cleopatra Robinson, "Farrakhan Gives Nod to Jesse," *The Hilltop*, November 18, 1983. Farrakhan's endorsement represented a shift that moved the Nation of Islam into formal political activity for the first time. For Black nationalists, this was a critical move; for the national media and the punditry, it reminded them of the perceived "danger" of Jackson. Jackson's loyalty to Farrakhan during the media-concocted controversies around his statements on Judaism would prove to be, for these pundits, a grave mistake. See Bob Faw and Nancy Skelton, *Thunder in America: The Improbable Presidential Campaign of Jesse Jackson in 1984* (Austin: Texas Monthly Press, 1986), 107–118; and Frady, *Jesse*, 349–354. These issues would recur during the New York primary in 1988, after Jackson had surprised many with his victory in Michigan. See Colton, *The Jackson Phenomenon*, 202–215.

70 Gerald Massengill, "Jackson Forum," *The Hilltop*, February 10, 1984; and Joyce Harris, "HUSA Voter Registration Drive Reaches 5,000 Mark, Support from Howard Students Lacking," *The Hilltop*, February 10, 1984. At the time of these articles, the leaders of the Howard University Student Association (HUSA) effort, Mark Hall and Andre Owens, stated that only about 20 percent of this figure were Howard students, which demonstrated that the excitement often did not translate into votes. It must be remembered, however, that many Howard students—a body that has always been national—had perhaps registered to vote in their home states. Jackson issues director and Howard professor Ronald Walters was at the center of many of these voter registration efforts, which reflected one of the most important aspects of Jackson's run. See Paul Delaney, "Voting: The New Black Power," *New York Times*, November 27, 1983; Chappell, *Waking from the Dream*, 145; Adolph L. Reed, *The Jesse Jackson Phenomenon: The Crisis of Purpose in Afro-American Politics* (New Haven, CT: Yale University Press, 1986), 17–22; and Rod Bush, ed., *The New Black Vote: Politics and Power in Four American Cities* (San Francisco: Synthesis Publications, 1984).

71 Steve Howard, "More than 2,000 Attend Fundraiser for Jackson," *Washington Informer*, April 11, 1984; Edward D. Sargent, "Jackson Backers Attend Fund-Raiser at Howard," *Washington Post*, April 2, 1984; and Gerald Massengill, "D.C. Women Boost Jackson," *The Hilltop* April 6, 1984. Black women, particularly activists like Rosa Parks, were among Jackson's most ardent supporters. On the significance of this support, see Miriam Louie and Gloria Quinones, "Women's Stake in the Rainbow Coalition," *Black Scholar* 15 (September/October 1984): 27–32.

72 Oscar H. Gandy, Jr., and Larry G. Coleman, "Watch Jesse Run and Tell Me What You See: A First Look at Student Perceptions of the Jesse Jackson Presidential Candidacy," *Journal of Black Studies* 16 (March 1986): 293–306.

73 "Run (Again) Jesse, Run," *The Hilltop*, April 17, 1987.

74 Ona Alston, "Howard Co-hosts Conference," *The Hilltop*, October 2, 1987.

75 Yolanda A. Plummer, "Students Seek Unity," *The Hilltop*, October 30, 1987.

76 "Jackson Made Bad Move," *The Hilltop*, October 30, 1987.

77 "Racism Raising its Head," *The Hilltop*, February 19, 1988; Sheila Maxwell, "Black Students at UMass Stage Protest," *The Hilltop*, February 19, 1988; and "A Black College Plus," *The Hilltop*, May 13, 1988. On the national context, see Vellela, *New Voices*, 86–117.

78 Rebecca Little, "Panelists Address Blacks' Problems," *The Hilltop*, March 4, 1988; and Robert J. Vickers, "Jackson Brings Message to D.C.," *The Hilltop*, March 18, 1988.

79 Tanya Alexander, "Omegas Sponsor Run to Benefit Jesse," *The Hilltop*, April 8, 1988; and Bill Peterson, "Jackson Translating Popularity on Campus into Student Votes," *Washington Post*, March 28, 1988.

80 Frances M. Beale, "U.S. Politics Will Never Be the Same," *Black Scholar* 15 (September/October 1984): 10–11; and Cornel West, "Black Politics Will Never Be the Same," *Christianity and Crisis* 44 (August 13, 1984): 302–305. On the legacies of Jackson's campaigns, see Smith, *We Have No Leaders*, 229–253; Chappell, *Waking from the Dream*, 143–147; and Sam Tanenhaus, "Jesse Jackson Created the Modern Democratic Party," *Bloomberg*, August 26, 2015, www.bloomberg.com.

CHAPTER 4. A FORCE

1 Memorandum, "The Meaning of Force," Black Nia F.O.R.C.E, March 13, 1988, Akanke Washington Collection, private collection.

2 Cedric Robinson, *Black Marxism: The Making of the Black Radical Tradition* (Chapel Hill: University of North Carolina Press, 2000), 316.

3 On the deepening inequity of American society and the continuing struggle against colonialism in Southern Africa, see the discussions in chaps. 2 and 3, in this volume, respectively. On the development of the Black university concept, see the work of the Howard chapter of the Save and Change Black Schools Committee, a national effort founded by Nelson Johnson and activists affiliated with the Student Organization for Black Unity: Daryl Gaines, "Save Black Schools Retreat," *The Hilltop*, July 11, 1973; Donald Isaac, "Save Our Schools," *The Hilltop*, February 1, 1974; Roger Glass, "Seminar on the Essence of Black Education," *The Hilltop*, November 20, 1973; the proceedings of "Howard in the Decade of the 1970s: A Symposium in Celebration of the 90th Birthday of Andrew Billingsley," Howard University, Washington, D.C., April 20–22, 2016; and Robert C. Smith, *Ronald W. Walters and the Fight for Black Power* (Albany: State University of New York Press, 2018), 69–72.

4 Richard Iton, *In Search of the Black Fantastic: Politics and Popular Culture in the Post–Civil Rights Era* (New York: Oxford University Press, 2009); Cedric Johnson, *Revolutionaries to Race Leaders: Black Power and the Making of African American Politics* (Minneapolis: University of Minnesota Press, 2007); Adolph Reed, Jr., *Stirrings in the Jug: Black Politics in the Post-segregation Era* (Minnesota: University of Minnesota Press, 1999); Ronald W. Walters, *Pan Africanism in the African Diaspora: An Analysis of Modern Afrocentric Political Movements* (Detroit: Wayne State University Press, 1993), 149–150.

5 Johnson, *Revolutionaries to Race Leaders*, 131–172.

6 For a discussion of the 1970s era iteration, see, generally, Michael Dawson, *Black Visions: The Roots of African American Political Ideologies* (Chicago: University of Chicago Press, 2001), 198–221; Rod Bush, *We Are Not What We Seem: Black Nationalism and Class Struggle in the American Century* (New York: New York University Press, 1999), 193–213; Jeffrey O. G. Ogbar, *Black Power: Radical Politics and African American Identity* (Baltimore: Johns Hopkins University Press, 2004), 93–122; Peniel Joseph, *Waiting 'til the Midnight Hour: A Narrative History of Black Power in America* (New York: Henry Holt, 2006), 241–247; Scot Brown, *Fighting for Us: Maulana Karenga, the US Organization and Black Cultural Nationalism* (New York: New York University Press, 2003); Komozi Woodard, *A Nation within a Nation: Amiri Baraka (LeRoi Jones) and Black Power Politics* (Chapel Hill: University of North Carolina Press, 1999); James Edward Smethurst, *The Black Arts Movement: Cultural Nationalism in the 1960s and 1970s* (Chapel Hill: University of North Carolina Press, 2005); Russell Rickford, *We Are an African People: Independent Education, Black Power, and the Radical Imagination* (New York: Oxford University Press, 2016); and Johnson, *Revolutionaries to Race Leaders*, 131–172. For a discussion of the present, see Keeanga-Yamahtta Taylor, *From #BlackLivesMatter to Black Liberation* (Chicago: Haymarket Books, 2016).

7 Walters, *Pan Africanism in the African Diaspora*, 72–74; Joseph, *Waiting 'til the Midnight Hour*, 289–293; Bush, *We Are Not What We Seem*, 212–213; and Johnson, *Revolutionaries to Race Leaders*, 153–155.

8 On Kwame Ture at the Howard conference, see Walters, *Pan Africanism and the African Diaspora*, 72–85; and Peniel Joseph, *Stokely: A Life* (New York: Basic Books, 2014), 277–304. Baraka's evolution was critical, given his stature among cultural nationalists and the significance of the Congress of African People, of which he was a key leader. See Dawson, *Black Visions*, 214–220. For Ture and Baraka's own reading of their quests toward ideological clarity, see Amiri Baraka, *The Autobiography of LeRoi Jones* (Chicago: Lawrence Hill, 1997), 433–445; Stokely Carmichael with Ekwueme Michael Thelwell, *Ready for Revolution: The Life and Struggles of Stokely Carmichael [Kwame Ture]* (New York: Scribner & Sons, 2003), 607–679; Amiri Baraka, "Toward Ideological Clarity: Nationalism, Pan Africanism, Socialism," *Black World*, November 1974, 24–33, 84–95, and "'Why I Changed My Ideology': Black Nationalism and Socialist Revolution," *Black World*, July 1975, 30–42; and Stokely Carmichael, "Pan-Africanism," in *Stokely Speaks: From Black Power to Pan-Africanism* (Chicago: Lawrence Hill, 2007), 183–220.

9 Walters, *Pan Africanism in the African Diaspora*, 174–181. On the earlier eras, see Jonathan Scott Holloway, *Confronting the Veil: Abram Harris, Jr., E. Franklin Frazier, and Ralph Bunche, 1919–1941* (Chapel Hill: University of North Carolina Press, 2002); and Robert Vitalis, *White World Order, Black Power Politics: The Birth of American International Relations* (Ithaca, NY: Cornell University Press, 2015).

10 These ideas include Umoja (unity), Ujima (collective work and responsibility), Kuji-chagulia (self-determination), Ujamaa (cooperative economics), Kuumba (creativity), Nia (purpose), and Imani (faith).

11 "Ubiquity Seeks Recognition," *The Hilltop*, October 25, 1974.

12 See Sheron L. Covington, "Students Organize to Save Black Colleges," *Atlanta Daily World*, December 7, 1979; Dorothy Gilliam, "Controversial March for Black Colleges," *Washington Post*, September 29, 1980; and James Dodson, "NOBUCS Hosts National Caucus," *The Hilltop*, November 6, 1981.

13 Dawson, *Black Visions*, 104–133; Johnson, *Revolutionaries to Race Leaders*, 166–167; Reed, *Stirrings in the Jug*; and Robert C. *African Americans in the Post–Civil Rights Era* (Albany: State University of New York Press, 1996), 100–105.

14 Clifton Marsh, *The Lost-Found Nation of Islam in America* (Lanham, MD: Scarecrow Press, 2000), 94–128; and Matthias Gardell, *In the Name of Elijah Muhammad: Louis Farrakhan and the Nation of Islam* (Durham, NC: Duke University Press, 1996), 135–143.

15 Ernest Allen, Jr., "Making the Strong Survive: The Contours and Contradictions of Message Rap," in *Droppin' Science: Critical Essays on Rap Music and Hip Hop Culture*, ed. William Eric Perkins (Philadelphia: Temple University Press, 1996), 184–188; Felicia M. Miyakawa, *Five Percenter Rap: God Hop's Music, Message, and Black Muslim Mission* (Bloomington: Indiana University Press, 2005), 21–22; and Gardell, *In the Name of Elijah Muhammad*, 293–301.

16 Haqq Islam, interview by the author, January 24, 2018; Kelly Marbury, "Minister Farrakhan Addresses the Role of Today's Youth," *The Hilltop*, February 10, 1984; and Tracey R. Mitchell and Freda Satterwhite, "Farrakhan Stresses World Unity," *The Hilltop*, September 28, 1984.

17 Joyce Harris, "Kwame Ture Urges Political Education," *The Hilltop*, November 2, 1984.

18 Haqq Islam, interview by the author, January 24, 2018; Christopher Cathcart, interview by the author, January 31, 2018; Robin McGinty, "Newell: The Student and the Politician," *The Hilltop*, January 28, 1983; Carlton Lockhard and Joyce Harris, "Students Demand Pres. Cheek's Resignation," *The Hilltop*, February 11, 1983; and "60 Students Continue Sit-in," *Washington Post*, February 18, 1983.

19 Kelly Marbury, "Hundreds Gather for Bobby Seale Panther Forum," *The Hilltop*, September 30, 1983; "What Was Bobby Seale So Afraid Of?" *The Hilltop*, October 7, 1983; "Who Is Bobby Seale and What Is He Afraid Of?" *Young Spartacus* 112 (October 1983): 4, 10; Manotti L. Jenkins, "SYL Needs New Approach," *The Hilltop*, January 20, 1984; "SYL Seeks Recognition at Howard," *The Hilltop*, January 27, 1984; and "Marxism vs. Black Nationalism," *Young Spartacus* 116 (March 1984): 3, 9.

20 Haqq Islam, interview by the author, January 24, 2018.

21 The influence of Lewis was revealed to me by University of Pennsylvania student activist and eventual student leader Conrad Tillard, who also saw the links between this sort of admiration and the need for African Americans to achieve financial independence. As discussed below, Tillard helped develop what became known as "hip-hop activism," and this notion of Black economics became a central thread of that work. See Conrad Tillard, interview by the author, December 7, 2017. See also Lester Spence, *Stare in the Darkness: The Limits of Hip-Hop and Black Politics* (Minneapolis: University of Minnesota Press, 2011); and S. Craig Watkins, *Hip Hop Matters: Politics, Pop Culture, and the Struggle for the Soul of a Movement* (Boston: Beacon Press, 2005).

22 For Jenkins's comments, see "Meet HUSA Candidates," *The Hilltop*, March 2, 1984.

23 "Cathcart for President," *The Hilltop*, March 2, 1984.

24 Alison Bethel, "A Look at HUSA," *The Hilltop*, September 7, 1984.

25 For "cultural void," see ibid. See also Christopher Cathcart, interview by the author, January 31, 2018. Given the influences of Ture upon this generation, perhaps it is no surprise that in his era as a Howard student activist, the same tactics of utilizing student government were employed. It would be the case again with Black Nia F.O.R.C.E. See Carmichael with Thelwell, *Ready for Revolution*, 149–154.

26 Deron Snyder, "HUSA Campaigns to Mandate Class," *The Hilltop*, February 15, 1985; and Alison Bethel, "Group to Examine Mandatory Initiative," *The Hilltop*, April 12, 1985. For a discussion of Howard and anti-apartheid see chap. 3, in this volume.

27 See Frantz Fanon, *The Wretched of the Earth* (New York: Grove Press, 2004), 145.

28 Fritz Jean, interview by the author, January 7, 2018; and Haqq Islam, interview by the author, January 27, 2018.

29 Aaron Johnson, interview by the author, July 18, 2017; and Stephen Jackson, interview by the author, February 19, 2018. See also Gary Smith, "I Almost Trained a Schizo," *Washington Post*, November 29, 1987.

30 Carlisle Sealy, interview by the author, July 7, 2017; Charles "Chuck" Webb, interview by the author, June 26, 2017; Anthony Dandridge, interview by the author, December 18, 2017; and R. K. Byers, *The Real HU* (New York: Banned Books, 2012).

31 Charles "Chuck" Webb, interview by the author, June 26, 2017.

32 Aaron Johnson, interview by the author, July 18, 2017.

33 Amiri Baraka, *The Autobiography of LeRoi Jones*, 447–448.

34 Ras J. Baraka, interview by the author, August 25, 2017; and Shawn Houston, interview by the author, December 18, 2017.

35 Aaron Johnson, interview by the author, July 18, 2017; Carlisle Sealy, interview by the author, July 7, 2017; and Byers, *The Real HU*.

36 Carlisle Sealy, interview by the author, July 7, 2017; and Charles "Chuck" Webb, interview by the author, June 26, 2017.

37 Carlisle Sealy, interview by the author, July 7, 2017; and Ras J. Baraka, interview by the author, August 25, 2017.

38 Carlisle Sealy, interview by the author, July 7, 2017; and Ras J. Baraka, interview by the author, August 25, 2017.

39 See Dawson, *Black Visions*, 102–120; Bush, *We Are Not What We Seem*; and Sterling Stuckey, *Slave Culture: Nationalist Theory and the Origins of Black America* (New York: Oxford University Press, 1987).

40 Rich Byers, interview by the author, September 15, 2017; and Byers, *The Real HU*.

41 Aaron Lloyd, interview by the author, July 22, 2017; Kevin Williams, interview by the author, July 9, 2017; Ras J. Baraka, interview by the author, August 25, 2017; Carlisle Sealy, interview by the author, July 7, 2017; Charles "Chuck" Webb, interview by the author, June 26, 2017; and Aaron Johnson, interview by the author, July 18, 2017.

42 Carlisle Sealy, interview by the author, July 7, 2017.

43 Curtrice Garner, "Students Work for Awareness," *The Hilltop*, February 26, 1988.

44 Charles "Chuck" Webb, interview by the author, June 26, 2017; and Ras J. Baraka, interview by the author, August 25, 2017.

45 Tillard's brainchild was extended by Howard activists in HUSA, such as Fritz Jean, Wayne Carter, and Ona Alston. The manifestation was a theme focusing upon "Seizing Power in the 21st Century." See Ona Alston, "Howard Co-Hosts Conference," *The

Hilltop, October 2, 1987; Robert Frelow, Jr., "Unity Day Attracts 2,000 Students," *The Hilltop*, October 23, 1987; Conrad Tillard, interview by the author, December 7, 2017; and Fritz Jean, interview by the author, January 7, 2018.

46 "Garvey Scholar Honored by Black Students," *Columbus Times*, November 29, 1987.

47 Louis Farrakhan, *Seizing Power in the 21st Century* (DVD, Chicago: Final Call, 1987); Lori Buckner, "Islamic Leader Promotes Self-Pride," *The Hilltop*, October 30, 1987.

48 Public Enemy, *Yo! Bum Rush the Show* (New York: Def Jam Recordings/Columbia Records, 1987).

49 Bill Stephney, personal communication, October 18, 2017.

50 Jeff Chang, *Can't Stop, Won't Stop: A History of the Hip-Hop Generation* (New York: Picador, 2005), 275.

51 April Silver, interview by the author, September 1, 2017. On February 26, 1988, HUSA invited Stephney, Souljah, and others—including Ras Baraka, Chuck D, Daddy-O, Stephen Jackson, and Haqq Islam—to speak on the state of Black America. See "The Howard University Student Association Presents 'The State of Black America: A Youth Perspective,'" February 26, 1988, April Silver Collection, private collection; and Rebecca Little, "Panelists Address Blacks' Problems," *The Hilltop*, March 4, 1988.

52 Ras J. Baraka, interview by the author, August 25, 2017.

53 Ibid.; and Byers, *The Real HU*.

54 Byers, *The Real HU*, Kindle section location 1400.

55 Lynn Duke and Martin Weil, "Crowds Flock to Georgetown for Halloween," *Washington Post*, November 1, 1987.

56 Kevin Williams, interview by the author, July 9, 2017; and Shawn Houston, interview by the author, December 18, 2017.

57 Ras J. Baraka, interview by the author, August 25, 2017; and Byers, *The Real HU*.

58 Ras J. Baraka, interview by the author, August 25, 2017.

59 Gail Sharps-Myers, interview by the author, October 2, 2017. Amid the critiques launched by Black women in the previous iterations of the Black liberation struggle, there was by this period an emphasis on the idea that "black men should show greater "respect" for Black women." See Dawson, *Black Visions*, 127. This was also present at Howard University. Haqq Islam's organizing included a series of programs during the 1980s entitled "Salute to Black Women." See Tracy L. Smith, "UGSA Salutes Black Women," *The Hilltop*, November 5, 1982; Crystal Chissell, "Banquet Honors Black Women," *The Hilltop*, November 18, 1983; and Alison Bethel and Gerald Massergill, "Students Salute Ten Women," *The Hilltop*, November 16, 1984. On gender and nationalism during this period, see Charise Cheney, *Brothers Gonna Work It Out: Sexual Politics in the Golden Age of Rap Nationalism* (New York: New York University Press, 2005); and Bakari Kitwana, *The Rap on Gangsta Rap* (Chicago: Third World Press, 1994).

60 Killa Patterson, interview by the author, January 22, 2018.

61 Carlisle Sealy, interview by the author, July 7, 2017; and Ras J. Baraka, interview by the author, August 25, 2017.

62 Ras J. Baraka, interview by the author, August 25, 2017.

63 Byers, *The Real HU*, Kindle section locations 1614–1621; and "Guidelines and Policies of Black Nia F.O.R.C.E (Freedom Organization for Racial and Cultural Enlightenment)," n.d., 3, April Silver Collection, private collection.

64 Charles "Chuck" Webb, interview by the author, June 26, 2017; and Carlisle Sealy, interview by the author, July 7, 2017.

65 Charles "Chuck" Webb, interview by the author, June 26, 2017; and Ras J. Baraka, interview by the author, August 25, 2017.

66 Aaron Lloyd, interview by the author, July 22, 2017. Also see Louis Camphor III to April Silver, February 22, 1989, April Silver Collection, private collection.

67 On the Black Panther Party's organizational structure, see Curtis Austin, *Up against the Wall: Violence in the Making and Unmaking of the Black Panther Party* (Fayetteville: University of Arkansas Press, 2006), 36–40.

68 Aaron Lloyd, interview by the author, July 22, 2017. On the gender dynamics of the Nation of Islam, see Ula Yvette Taylor, *The Promise of Patriarchy: Women and the Nation of Islam* (Chapel Hill: University of North Carolina Press, 2017).

69 Stephen Jackson, interview by the author, February 19, 2018; and Ras J. Baraka, interview by the author, August 25, 2017.

70 Aaron Lloyd, interview by the author, July 22, 2017; and Ras J. Baraka, interview by the author, August 25, 2017.

71 Shawn Houston, interview by the author, December 18, 2017.

72 Carlisle Sealy, interview by the author, July 7, 2017; and Ras J. Baraka, interview by the author, August 25, 2017. See Malcolm X, *The Autobiography of Malcolm X*, with Alex Haley (New York: Grove Press, 1965); Anthony Browder, *From the Browder File: 22 Essays on the African American Experience* (Washington, DC: Institute of Karmic Guidance, 1989); Yosef Ben-Jochannan, *Black Man of the Nile and his Family* (New York: Alkebulan, 1970); Maulana Karenga, *Introduction to Black Studies* (Los Angeles: University of Sankore Press, 1982); and Baba Zak Kondo, *The Black Student's Guide to Positive Education* (Washington, DC: Nubia Press, 1987).

73 Garner, "Students Work for Awareness."

74 Dawson, *Black Visions*, 120–121.

75 Sekou Franklin, *After the Rebellion: Black Youth, Social Movement Activism, and the Civil Rights Generation* (New York: New York University Press, 2014), 95–252.

76 Aaron Lloyd remembers that this idea came from the women. See Aaron Lloyd, interview by the author, July 22, 2017.

77 Ras J. Baraka, interview by the author, August 25, 2017; and April Silver, interview by the author, September 1, 2017.

78 Carlisle Sealy, interview by the author, July 7, 2017.

79 Aaron Lloyd, interview by the author, July 22, 2017; April Silver, interview by the author, September 1, 2017; Gail Sharps-Myers, interview by the author, October 2, 2017; and Akanke Washington, interview by the author, December 17, 2017.

80 Garner, "Students Work for Awareness."

81 Charles "Chuck" Webb, interview by the author, June 26, 2017; and Ras J. Baraka, interview by the author, August 25, 2017. See also Amiri Baraka, "Black People and Jesse Jackson II," in *The LeRoi Jones/Amiri Baraka Reader*, ed. William J. Harris (Chicago: Lawrence Hill Books, 1999), 458–460.

82 Martin Robison Delany, *Blake; or, The Huts of America* (Cambridge, MA: Harvard University Press, 1970).

83 April Silver, interview by the author, September 1, 2017.

84 Ibid. For the interrelated politics of fashion and beauty on the movement, see Tanisha C. Ford, *Liberated Threads: Black Women, Style, and the Global Politics of Soul* (Chapel Hill: University of North Carolina Press, 2015).

85 April Silver, "Education Should be a Priority," *The Hilltop*, February 5, 1988.

86 Charles "Chuck" Webb, interview by the author, June 26, 2017; Carlisle Sealy, interview by the author, July 7, 2017; and "Black Nia F.O.R.C.E Meeting Notes," October 14, 1988, April Silver Collection, private collection.

87 Notable women in leadership in both critical student campus organizations and student movement work included Adrienne Manns, *Hilltop* editor in chief and a leader of the 1968 Administration Building protest; the aforementioned Janice McKnight, *Hilltop* editor in chief from 1982 to 1983; and Ona Alston, who served as HUSA president during the 1986–1987 term.

88 See Kondo, *The Black Student's Guide to Positive Education*, 45.

89 Charles "Chuck" Webb, interview by the author, June 26, 2017; and Carlisle Sealy, interview by the author, July 7, 2017.

CHAPTER 5. THE CONFRONTATION

1 Amiri Baraka, "Howard University, 'Cap Stone,'" *New York Amsterdam News*, April 1, 1989.

2 Frederick Douglass, "West India Emancipation Speech," in *Frederick Douglass: Selected Speeches and Writings*, ed. Philip S. Foner and Yuval Taylor (Chicago: Chicago Review Press, 2000), 367.

3 "Dream sequence" is from Acklyn Lynch, one of the organizers of the Toward a Black University Conference in November 1968. See his *Riffing on a Blue Nite . . . Sometimes I Wander* (Baltimore, MD: Afrikan World Books, 2017); and Joshua Myers, "Howard University and the Dream Sequence," *Black Perspectives*, March 23, 2017, posted at African American Intellectual History Society, www.aaihs.org. On the idea of dreaming and imagination and Black political struggle, see Robin D. G. Kelley, *Freedom Dreams: The Black Radical Imagination* (Boston: Beacon Press, 2002).

4 John Henrik Clarke, ed., *Harlem, USA* (Berlin: Seven Seas, 1964); Harold Curse, *The Crisis of the Negro Intellectual* (New York: Morrow, 1967), 64–95; Sharifa Rhodes-Pitts, *Harlem Is Nowhere: Journey to the Mecca of Black America* (New York: Back Bay Books, 2011); and Minkah Makalani, *In the Cause of Freedom: Radical Black Internationalism from Harlem to London, 1917–1939* (Chapel Hill: University of North Carolina Press, 2011).

5 "Howard University Trustee Named," *Washington Post*, February 1, 1989.

6 Aarian Pope Punter, interview by the author, December 12, 2017.

7 Minutes of Black Nia F.O.R.C.E Closed Meeting, February 17, 1989, April Silver Collection, private collection.

8 Aaron Lloyd, interview by the author, July 22, 2017; and Sheri Warren, interview by the author, December 16, 2017.

9 Flyer, "Why We Don't Want Harvey Lee Atwater (Co-chairperson of the Republican National Committee) at Howard?" March 3, 1989, April Silver Collection, private collection. There were a number of BNF members who were responsible for carrying out research on Atwater. See Minutes of Black Nia F.O.R.C.E Closed Meeting, February 24, 1989, April Silver Collection, private collection.

10 Eric Smith, "Atwater Elected Newest Trustee," *The Hilltop*, February 10, 1989; "President Cheek Issues Open Letter," *The Capstone*, March 20, 1989; Dorothy Gilliam, "Howard U. Romances the GOP," *Washington Post*, February 16, 1989.

11 Garfield Swaby and Daniel Goodwin, both quoted in Smith, "Atwater Elected Newest Trustee."

12 "Atwater Is All Wet," *The Hilltop*, February 10, 1989.

13 Along with Atlanta University, under the leadership of Mack Jones, Howard's politi-cal science department was where one went to concentrate in the bourgeoning field of Black politics. On its development via the life of its longtime department chair Ronald W. Walters, see Robert C. Smith, Cedric Johnson, and Robert G. Newby, eds., *What Has This Got to Do with the Liberation of Black People? The Impact of Ronald W. Walters on African American Thought and Leadership* (Albany: State University of New York Press, 2014); and Robert C. Smith, *Ronald W. Walters and the Fight for Black Power, 1969–2010* (Albany: State University of New York Press, 2018).

14 Gail Sharps-Myers, interview by the author, October 2, 2017; and Ras J. Baraka, inter-view by the author, August 25, 2017.

15 Smith, "Atwater Elected Newest Trustee"; and Alvin Thornton, interview by the author, May 15, 2018.

16 Steve Piacente, "Atwater Rocks National Politics," *Sunday Post-Courier*, March 19, 1989.

17 Joseph McCormick, "Notes for Proposed Manuscript," April 29, 1989, manuscript copy in author's possession.

18 Anne Simpson, "Atwater's Election as Howard University's Trustee Sparks Dissension," *Washington Post*, February 23, 1989.

19 Alonza Robertson, quoted in ibid. On Reed, see Thomas Lake, "Fixer, Charmer, Builder, Mayor," *Atlanta Magazine*, October 2010, www.atlantamagazine.com.

20 Minutes of Black Nia F.O.R.C.E Closed Meeting, February 24, 1989, April Silver Col-lection, private collection; and April Silver, interview by the author, January 29, 2017.

21 Minutes of Black Nia F.O.R.C.E Closed Meeting, February 24, 1989, April Silver Col-lection, private collection.

22 Ibid.; and Brooke A. Masters, "Ex-Farrakhan Aide Gets Mixed Reaction on Campus," *Washington Post*, February 24, 1994. In the early nineties, PSM would morph into the nationalist student group Unity Nation.

23 Shawn Houston, interview by the author, December 18, 2017; Aaron Lloyd, interview by the author, May 4, 2018. There are at least two occasions when this group tried to exert leadership of the protest. The first was the Charter Day takeover, discussed in this chapter. According to Rich Byers, Lewis tried to seize the microphone before being fought off. Kevin Williams also related that he brought his own microphone into the A-Building as that takeover was in its beginning stages. Black Nia F.O.R.C.E members confiscated the equipment. See R. K. Byers, *The Real HU* (New York: Banned Books, 2012), Kindle section location 1651; and Kevin Williams, interview by the author, May 7, 2018.

24 Sheri Warren, interview by the author, December 16, 2017.

25 Sandra Upshur, "Charter Day Disrupted," *The Hilltop*, March 4, 1983; Lawrence Fein-berg, "Chanting Students Drown Out Howard University Ceremony," *Washington Post*, March 3, 1983; and Paul S. Burley, "Students Protest for Afro-American Studies," *The Hilltop*, March 7, 1986.

26 See chap. 1, in this volume. See also Sophia Tignor, "Symbolic Siege Reenacts Past," *The Hilltop*, April 1, 1988; and Sheila Maxwell, "1,500 Join Symbolic Takeover," *The Hilltop*, April 8, 1988.

27 Garfield Bright, interview by the author, April 4, 2018; and Jam Shakwi, interview by the author, December 14, 2017.

28 Jam Shakwi, interview by the author, December 14, 2017.

29 Ibid.

30 Keith Alexander, "Students Prevail in Three-Day Takeover," *The Hilltop*, March 10, 1989.

31 Ibid.; April Silver, interview by the author, January 29, 2017.

32 HU Student Demands," March 3, 1989, April Silver Collection, private collection.

33 Flyer, "Why We Don't Want Harvey Lee Atwater (Co-chairperson of the Republican National Committee) at Howard?" March 3, 1989, April Silver Collection, private collection.

34 "HU Student Demands," March 3, 1989, April Silver Collection, private collection.

35 On the impact of Black Studies on the academy, see Martha Biondi, *The Black Revolution on Campus* (Berkeley: University of California Press, 2012), 268–278. On the incorporation of Black Studies, see Roderick Ferguson, *The Reorder of Things: The University and Its Pedagogies of Minority Difference* (Minneapolis: University of Minnesota Press, 2012).

36 Brigette Rouson, "Howard University: The Power in the Protest," *Black Networking News* 1 (April 1989): 6.

37 April Silver, interview by the author, January 29, 2017; and Carlisle Sealy, interview by the author, July 7, 2017.

38 On the relationship between Afrocentricity and Africana Studies, see Molefi Asante, *The Afrocentric Idea* (Philadelphia: Temple University Press, 1987), and *Kemet, Afrocentricity, and Knowledge* (Trenton, NJ: Africa World Press, 1990). Also see Lucius T. Outlaw, Jr., *On Race and Philosophy* (New York: Routledge, 1996), 97–134.

39 "HU Student Demands," March 3, 1989, April Silver Collection, private collection.

40 Admittedly, "service learning"—the name given to this practice—as imagined by BNF, is qualitatively different from the sorts of liberal deliberative models of community engagement that have been incorporated into the contemporary academy. See Robert G. Bringle and Julie A. Hatcher, "Institutionalization of Service Learning in Higher Education," *Journal of Higher Education* 71 (May/June 2000): 273–290; Ernest L. Boyer, "The Scholarship of Engagement," *Journal of Public Service and Outreach* 1 (1996): 11–20; and Harry C. Boyte, ed., *Democracy's Education: Public Work, Citizenship, and the Future of Colleges and Universities* (Nashville, TN: Vanderbilt University Press, 2015). On the relationship between service learning, conceptions of community service, and the larger bases of Black Studies and race, see Stephanie Y. Evans et al., eds., *African Americans and Community Engagement in Higher Education* (Albany: State University of New York Press, 2009).

41 Devin Fergus, *Land of the Fee: Hidden Costs and the Decline of the Middle Class* (New York: Oxford University Press, 2018); Sara Goldrick-Rab, *Paying the Price: College Costs, Financial Aid, and the Betrayal of the American Dream* (Chicago: University of Chicago Press, 2016); Andrew P. Kelly and Sara Goldrick-Rab, *Reinventing Financial Aid: Charting a New Course to College Affordability* (Cambridge, MA: Harvard Education Press, 2014); Sheila Slaughter, "Federal Policy and Supply-Side Institutional Resource Allocation at Public Research Universities," *Review of Higher Education* 21 (Spring 1998): 209–244; and Maurice A. St. Pierre, "Reaganomics and Its Implications for African American Family Life," *Journal of Black Studies* 21 (March 1991): 325–340.

42 April Silver, interview by the author, January 29, 2017. Over 80 percent of Howard students were receiving some form of federal aid in the academic year 1987–1988. See U.S. Congress, House, Subcommittee of the Committee on Appropriations, "Departments

of Labor, Health and Human Services, Education, and Related Agencies Appropriations for 1990," 101st Congress, 1st Session (1989), 1567.

43 "HU Student Demands," March 3, 1989, April Silver Collection, private collection.

44 Rouson, "Howard University: The Power in the Protest," 6.

45 "HU Student Demands," March 3, 1989, April Silver Collection, private collection. Also
see April Silver, interview by the author, January 29, 2017; and Aaron Lloyd, interview
by the author, May 4, 2018.

46 "HU Student Demands," March 3, 1989, April Silver Collection, private collection.

47 Kevin Williams, interview by the author, May 7, 2018; April Silver, interview by the
author, January 29, 2017; "Security at Howard?" Leaflet, n.d., April Silver Collection,
private collection. In recent years, student activists have been less willing to directly
support increased funding for policing functions, whether they be private or public
forces. Instead, they have pushed for measures like disarmament and abolition. It
appears, however, that for the organizers at Howard in 1989, they saw more of a connection between public safety and policing, while also attempting to speak directly to
the human needs of those community members employed by the police and security
forces. See Jordan T. Camp and Christina Heatherton, eds., *Policing the Planet: Why
the Policing Crisis Led to Black Lives Matter* (London: Verso, 2016); Alex Vitale, *The
End of Policing* (London: Verso, 2017); and Maya Schenwar, Joe Macare, and Alana Yu-
lan Price, eds., *Who Do You Serve, Who Do You Protect? Police Violence and Resistance
in the United States* (Chicago: Haymarket Books, 2016). This was akin to the forms
of solidarities seen between students and staff in more recent iterations of campus
struggle. For an example of recent student protests and the attention to labor as it
relates to campus staff, see the discussion in Robin D. G. Kelley, "Black Study, Black
Struggle," forum, *Boston Review*, March–April 2016, 9–20, http://bostonreview.net.

48 "HU Student Demands," March 3, 1989, April Silver Collection, private collection.

49 This variation of the mission was adopted on September 24, 1988. See the Howard
University Commission, *Investing for Excellence: Strategically Repositioning How-
ard University to Face the Challenges of the 21st Century* (Washington, DC: Howard
University, November 18, 1990), 13, Howard University Archives, Moorland-Spingarn
Research Center.

50 Eric Smith and Stacey J. Phillips, "Protest Slated for Today," *The Hilltop*, March 3, 1989.

51 Spike Lee, director, *School Daze* (Culver City, CA: Columbia Pictures, 1988).

52 V. Jimale Ridgeway, interview by the author, March 26, 2018; and Sheri Warren, interview by the author, December 16, 2017.

53 Michael Winston, "The Story behind Howard's Seal," *The Hilltop*, December 3, 1976.

54 On academic rituals and their ecclesiastical origins, see William Clark, *Academic
Charisma and the Origins of the Research University* (Chicago: University of Chicago
Press, 2006); and Julie A. Reuben, *The Making of the Modern University: Intellectual
Transformation and the Marginalization of Morality* (Chicago: University of Chicago
Press, 1996).

55 *The Cosby Show* (television show; New York: NBC, 1984–1992).

56 On the cultural significance of *The Cosby Show* and the complex, though ultimately
conservative, political message, see Sut Jhally and Justin Lewis, *Enlightened Racism:
The Cosby Show, Audiences, and the Myth of the American Dream* (Boulder, CO:
Westview Press, 1992); and Ashon Crawley, "By the Content of Pam's Character," *Seven
Scribes*, July 13, 2016, http://sevenscribes.com.

57 Byers, *The Real HU*, Kindle section location 1646. Also see Sidney Poitier, director, *Let's Do It Again* (film; Burbank, CA: Warner Bros., 1975); and Bill Cosby, *More of the Best of Bill Cosby* (album; Burbank, CA: Warner Bros., 1970).

58 *A Different World* (television show; New York: NBC, 1987–1993).

59 Phylicia Rashad, "Charter Day Address," Howard University, Washington, DC, March 13, 2009; and Robin R. Means Coleman and Andrew Calvacante, "Two Different Worlds: Television as the Producer's Medium," in *Watching While Black: Centering the Television of Black Audiences*, ed. Beretta E. Smith-Shomade (New Brunswick, NJ: Rutgers University Press, 2012), 33–48.

60 Lee A. Daniels, "A Black College Gets Cosby Gift of $20 Million," *New York Times*, November 8, 1988; Dinesh D'Souza, *Illiberal Education: The Politics of Race and Sex on Campus* (New York: Free Press, 1991), 98–99; Courtland Milloy, "Revolution by Flunking Out," *Washington Post*, March 7, 1989; and Byers, *The Real HU*, Kindle section location 1649.

61 April Silver, interview by the author, January 29, 2017; and Jacqueline Trescott, "Howard Protesters Take Over Ceremony," *Washington Post*, March 4, 1989.

62 Rouson, "Howard University: The Power in the Protest," 6.

63 Trescott, "Howard Protestors Take Over Ceremony"; Sherri Milner and Korva DeMarr Coleman, "'Mecca' Stands Up to be Heard as 60's Activism Is Revived," *Washington Afro-American*, March 11, 1989.

64 Byers, *The Real HU*, Kindle section location 1644–1651.

65 April Silver, interview by the author, January 29, 2017.

66 Shawn Houston, interview by the author, December 18, 2017; and Jam Shakwi, interview by the author, December 14, 2017.

67 April Silver, interview by the author, January 29, 2017.

68 Trescott, "Howard Protestors Take Over Ceremony"; and Keith L. Alexander and Tina Travers, "Protestors Show There's Strength in Numbers," *The Hilltop*, March 10, 1989.

69 Akanke Washington, interview by the author, December 17, 2017.

70 Garfield Bright, interview by the author, April 4, 2018; and Memorandum, "The Meaning of Force," Black Nia F.O.R.C.E, March 13, 1988, Akanke Washington Collection, private collection.

71 Akanke Washington, interview by the author, December 17, 2017.

72 Kellye Lynne and James Walker, "Cosby: I'll Be Back," *Community News*, March 9, 1989.

73 Aaron Lloyd, interview by the author, May 4, 2018. This was not enough to stem the criticism of faculty and students who had come to hear Cosby. See Alexander and Travers, "Protestors Show There's Strength in Numbers." Divinity student Michael O. Grafton, in a hyperbolic statement, called the disruption of Cosby a "lynching." See Michael O. Grafton, "Lynching Cosby," *The Hilltop*, March 10, 1989.

74 Alexander, "Students Prevail in Three-Day Takeover"; and Alexander and Travers, "Protestors Show There's Strength in Numbers."

75 Kevin Williams, interview by the author, May 7, 2018.

76 Milner and Coleman, "'Mecca' Stands Up."

77 Kevin Williams, interview by the author, May 7, 2018; Aaron Lloyd, interview by the author, May 4, 2018; and Byers, *The Real HU*, Kindle section location 1657.

78 Minutes of Black Nia F.O.R.C.E Closed Meeting, March 3, 1989, April Silver Collection, private collection.

79 Alexander, "Students Prevail in Three-Day Takeover"; and Sandra G. Boodman, "Howard Parley Leaves Dispute Unresolved," *Washington Post*, March 5, 1989.
80 Sheri Warren, interview by the author, December 16, 2017.

CHAPTER 6. OCCUPATION

1 Tunji Turner, interview by the author, December 18, 2017.
2 On order, see Cedric Robinson, *The Terms of Order: Political Science and the Myth of Leadership* (Chapel Hill: University of North Carolina Press, 2016). On the notion of a "fantastic," see Richard Iton, *In Search of the Black Fantastic: Politics and Popular Culture in the Post–Civil Rights Era* (New York: Oxford University Press, 2008).
3 See Stefano Harney and Fred Moten, "Improvement and Preservation: Or, Usufruct and Use," in *Futures of Black Radicalism*, ed. Gaye Theresa Johnson and Alex Lubin (London: Verso, 2017); and Carl Schmitt, *The Nomos of the Earth in the International Law of the Jus Publicum Europaeum* (New York: Telos Press, 2003).
4 Alvin Thornton, interview by the author, May 15, 2018; Michael Dawson, *Black Visions: The Roots of Contemporary African American Political Ideologies* (Chicago: University of Chicago Press, 2001); and Bakari Kitwana, *The Hip Hop Generation: Young Blacks and the Crisis in African American Culture* (New York: Basic Books, 2002). It is important to note that elements of hip-hop activism would soon be incorporated into that neoliberal hegemon; see Lester Spence, *Stare in the Darkness: The Limits of Hip-Hop and Black Politics* (Minneapolis: University of Minnesota Press, 2011).
5 April Silver, interview by the author, May 6, 2018.
6 "President Cheek Issues Open Letter," *The Capstone*, March 15, 1989; Laura Sessions Stepp and Jacqueline Trescott, "Student Protest at Howard Bares Holes in Ivory Tower," *Washington Post*, March 13, 1989.
7 Kevin Williams, interview by the author, May 7, 2018.
8 Aaron Lloyd, interview by the author, May 4, 2018.
9 V. Jimale Ridgeway, interview by the author, March 26, 2018.
10 Michael Abramowitz and Lawrence Feinberg, "Howard Protestors Defy Court Order to Leave Building," *Washington Post*, March 7, 1989.
11 Aaron Lloyd, interview by the author, May 4, 2018; and Flyer, "Why We Don't Want Harvey Lee Atwater (Co-chairperson of the Republican National Committee) at Howard?" March 3, 1989, April Silver Collection, private collection.
12 Charles "Chuck" Webb, interview by the author, June 26, 2017.
13 Ibid.
14 Aaron Lloyd, interview by the author, May 4, 2018, and July 22, 2017; and Louis Camphor to Black Nia F.O.R.C.E, "Appointment of Aaron Lloyd as Minister of Defense," February 22, 1989, April Silver Collection, private collection.
15 April Silver, "Pre-protest Notes," n.d., April Silver Collection, private collection.
16 April Silver, "Howard U Student Protest of 1989: The Takeover, 25 Years Later," *Liberator Magazine*, July 2014, posted at the *Live from Planet Earth* website, www.livefromplanetearth.org.
17 Lloyd, interview by the author, May 4, 2018. Cheek also mentioned this in his open letter. See "President Cheek Issues Open Letter."
18 Kevin Williams, interview by the author, May 7, 2018.
19 Ibid.

20 V. Jimale Ridgeway, interview by the author, March 26, 2018.

21 Ibid.; Kevin Williams, interview by the author, May 7, 2018; and Jam Shakwi, interview by the author, December 14, 2017.

22 Kevin Williams, interview by the author, May 7, 2018; Jam Shakwi, interview by the author, December 14, 2017; and Abramowitz and Feinberg, "Howard Protestors Defy Court Order."

23 Shrona Foreman, "HU Security Calls in Sick," *The Hilltop*, March 10, 1989.

24 Abramowitz and Feinberg, "Howard Protests Defy Court Order"; Onika L. Johnson and Sheila Maxwell, "A Day-to-Day Account of the '89 Student Movement," *The Hilltop*, March 10, 1989; Gale P. Mitchell, "Sights and Sounds of a Sit-in," *The Hilltop*, March 10, 1989; and "Ovation," *The Hilltop*, March 10, 1989.

25 Jam Shakwi, interview by the author, December 14, 2017; and Kevin Williams, interview by the author, May 7, 2018.

26 V. Jimale Ridgeway, interview by the author, March 26, 2018.

27 Ibid.

28 April Silver, "Pre-protest Notes," n.d., April Silver Collection, private collection.

29 Suzanne C. Alexander, "Local Business Offer Support for Cause," *The Hilltop*, March 10, 1989; and Garfield Bright, interview by the author, April 4, 2018.

30 Sheri Warren, interview by the author, December 16, 2017; and Jam Shakwi, interview by the author, December 14, 2017.

31 Kevin Williams, interview by the author, May 7, 2018.

32 R. K. Byers, *The Real HU* (New York: Banned Books, 2012), Kindle section location 1701.

33 Mitchell, "Sights and Sounds of a Sit-in"; Akanke Washington, interview by the author, December 17, 2017; Shawn Houston, interview by the author, December 18, 2017; and Aarian Pope Punter, interview by the author, December 12, 2017.

34 Jacqueline Trescott, "Howard Protesters Take Over Ceremony," *Washington Post*, March 4, 1989.

35 Paul Hendrickson, "Behind the Howard Barricades," *Washington Post*, March 8, 1989.

36 Jam Shakwi, interview by the author, December 14, 2017.

37 Joseph Jordan, interview by the author, March 30, 2017.

38 Kevin Williams, interview by the author, May 7, 2018.

39 Abramowitz and Feinberg, "Howard Protestors Defy Court Order"; and "President Cheek Issues Open Letter."

40 Johnson and Maxwell, "A Day-to-Day Account."

41 Kevin Williams, interview by the author, May 7, 2018.

42 Johnson and Maxwell, "A Day-to-Day Account."

43 Kevin Williams, interview by the author, May 7, 2018; Matt Middleton, interview by the author, January 2, 2018; and Kamal Harris, interview by the author, May 24, 2018.

44 Jam Shakwi, interview by the author, December 14, 2017; and Johnson and Maxwell, "A Day-to-Day Account."

45 Johnson and Maxwell, "A Day-to-Day Account"; and Aarian Pope Punter, interview by the author, June 6, 2018.

46 Akanke Washington, interview by the author, December 17, 2017.

47 Hendrickson, "Behind the Howard Barricades."

48 Jam Shakwi, interview by the author, December 14, 2017.

49 On Barry's life and activism, see Clayborne Carson, *In Struggle: SNCC and the Black Awakening of the 1960s* (Cambridge, MA: Harvard University Press, 1981); Howard

Zinn, *SNCC: The New Abolitionists* (Boston: South End Press, 1964); "Marion Barry," *SNCC Digital Gateway*, https://snccdigital.org; Marion Barry and Omar Tyree, *Mayor for Life: The Incredible Story of Marion Barry, Jr.* (Largo, MD: Strebor Books, 2014); and Chris Myers Asch and George Derek Musgrove, *Chocolate City: A History of Race and Democracy in the Nation's Capital* (Chapel Hill: University of North Carolina Press, 2017), 390–424. On the attempts to bring Black Power into city halls across urban America, see J. Phillip Thompson, *Double Trouble: Black Mayors, Black Communities, and the Call for a Deep Democracy* (New York: Oxford University Press, 2005).

50 Garfield Bright, interview by the author, April 4, 2018; and Shawn Houston, interview by the author, December 18, 2017.

51 Matt Middleton, interview by the author, January 2, 2018.

52 Kevin Williams, interview by the author, May 7, 2018.

53 Rene Sanchez and Patrice Gaines-Carter, "Howard U. Becomes a Bustling Nest for Student Demonstrators," *Washington Post*, March 8, 1989.

54 Jam Shakwi, interview by the author, December 14, 2017.

55 Shawn Houston, interview by the author, December 18, 2017.

56 Akanke Washington, interview by the author, December 17, 2017.

57 Jam Shakwi, interview by the author, December 14, 2017.

58 Kevin Williams, interview by the author, May 7, 2018.

59 Jam Shakwi, interview by the author, December 14, 2017. The MOVE bombing was a mere four years earlier and was a bracing reminder of the capacity of the state to enact violence on Black people. See John Anderson and Hilary Hevenor, *Burning Down the House: MOVE and the Tragedy of Philadelphia* (New York: W. W. Norton & Co., 1990).

60 Martha Biondi, *The Black Revolution on Campus* (Berkeley: University of California Press, 2012).

61 Akanke Washington, interview by the author, December 17, 2017.

62 Garfield Bright, interview by the author, April 4, 2018.

63 Killa Patterson, interview by the author, January 22, 2018.

64 Charles "Chuck" Webb, interview by the author, June 26, 2017.

65 Akanke Washington, interview by the author, December 17, 2017.

66 Garfield Bright, interview by the author, April 4, 2018.

67 Chris Booker, "Howard, You Won!" *Guardian: Independent Radical Newsweekly*, March 15, 1989.

68 Jam Shakwi, interview by the author, December 14, 2017; and Sari Horwitz and Jeffrey Goldberg, "Atwater Resigns from the Board," *Washington Post*, March 8, 1989.

69 Yvonne Brooks, "Atwater Quits Howard Post, Citing Protest," *Boston Globe*, March 8, 1989.

70 Lloyd, interview by the author; and Kevin Williams, interview by the author, May 7, 2018.

71 "Atwater States Reasons for Resignation," *The Hilltop*, March 10, 1989.

72 John Brady, *Bad Boy: The Life and Politics of Lee Atwater* (Reading, MA: Addison-Wesley, 1997), 212. Atwater, who elsewhere described the protest as a "kick in the teeth," also met with a group of fifteen student Republicans and independents, including M. Kasim Reed. See Ralph Z. Hallow, "Atwater Bloodied by Howard Furor, but Still Resolute," *Washington Times*, March 7, 1989.

73 Lee Atwater, "What I Would Have Told the Howard Students," *Washington Post*, March 10, 1989. It was read into the *Congressional Record* on March 14, 1989. The concerns dealt with these issues, but students asked more pointed questions about Atwater's support of Reagan's "veto of Congressional sanctions," his "position on the invasion of

Grenada," and his role in "executing elements of the Southern Strategy." See Howard University Student Associates to Lee Atwater, n.d., copy in author's possession.

74 Emphasis added. See "Howard Student Speaks Out: 'Too Black, Too Strong,'" *Revolutionary Worker*, March 13, 1989.

75 Jesse H. Walker, "GOP Chairman Will Reach for Blacks," *New York Amsterdam News*, February 11, 1989; Thomas B. Edsall, "Atwater and the Politics of Race," *Washington Post*, March 13, 1989; and Brady, *Bad Boy*, 235–236.

76 Atwater, "What I Would Have Told the Howard Students." On these issues, see Edsall, "Atwater and the Politics of Race"; Steven A. Shull, *A Kinder, Gentler Racism? The Reagan-Bush Civil Rights Legacy* (Armonk, NY: M. E. Sharpe, 1993); and Ron Nixon, *Selling Apartheid: South Africa's Global Propaganda War* (London: Pluto Press, 2016), 169–170. On Atwater's involvement in the advertisements, see the discussion in chap. 2, in this volume; and Brady, *Bad Boy*, 204–210.

77 Brady, *Bad Boy*, 212; and "He Is the Blues," *Southern Changes* 11 (1989): 22.

78 Horwitz and Goldberg, "Atwater Resigns."

79 James L. Walker and Kellye Lynne, "Q&A: Cheek Says Job Lacks Prestige," *The Hilltop*, March 10, 1989; "A Candid Conversation with James Edward Cheek," *New Directions* 16 (July 1989): 33–35; Suzanne Alexander, "Cheek Reflects on 20 Years of Leading "The Mecca," *The Hilltop*, May 12, 1989.

80 "President Cheek Issues Open Letter."

81 Sandra G. Boodman, "Howard Parley Leaves Dispute Unresolved," *Washington Post*, March 5, 1989.

82 Lauren Sessions Stepp and Lawrence Feinberg, "Howard Trustees Fault Top Administrators in Student Uprising," *Washington Post*, March 16, 1989.

83 Horwitz and Goldberg, "Atwater Resigns."

84 Yvonne Brooks, "Howard Students Drive Atwater to Quit as Trustee," *Boston Globe*, March 8, 1989.

85 Killa Patterson, interview by the author, January 22, 2018.

86 Kevin Williams, interview by the author, May 7, 2018.

87 Ibid.

88 Ibid.; Brooks, "Howard Students Drive Atwater to Quit."

89 Akanke Washington, interview by the author, December 17, 2017.

90 Johnson and Maxwell, "A Day-to-Day Account."

91 Ibid.

92 Philip Shenon, "Howard University President Threatens to Arrest Student Protestors," *New York Times*, March 9, 1989.

93 Shawn Houston, interview by the author, December 18, 2017.

94 Byers, *The Real HU*, Kindle section locations 1664–1670.

95 Shawn Houston, interview by the author, December 18, 2017.

96 Johnson and Maxwell, "A Day-to-Day Account"; Jeffrey Goldberg and Rene Sanchez, "Howard Students Step up Disruption, Meet with Jackson," *Washington Post*, March 9, 1989.

97 Shawn Houston, interview by the author, December 18, 2017.

98 Byers, *The Real HU*, Kindle section locations 1670.

99 Shenon, "Howard University President Threatens to Arrest Student Protestors"; Goldberg and Sanchez, "Howard Students Step up Disruption"; and Laura Christion "Faculty, Alumni, Support Protest," *Community News*, March 9, 1989.

100 Johnson and Maxwell, "A Day-to-Day Account."

101 April Silver, interview by the author, September 1, 2017.

102 Shawn Houston, interview by the author, December 18, 2017.

103 Brady, *Bad Boy*, 212.

104 Ibid., 213; and "Howard Protest Shows GOP's Image Problem," *Hartford (CT) Courant*, March 9, 1989.

105 Brady, *Bad Boy*, 213.

106 Johnson and Maxwell, "A Day-to-Day Account"; and Jeffrey Goldberg and Lawrence Feinberg, "Victorious Howard Students End Siege of Building," *Washington Post*, March 10, 1989.

107 Shawn Houston, interview by the author, December 18, 2017; and Kevin Williams, interview by the author, May 7, 2018.

108 Under Jackson's leadership, Operation Breadbasket led successful boycotts of large corporations unwilling to accede to its demands and executed what it called "covenants," where businesses like A&P Grocery agreed to hire and train Black employees for managerial positions, stock Black-created consumer items, utilize Black-owned service agencies, and to invest funds in Black-owned banks. See Barbara Reynolds, *Jesse Jackson: America's David* (Washington, DC: JFJ Associations, 1985), 105–183.

109 "A Covenant between Howard University and the Coalition of Concerned Howard University Students," March 9, 1989, April Silver Collection, private collection.

110 Eric Smith, "Jackson Visit Aids in Negotiations," *The Hilltop*, March 10, 1989.

111 Shawn Houston, interview by the author, December 18, 2017.

112 Kevin Williams, interview by the author, May 7, 2018.

113 Minutes of Black Nia F.O.R.C.E Closed Meeting, March 10, 1989, April Silver Collection, private collection; and V. Jimale Ridgeway, interview by the author, March 26, 2018.

114 Minutes of Black Nia F.O.R.C.E Closed Meeting, March 10, 1989, April Silver Collection, private collection; Courtland Milloy, "Revolution by Flunking Out," *Washington Post*, March 7, 1989; and Cal Thomas, "Blacks Must Give New Conservatives a Chance," *Tennessean*, March 10, 1989.

115 April Silver, interview by the author, May 6, 2018.

116 Amiri Baraka, "Howard University 'Cap Stone,'" *New York Amsterdam News*, April 1, 1989.

117 "Ovation," *The Hilltop*, March 10, 1989.

118 Cartoon, *The Hilltop*, March 10, 1989.

119 Retha Powers, "Student Power!" *Essence*, August 1989, 122.

120 Jacqueline Trescott, "We Stood Up Because We Love This Black School," *Washington Post*, March 10, 1989.

121 Sheri Warren, interview by the author, December 16, 2017.

122 Jam Shakwi, interview by the author, December 14, 2017; and Tina Travers, "Takeover Leaves Trail of Cleaning Bills," *The Hilltop*, March 17, 1989.

123 Goldberg and Feinberg, "Victorious Howard Students End Siege of Building."

124 Jonathan Scott Holloway, *Confronting the Veil: Abram Harris, Jr., E. Franklin Frazier, and Ralph Bunche, 1919–1941* (Chapel Hill: University of North Carolina Press, 2002), 77.

125 Goldberg and Feinberg, "Victorious Howard Students End Siege of Building"; and U.S. Congress, House, Subcommittee of the Committee on Appropriations, "Departments of Labor, Health and Human Services, Education, and Related Agencies Appropriations for 1990," 101st Congress, 1st Session (1989), 1557–1629.

126 Sheri Warren, interview by the author, December 16, 2017.

127 Ibid.

128 Aaron Lloyd, interview by the author, May 4, 2018; V. Jimale Ridgeway, interview by the author, March 26, 2018; and Akanke Washington, interview by the author, January 24, 2017.

129 April Silver, interview by the author, May 6, 2018.

130 David Nicholson, "Why Howard University Exploded Last Week," *Washington Post*, March 12, 1989.

131 Telegram from Toni Cade Bambara, March 8, 1989, April Silver Collection, private collection. Karma Bambara was interviewed in Trescott, "We Stood Up Because We Love This Black School." See also the telegram from Al Sharpton, March 8, 1989, April Silver Collection, private collection.

132 Telegram from Al Sharpton, March 8, 1989; Third Annual Melanin Conference Program, April 6–8, 1989, Washington, DC; "Black United Youth Presents: Student Activism: Where Do We Go From Here?!" March 14, 1989, Washington, DC; "Ladies of the Howard University Quad and the All-African People's Revolutionary Party Presents 'A Woman's Place in the Struggle,'" April 1, 1989, Washington, DC; and "Draft Letter Re: Appearance on Geraldo," November 29, 1989, all in the April Silver Collection, private collection.

133 April Silver, interview by the author, June 2, 2018.

134 Jill Nelson, "At Howard, 3 Forces behind a 'Revolution,'" *Washington Post*, March 14, 1989.

135 See Brady, *Bad Boy*, 266–322; and Lee Atwater and Todd Brewster, "Lee Atwater's Last Campaign," *Life*, February 1991, 58–67.

136 Glenda Fauntleroy, "Silver Exemplifies Strength, Modesty," *The Hilltop*, March 10, 1989.

CHAPTER 7. NEW HOWARD

1 Aarian Pope Punter, interview by the author, June 6, 2018.

2 Ameera Sheckles, "From New to Newer: How Gentrification Is Contributing to the Shift in Howard Culture," *The Hilltop*, September 23, 2016, http://thehilltoponline.com; Brakkton Booker, "When a Historically Black University's Neighborhood Turns White," National Public Radio, July 25, 2017, www.npr.org. See also Derek S. Hyra, *Race, Class, and Politics in the Cappuccino City* (Chicago: University of Chicago Press, 2017); and Sabiyha Prince, *African Americans and Gentrification in Washington, D.C.: Race, Class, and Social Justice in the Nation's Capital* (New York: Routledge, 2014).

3 "Mission and Core Values," *Howard University*, www2.howard.edu.

4 Ibid. For references to "African diaspora," see Alvin Thornton et al. of the Presidential Commission on Academic Renewal, *Defining the Future: Enriching the Ground on Which We Stand* (Washington, DC: Howard University, 2010); Howard University, *2009 Self-Study Report to the Middle States Association of Colleges and Schools Commission on Higher Education* (Washington, DC: Howard University, 2009), www2.howard.edu; and J. Lorand Matory, *Stigma and Culture: Last-Place Anxiety in Black America* (Chicago: University of Chicago Press, 2015), 134–135.

5 Matory, *Stigma and Culture*, 63.

6 Rayford Logan, *Howard University: The First Hundred Years, 1867–1967* (New York: New York University Press, 1968), 558–564; and Alvin Thornton, interview by the author, May 15, 2018.

7 On the idea of post-1989 triumphalism—which speaks to the fall of the Berlin Wall and the so-called end of history—and its relationship to Black politics, see Richard Iton, "Still Life," *Small Axe* 17 (March 2013): 35, and *In Search of the Black Fantastic: Politics and Popular Culture in the Post–Civil Rights Era* (New York: Oxford University Press, 2008), 126–128.

8 "Letter to the Students," *The Hilltop*, March 31, 1989.

9 Charles Webb, "This Is a Revolutionary 'Thang,'" *The Hilltop*, March 17, 1989.

10 Marea Battle, "Milloy Says His Columns Galvanized Movement," *The Hilltop*, April 7, 1989. Sponsored by the Society of Professional Journalists, this forum was particularly noteworthy, given that, as a Black columnist, Courtland Milloy's condemnation of the protest and singling out of Ras Baraka was seen as an egregious betrayal. See also "Really, Mr. Milloy," *The Hilltop*, March 17, 1989; LaSandra Bowman, "Courtland's Shuffle," *The Hilltop*, April 7, 1989; Tony Brown, "A Lesson in the Victory at Howard," *Tri-State Defender*, March 29, 1989; and Statement from Coalition of Concerned Howard University Students, "On Courtland Milloy," n.d., April Silver Collection, private collection.

11 James K. Stovall, "Student Follow Up on Protest Demands," *The Hilltop*, April 7, 1989; and D. Malcolm Carson, "Making an Afro-centric 'Mecca,'" *The Hilltop*, April 7, 1989. Stovall's report in *The Hilltop* indicated that additional suggestions to the board made sometime after the coalition's letter included Amiri Baraka, Ron Brown, Alim Muhammad, Kwame Ture, and Walter Fauntroy. The names on the initial list did not appear in this report and can be found in Coalition of Concerned Howard University Students to Daniel Goodwin, March 14, 1989, April Silver Collection, private collection.

12 "Coalition of Concerned Howard University Students Meeting Notes," n.d., April Silver Collection, private collection; "Coalition of Concerned Howard University Students Meeting with Administration Notes," March 31, 1989, April Silver Collection, private collection; Minutes of Black Nia F.O.R.C.E Closed Meeting, April 14, 1989, April Silver Collection, private collection; and Gale P. Mitchell, "Alumni Calls for Cheek's Ouster," *The Hilltop*, March 17, 1989.

13 Minutes of Black Nia F.O.R.C.E Closed Meeting, April 14, 1989, April Silver Collection, private collection.

14 Coalition of Concerned Howard University Students, "Mass Student Rally and Candlelight Vigil," press release, n.d., April Silver Collection, private collection.

15 Flyer, "Cheek Rally and Vigil," April 21, 1989, April Silver Collection, private collection.

16 Nicole Brown, interview by the author, June 2, 2018.

17 Minutes of Black Nia F.O.R.C.E Closed Meeting, March 10, 1989, April Silver Collection, private collection.

18 "Paying the Price," *The Hilltop*, March 17, 1989. See also "Cheek's Intolerable Action," *The Hilltop*, March 10, 1989.

19 "Howard's Cheek to End Twenty-Year Career There to Take New Ambassadorship," *Jet*, April 24, 1989, 5.

20 "A Candid Conversation with James Edward Cheek," *New Directions* 16 (July 1989): 29.

21 Ibid., 30–33.

22 Ibid., 30.

23 Lawrence Feinberg and Jeffrey Goldberg, "Cheek to Retire in June as Howard U. President," *Washington Post*, April 23, 1989.

24 Douglas Martin, "James E. Cheek, Forceful University President, Dies at 77," *New York Times*, January 31, 2010.

25 Suzanne Alexander, "Cheek Reflects on 20 Years of Leading the 'Mecca,'" *The Hilltop*, May 12, 1989.

26 Jacqueline Trescott, "At Howard, Praise for a President," *Washington Post*, July 1, 1989.

27 Michael R. Winston, "On the Sesquicentennial of Howard University," *Howard Magazine* 26 (Winter 2017): 5.

28 Jelani Cobb, "Hard Tests," *New Yorker*, January 15, 2018, 49.

29 Carlisle Sealy, interview by the author, July 7, 2017; and Jam Shakwi, interview by the author, December 14, 2017.

30 Feinberg and Goldberg, "Cheek to Retire."

31 Bayard Rustin, "From Protest to Politics," *Commentary* 39 (February 1965): 25–31; and Cedric Johnson, *Revolutionaries to Race Leaders: Black Power and the Making of African American Politics* (Minneapolis: University of Minnesota Press, 2007).

32 V. Jimale Ridgeway, interview by the author, March 26, 2018; and Aaron Lloyd, interview by the author, May 4, 2018.

33 Aaron Lloyd, interview by author, May 4, 2018; Sheri Warren, interview by the author, December 16, 2017; and "Black Nia F.O.R.C.E Questionnaire," n.d., April Silver Collection, private collection.

34 Carslile Sealy to April Silver, August 3, 1989, April Silver Collection, private collection; and "By-Laws, Black Nia F.O.R.C.E (Draft)," n.d., April Silver Collection, private collection.

35 "Guidelines and Policies of Black Nia F.O.R.C.E (Freedom Organization for Racial and Cultural Enlightenment)," n.d., 1, April Silver Collection, private collection.

36 "Guidelines and Policies of Black Nia F.O.R.C.E (Freedom Organization for Racial and Cultural Enlightenment)," n.d., page 7A, Akanke Washington Collection, private collection.

37 Minutes of Black Nia F.O.R.C.E Closed Meeting, September 22, 1989, April Silver Collection, private collection.

38 Flyer, "Zak Kondo: Positive Education as a Weapon," October 20, 1989, April Silver Collection, private collection.

39 April Silver, interview by the author, June 2, 2018.

40 "To the Brothers of Black Nia F.O.R.C.E," December 12, 1989, April Silver Collection, private collection.

41 "Agenda Notes," September 7, 1989, April Silver Collection, private collection.

42 Carlisle Sealy, interview by the author, July 7, 2017; and Flyer, "Black Nia F.O.R.C.E Presents a Cultural Festival," November 18, 1989, April Silver Collection, private collection.

43 Pierre Thomas and Steve Bates, "Virginia Beach Festival Erupts into a Riot," *Washington Post*, September 4, 1989; and Robert Vickers and Tracy Carr, "Students Claim Harassment in Virginia Beach Unrest," *The Hilltop*, September 8, 1989.

44 April Silver, interview by the author, June 2, 2018; Paula M. White, "Concerned Students Forced to Postpone Meeting," *The Hilltop*, September 29, 1989; and William Simms, "Fighting Back," *The Hilltop*, November 3, 1989.

45 Dora Stewart, "Students Give Support to D.C. Mayor Barry," *The Hilltop*, January 26, 1990; Kassandra Fleming, "HU Students Support Barry in Rally," *The Hilltop*, February 2, 1990; Sonsyrea Tate, "Howard U. Students Defend Barry at Rally," *Washington Times*, February 1, 1990; Sharon LaFraniere, "Barry Arrested on Cocaine Charges in Undercover FBI, Police Operation," *Washington Post*, January 19, 1990; "Hastings:

Impeachment Hearing Based on Racism," *Los Angeles Sentinel*, October 12, 1990; April Silver, interview by the author, June 2, 2018; and Ras J. Baraka, interview by the author, August 25, 2017.

46 Flyer, "Leadership for the Masses," February 28, 1990, April Silver Collection, private collection; and Sonsyrea Tate, "Leadership from the Masses," *Washington Times*, March 2, 1990.

47 Garfield Bright, interview by the author, April 4, 2018.

48 April Silver, interview by the author, June 2, 2018.

49 Paula White, "Candidates Put to the Test," *The Hilltop*, February 23, 1990.

50 Shawn Houston, interview by the author, December 18, 2017.

51 Ibid.

52 Flyer, "Leadership for the Masses," February 28, 1990, April Silver Collection, private collection; and Kassandra Fleming, "Silver, Baraka Promote Unification of the Masses," *The Hilltop*, February 23, 1990.

53 Paula White, "Silver, Beacham Slates Face Run-off Election," *The Hilltop*, March 2, 1990; and Tate, "Leadership from the Masses."

54 Ras Baraka, "No Apologies: Just Truth," *The Hilltop*, March 2, 1990.

55 Tracy Hopkins, "Students Weigh Fruits of Spring '89 Uprising," *The Hilltop*, March 2, 1990; and Rene Sanchez, "Howard Students Wait for Promises to Turn to Action," *Washington Post*, March 4, 1990.

56 Tracy Hopkins, "Protest Effected [*sic*] Changes on Campus," *The Hilltop*, March 9, 1990; and Paula White, "Jenifer Takes the Helm," *The Hilltop*, April 6, 1990.

57 Paula White, "'Masses' Wins HUSA Runoff Vote," *The Hilltop*, March 9, 1990; and Sanchez, "Howard Students Wait for Promises to Turn to Action."

58 "Leadership for the Masses," *The Hilltop*, March 9, 1990.

59 April Silver, "For the Liberation of Us All," *The Hilltop*, May 12, 1990.

60 For these varied perspectives, see James Davison Hunter, *Culture Wars: The Struggle to Define America* (New York: Basic Books, 1991); Frederic Jameson, *Postmodernism, or The Cultural Logic of Late Capitalism* (Durham, NC: Duke University Press, 1991); and Allan Bloom, *The Closing of the American Mind: How Higher Education Has Failed Democracy and Impoverished the Souls of Today's Students* (New York: Simon & Schuster, 1987). The conservative writer Dinesh D'Souza saw events at Howard along these lines, devoting a chapter to Howard and the protest titled, "In Search of Black Pharaohs," in his contribution to this literature. It was universally condemned on campus. See Dinesh D'Souza, *Illiberal Education: The Politics of Race and Sex on Campus* (New York: Free Press, 1991), 94–123.

61 On the historical particulars of this moment, see Andrew Hartman, *A War for the Soul of America: A History of the Culture Wars* (Chicago: University of Chicago Press, 2015); John Ehrman, *The Eighties: America in the Age of Reagan* (New Haven, CT: Yale University Press, 2005), 193–204; and Robert M. Collins, *Transforming America: Politics and Culture during the Reagan Years* (New York: Columbia University Press, 2007), 179–186. On the relationship between the battle over multiculturalism and the perceived universalisms of the American creed/Western tradition and their contradictions, see Nikhil Pal Singh, "Culture/Wars: Recoding Empire in an Age of Democracy," *American Quarterly* 50 (September 1998): 471–522; as well as Cedric Robinson, "Manichaeism and Multiculturalism," in *Mapping Multiculturalism*, ed. Avery Gordon and Christopher Newfield (Minneapolis: University of Minnesota Press, 1996), 116–124. What troubled many African-centered

thinkers was not their lack of inclusion but the fundamental epistemological structures of Western thought. In an example of an African-centered argument, Jacob Carruthers argued that "cultural democracy" would not be possible "as long as the curriculum is enthralled in Western historiography and the broader modern European philosophy from which it is derived." See Jacob Carruthers, "The Battle over the Multicultural Curriculum," in his *Intellectual Warfare* (Chicago: Third World Press, 1999), 91.

62 Molefi Kete Asante, *Afrocentricity: The Theory of Social Change* (Buffalo, NY: Amulefi Publishing Co., 1980).

63 Greg Carr, "What Black Studies Is Not: Moving from Crisis to Liberation in Africana Intellectual Work," *Socialism and Democracy* 25 (March 2011): 181.

64 See Molefi Asante, *The Afrocentric Idea* (1987; reprint, Philadelphia: Temple University Press, 1998), and *Kemet, Afrocentricity, and Knowledge* (Trenton, NJ: Africa World Press, 1990). See also Ama Mazama, ed., *The Afrocentric Paradigm* (Trenton, NJ: Africa World Press, 2003); and Molefi Kete Asante, *An Afrocentric Manifesto* (Malden, MA: Polity Press, 2007). My thinking on Afrocentricity and Africana Studies (or Africology) has been enhanced by Lucius T. Outlaw, Jr., "Africology and Normative Theory," in his *On Race and Philosophy* (New York: Routledge, 1996), 97–134; and Greg Carr, "African Philosophy of History in the Contemporary Era: Its Antecedents and Methodological Implications for the African Contribution to World History" (PhD diss., Temple University, 1998), 114–132.

65 It is important to distinguish "popular Afrocentrism" from the intellectual and conceptual formulation; see James Stewart, "Reaching for Higher Ground: Toward an Understanding of Black/Africana Studies," *Afrocentric Scholar* 1 (May 1992): 1–63; and Patricia Hill-Collins, *From Black Power to Hip Hop: Racism, Nationalism, Feminism* (Philadelphia: Temple University Press, 2006), 75–94.

66 Laura C. James, "Afrocentricity: A Trend or Tradition?" *The Hilltop*, March 8, 1991.

67 Tracy Hopkins, "'Last Leg' on Second Run," *The Hilltop*, April 13, 1990.

68 Silver, "For the Liberation of Us All."

69 Charles Whitaker, "The New Generation of the '90s," *Ebony*, August 1990, 32.

70 Quentina Johnson, "Silver Conveys a Message of 'Awareness,'" *The Hilltop*, August 31, 1990.

71 See, for instance, Russell L. Adams, "Intellectual Questions and Imperatives in African American Studies," *Journal of Negro Education* 53 (Summer 1984): 201–225. Later work includes his "African American Studies and the State of the Art," in *Africana Studies: A Survey of Africa and the African Diaspora*, ed. Mario Azevedo (Durham, NC: Carolina Academic Press, 2005), 33–52, and "Epistemological Considerations in Afro-American Studies," in *Out of the Revolution: The Development of Africana Studies*, ed. Delores P. Aldridge and Carlene Young (Lanham, MD: Lexington Books, 2000), 39–75.

72 Carson, "Making an Afro-centric 'Mecca.'"

73 Memorandum by Michael L. Blakey, "A Discussion of Afrocentrism for the Africana Studies Task Force," n.d., April Silver Collection, private collection. For Asante's critique of the rendering of Afrocentrism as opposed to Afrocentricity, see Asante, *An Afrocentric Manifesto*, 17.

74 "Report of the Howard University Task Force on Graduate African American Studies," draft, n.d., April Silver Collection, private collection.

75 Ibid. See also Eleanor Traylor, Alphonso A. Frost, and Leota S. Lawrence, *Broad Sympathy: The Howard University Oral Traditions Reader* (Needham, MA: Simon &

Schuster Custom Publishing, 1997); and Dana Williams, "Broad Sympathy: Howard University's DuBoisian Approach to Blackness and the Humanities," *International Journal of the Humanities* 2 (2004): 2509–2515.

76 Emphasis added. See "Report of the Howard University Task Force on Graduate African American Studies," draft, n.d., April Silver Collection, private collection.

77 Michael Blakey et al., "Report of the Howard University Task Force on Graduate African American Studies," January 2, 1991, 3, 5, April Silver Collection, private collection.

78 B. G. Neely, "President Gives 123rd Convocation Address," *The Hilltop*, August 31, 1990.

79 The Howard University Commission, *Investing for Excellence: Strategically Repositioning Howard University to Face the Challenges of the 21st Century* (Washington, DC: Howard University, November 18, 1990), Howard University Archives, Moorland-Spingarn Research Center.

80 See Paul Kennedy, *Preparing for the Twenty-First Century* (New York: Vintage, 1993); and Edward N. Luttwak, *The Endangered American Dream: How to Stop the United States from Becoming a Third-World Country and How to Win the Geo-economic Struggle for Industrial Supremacy* (New York: Touchstone, 1993), for examples of the thinking around global technological change, American decline, and the competition from Japan and Germany. For deeper historical context, see Collins, *Transforming America*, 113–115; and James T. Patterson, *Restless Giant: The United States from Watergate to Bush v. Gore* (New York: Oxford University Press, 2005), 203–204.

81 The Howard University Commission, *Investing for Excellence: Strategically Repositioning Howard University to Face the Challenges of the 21st Century* (Washington, DC: Howard University, November 18, 1990), 10, Howard University Archives, Moorland-Spingarn Research Center.

82 "The Man for Our Time," *The Hilltop*, December 8, 1989; "Swygert Plan Includes Afrocentric Emphasis," *The Hilltop*, December 1, 1989; "U Shudda Ben Dere," *The Hilltop*, December 1, 1989; and "Information, Please," *The Hilltop*, November 10, 1989.

83 The Howard University Commission, *Investing for Excellence: Strategically Repositioning Howard University to Face the Challenges of the 21st Century* (Washington, DC: Howard University, November 18, 1990), 120, Howard University Archives, Moorland-Spingarn Research Center; and Rochelle Tillery, "Student Committees Prepare Response to Commission Report," *The Hilltop*, December 7, 1990.

84 George Daniels, "There Was No Response to the Student Response," *The Hilltop*, March 8, 1991; Tillery, "Student Committees Prepare Response."

85 STEM = science, technology, engineering, and math. See Franklyn Jenifer, *Howard 2000: A Blueprint for Building a Stronger University to face the Challenges of the Year 2000 and Beyond* (Washington, DC: Howard University, April 27, 1991), Howard University Archives, Moorland-Spingarn Research Center. A shorter version, published in *New Directions*, 18 (Summer/Fall 1991): 1–14, is available via Digital Howard; see http://dh.howard.edu.

86 Franklyn Jenifer, *Howard 2000: A Blueprint for Building a Stronger University to face the Challenges of the Year 2000 and Beyond* (Washington, DC: Howard University, April 27, 1991), 6, Howard University Archives, Moorland-Spingarn Research Center; and the Howard University Commission, *Investing for Excellence: Strategically Repositioning Howard University to Face the Challenges of the 21st Century* (Washington, DC: Howard University, November 18, 1990), 11. For academic capitalism, see Sheila Slaughter and Larry L. Leslie, *Academic Capitalism: Politics, Policies, and the Entrepreneurial University* (Baltimore: Johns Hopkins University Press, 1997).

87 Franklyn Jenifer, *Howard 2000: A Blueprint for Building a Stronger University to face the Challenges of the Year 2000 and Beyond* (Washington, DC: Howard University, April 27, 1991), 9–20, Howard University Archives, Moorland-Spingarn Research Center; and Regina Mack, "Howard: A Research Institute?" *The Hilltop*, April 15, 1991.

88 Franklyn Jenifer, *Howard 2000: A Blueprint for Building a Stronger University to face the Challenges of the Year 2000 and Beyond* (Washington, DC: Howard University, April 27, 1991), 6, Howard University Archives, Moorland-Spingarn Research Center.

89 C. P. Snow, *The Two Cultures and the Scientific Revolution* (New York: Cambridge University Press, 1959). See also Jacob Carruthers, *Science and Oppression* (Chicago: Kemetic Institute, 1972).

90 Franklyn Jenifer, "Presidential Perspective: Defining Afrocentricity," *The Hilltop*, October 28, 1990. For the Task Force's discussion, see Michael Blakey et al., "Report of the Howard University Task Force on Graduate African American Studies," January 2, 1991, 5–7, April Silver Collection, private collection. On the "Howard School," see Robert Vitalis, *White World Order, Black Power Politics: The Birth of American International Relations* (Ithaca, NY: Cornell University Press, 2015).

91 See the 1991 Charter Day Address by Clifton R. Wharton, Jr., "Toward a Black Intellectual Agenda for the Nineties," *New Directions* 18 (Spring 1991): 6–9.

92 During Joyce Ladner's tenure as vice president, Asante was brought to campus to participate in a lecture series in 1993. See Molefi Kete Asante, "Afrocentric Approaches to History," lecture, Howard University, Washington, DC, February 15, 1993), hosted at C-SPAN, www.c-span.org. A more recent attempt to address the issue of "academic renewal" recommended a stronger emphasis on Africana Studies, although the recommendation has languished under a new administration. See Alvin Thornton et al. of the Presidential Commission on Academic Renewal, *Defining the Future*, 52. On Africana Studies at Howard today, see Greg Carr, "The Question of Academic Renewal at Howard University: Genealogy, Modalities, and Metrics," unpublished paper presented at Moorland-Spingarn Collection Symposium, Washington, DC, January 26, 2010; and Howard Dodson, Robert Edgar, Greg Carr, Sulayman S. Nyang, and Angel Baptiste, "African Studies at Howard University," panel discussion at the Library of Congress, Washington, DC, November 8, 2013, posted at the Library of Congress, www.loc.gov.

93 Tyya N. Turner, "Has HUSA Fulfilled a Promise Made a Year Ago?" *The Hilltop*, February 15, 1990; Brian Granville and Theodore Cummings, "Howard Assists in Va. Beach Boycott," *The Hilltop*, August 31, 1990; and Chet Lunner, "Virginia Beach Banks on 'Positive Holiday,'" *USA Today*, August 31, 1990.

94 Haqq Islam, interview by the author, January 23, 2018.

95 April Silver, interview by the author, January 29, 2017.

96 Turner, "Has HUSA Fulfilled a Promise Made a Year Ago?"; and April Silver, interview by the author, January 29, 2017.

97 Darrell Clark, "Each One Teach One," *Ear to the Streets*, n.d., Haqq Islam Collection, private collection; Gil Griffin, "Confab Hip to Evolution of Hip-Hop," *Billboard*, March 16, 1991; and David Mills, "The Hip-Hop Rap Session," *Washington Post*, February 25, 1991.

98 Mills, "The Hip-Hop Rap Session."

99 Griffin, "Confab Hip to Evolution of Hip-Hop."

100 Clark, "Each One Teach One"; and Gil Griffin, "More Hip Hop," *Washington Post*, March 1, 1991.

101 Gil Griffin, "Hip Hop Happening," *Washington Post*, March 1, 1991.

102 Ernest Allen, Jr., "Making the Strong Survive: The Contours and Contradictions of Message Rap," in *Droppin' Science: Critical Essays on Rap Music and Hip Hop Culture*, ed. William Eric Perkins (Philadelphia: Temple University Press, 1996), 159–191.

103 Tonya Pendleton, "Hip-Hop Conference Highlights Issues," *Philadelphia Tribune*, February 26, 1993.

104 Haqq Islam, interview by the author, January 23, 2018; V. Jimale Ridgeway, interview by the author, March 26, 2018; Matt Middleton, interview by the author, January 2, 2018; Garfield Bright, interview by the author, April 4, 2018; Aaron Lloyd, interview by the author, May 4, 2018; Lauryn Hill, *The Miseducation of Lauryn Hill* (album, New York: Ruffhouse Records and Columbia Records, 1998); and Laura Checkoway, "Inside 'The Miseducation of Lauryn Hill,'" *Rolling Stone*, August 26, 2008, www.rollingstone.com.

105 Islam's emphasis on the business aspect of hip hop and the impact it had in spawning the careers of many Howard-affiliated music industry insiders is neglected in Dan Charnas, *The Big Payback: The History of the Business of Hip Hop*; and S. Craig Watkins, *Hip Hop Matters: Politics, Pop Culture, and the Struggle for the Soul of a Movement* (Boston: Beacon Press, 2005). Marcus Reeves does mention the protest but does not mention the hip-hop conferences in his brief profile of Sean "Puff" Combs. See Marcus Reeves, *Somebody Scream! Rap Music's Rise to Prominence in the Aftershock of Black Power* (New York: Faber & Faber, 2008), 182–183.

106 Carl Bernstein, "Hershey Is Burned in Effigy," *Washington Post*, April 20, 1967; Lawrence B. de Graaf, "Howard: The Evolution of a Black Student Revolt," in *Protest! Student Activism in America*, ed. Julian Foster and Durward Long (New York: William Morrow & Co., 1968), 326–327; and Henry Hampton and Steve Fayer, with Sarah Flynn, "Howard University, 1967–1968: You Saw the Silhouette of Her Afro," 436–438.

107 Patterson, *Restless Giant*, 230–235; and Colin Powell, *An American Journey* (New York: Random House, 1998), 459–530.

108 D. Malcolm Carson, "Students March in Futile Attempt for Peace," *The Hilltop*, January 18, 1991; and Joel Achenbach, "Birth of a Protest Movement," *Washington Post*, January 17, 1991.

109 Erica Thompson and Christopher Conti, "Guerrilla Activists Burn 'Symbol of Oppression,'" *The Hilltop*, February 22, 1991; and D. Malcolm Carson, "Howard Anti-war Movement Gains Momentum in the Face of Ground War in the Persian Gulf," *The Hilltop*, February 22, 1991.

110 Carson, "Howard Anti-war Movement." There were obviously students who felt that the burning went too far, including George Daniels. See "Should We Burn the Flag?" *The Hilltop*, February 22, 1991.

111 Gwen McGill, "Silver and Baraka Lead Fight for Students Rights," *The Hilltop*, May 11, 1991. Black Nia F.O.R.C.E and Nation of Islam members Garfield Bright and Darnell Dinkins unsuccessfully attempted to continue this legacy as they were defeated in a runoff election in their HUSA run that spring. See Regina M. Mack and Tracy L. Wilson, "Bates/Grant Secure Top HUSA Offices," *The Hilltop*, March 8, 1991.

112 Alvin Thornton, interview by the author, May 15, 2018.

113 Joy-Ann Reid, *Fracture: Barack Obama, the Clintons, and the Racial Divide* (New York: HarperCollins, 2015), 65–70. See also Ronald W. Walters, *White Nationalism/Black Interests: Conservative Public Policy and the Black Community* (Detroit, MI: Wayne State University Press, 2003), 93–115, for a critique of Third Way politics.

114 See Walters, *White Nationalism/Black Interests*.

115 Joyce A. Ladner, ed., *The Death of White Sociology: Essays on Race and Culture* (Baltimore: Black Classic Press, 1998).

116 Juan Williams, "The Continuing Education of Franklyn Jenifer," *Washington Post*, September 20, 1992; Catherine S. Manegold, "Amid Criticism, Howard President Quits," *New York Times*, April 24, 1994; Brooke Masters, "Ex-Farrakhan Aide Gets Mixed Reactions on Howard Campus," *Washington Post*, February 25, 1994; Valerie Strauss, "At Howard U, Mandela the Man Lives Up to Mandela the Legend," *Washington Post*, October 8, 1994; Joseph Drew, "New Howard Head Vowing to Fight Tragedy of Hate," *Forward*, May 19, 1995; and "President Swygert Takes the Helm at Howard University," *Journal of Blacks in Higher Education* 8 (Summer 1995): 32–34.

CHAPTER 8. NIA

1 Ras Baraka, "In the Tradition Too," in *In the Tradition: An Anthology of Young Black Writers*, ed. Kevin Powell and Ras Baraka (New York: Harlem Rivers Press, 1992), 85.

2 Raymond Wolters, *The New Negro on Campus: Black College Rebellions of the 1920s* (Princeton, NJ: Princeton University Press, 1975); Ibram Kendi, *The Black Campus Movement: Black Students and the Racial Reconstitution of Higher Education, 1965–1972* (New York: Palgrave Macmillan, 2012); Martha Biondi, *The Black Revolution on Campus* (Berkeley: University of California Press, 2012); and Robin D. G. Kelley, "Black Study, Black Struggle," *Boston Review*, forum, March–April 2016, 9–20, http://bostonreview.net; and Alia Wong and Adrienne Greene, "Campus Politics: A Cheat Sheet," *Atlantic*, April 4, 2016, www.theatlantic.com.

3 Stacey J. Phillips, "Support from HU Battle Comes from Near and Far," *The Hilltop*, March 10, 1989.

4 Ann Hardie and Bill Montgomery, "Morris Brown Students Using Takeover to Make Demands," *Atlanta Journal-Constitution*, April 5, 1989; and Drew Jubera, "Alumni of a Revolution," *Atlanta Journal-Constitution*, May 9, 1991.

5 Alexander Wheatley, "Morris Brown Used to Enroll 2,500 Students. Now There are 40," *Atlanta Magazine*, April 2017, www.atlantamagazine.com.

6 Robert Lasker and Yul U. Tolbert, "Over 100 Rally to Support 'Study-in,'" *South End*, April 17, 1989; and Alexander Franzen, "The Black Student Protest That Woke Wayne State," *South End*, March 2, 2016, www.thesouthend.wayne.edu.

7 "Penn State Will Drop Charges against 89 Students," *New York Time*, April 19, 1988; and "Penn State Talks End," *Philadelphia Tribune*, July 8, 1988.

8 "BNF Closed Meeting Agenda," April 28, 1989, April Silver Collection, private collection; and Aarian Pope Punter, interview by the author, June 6, 2018.

9 James C. McKinley, Jr., "Some See Possible Tuition Rise at CUNY as Albany Betrayal," *New York Times*, May 2, 1989; and Kwame Okoampa-Ahoofe, Jr., "Protestors Say Poor Students Are Targets of Tuition Increase," *New York Amsterdam News*, May 6, 1989. On City College of New York, see Joseph Dorman, *Arguing the World: The New York Intellectuals in Their Own Words* (Chicago: University of Chicago Press, 2000), 41–66; Biondi, *The Black Revolution on Campus*, 114–141; and Allen B. Ballard, *Breaching Jericho's Walls: A Twentieth-Century African American Life* (Albany: State University of New York Press, 2011), 211–234. For Jordan's essay, see June Jordan, "Black Studies: Bringing Back the Person," *Evergreen Review* 17 (October 1969): 39–41; 71–72.

10 Kwame Okoampa-Ahoofe, Jr., "CCNY Prez Calls for White House Code," *New York Amsterdam News*, June 10, 1989; Kevin Powell, "CUNY Protests End Abruptly," *New York Amsterdam News*, May 4, 1991; and Amity Paye, "Students versus CUNY," *New York Amsterdam News*, December 5, 2013.

11 Wendy Brown, *Undoing the Demos: Neoliberalism's Stealth Revolution* (New York: Zone Books, 2015), 175–200; and Sara Goldrick-Rab, *Paying the Price: College Costs, Financial Aid, and the Betrayal of the American Dream* (Chicago: University of Chicago Press, 2016).

12 See *Adams v. Richardson* (1973); *United States v. Fordice* (1992); and Albert Samuels, *Is Separate Unequal? Black Colleges and the Challenge to Desegregation* (Lawrence: University Press of Kansas, 2004).

13 Brad Schmitt, "Activist Jeff Obafemi Carr's First Protest: Shutting Down TSU," *Tennessean*, March 30, 2017, www.tennessean.com.

14 Ibid.

15 Sheila Wissner and Rob Bingham, "Police Escort TSU Students from Sit-in," *Tennessean*, February 22, 1990; Rob Bingham, "Students Detail 'Unlivable Conditions,'" *Tennessean*, February 22, 1990; and Schmitt, "Activist Jeff Obafemi Carr's First Protest: Shutting Down TSU."

16 Rob Bingham, "Protest Moves Downtown," *Tennessean*, February 24, 1990; Kim Middlebrooks, "President Floyd's Lack of Response Leads to Second Student Sit-in," *Nashville Pride*, March 2, 1990.

17 Makola M. Abdullah, interview by the author, June 8, 2018; Jam Shakwi, interview by the author, December 14, 2017; Aarian Pope Punter, interview by the author, June 6, 2018; "Students Stage 60s-Style Protest at Tennessee State," *Atlanta Daily World*, February 27, 1990; and Rene Sanchez, "Howard Students Wait for Promises to Turn to Action," *Washington Post*, March 4, 1990.

18 Kassandra Fleming, "Silver, Baraka Promote Unification of the Masses," *The Hilltop*, February 23, 1990.

19 Rob Bingham, "TSU Students, Floyd Reach Agreement," *Tennessean*, March 9, 1990.

20 Dennis O'Brien, "Protests Uncover Silent Neglect at Morgan State," *Baltimore Sun*, March 18, 1990.

21 Melody Simmons, "200 Angry Students Seize Morgan Office," *Baltimore Sun*, March 6, 1990; and Amy Goldstein, "Morgan Campus Shut Down," *Washington Post*, March 9, 1990.

22 Amy Goldstein and Fern Shen, "Morgan Students, Schaefer Meet," *Washington Post*, March 10, 1990; Amy Goldstein, "Morgan State Students End Boycott of Classes," *Washington Post*, March 13 1990; and S. M. Khalid, "Morgan State to Review Police Actions during Melee at Dedication Ceremonies," *Baltimore Sun*, September 20, 1991.

23 Amy Goldstein and Leah Latimer, "Higher Fees Spur Protest at Bowie State University," *Washington Post*, April 27, 1990; and Amy Goldstein, "Bowie State Fees Are Set after Protest," *Washington Post*, June 1, 1990.

24 Jonetta Rose Barras and Michael Cromwell, "UDC Student Rally Turns Militant," *Washington Times*, September 27, 1990.

25 Quentina Johnson, "UDC Students Takeover A-Building," *The Hilltop*, September 28, 1990; and Brian Granville and Theodore Cummings, "Howard Assists in Va. Beach Boycott," *The Hilltop*, September 7, 1990.

26 Carlos Sanchez and Keith Harriston, "UDC Agrees to Most Demands as Student Protest Continues," *Washington Post*, October 1, 1990; Keith Harriston, "UDC Protestors

Aim to Build on Gains," *Washington Post*, October 7, 1990; and Kelby N. Brick, "UDC Protest Ends in Victory for Students; 42 Demands Met," *Buff and Blue*, October 8 1990.

27 Brian Kamanzi, "#FeesMustFall: Decolonizing Education," *Al Jazeera*, November 3, 2016, www.aljazeera.com; and Pramila Jayapal, "Why I Introduced the College for All Act," *Nation*, April 4, 2017.

28 Keith Harriston, "Black Students Hope March Will Boost Activism," *Washington Post*, June 16, 1990.

29 Michael Dawson, *Black Visions: The Roots of Modern African American Political Ideologies* (Chicago: University of Chicago Press, 2001), 101.

30 "Leadership Retreat Agenda," March 17, 1991, April Silver Collection, private collection.

31 V. Jimale Ridgeway, interview by the author, March 26, 2018.

32 BNF National Executive Board to Sevie Zawdie, October 13, 1991; "Guidelines and Policies of Black Nia F.O.R.C.E (Freedom Organization for Racial and Cultural Enlightenment," n.d.; and April Silver to BNF Membership, December 14, 1992, all in Akanke Washington Collection, private collection.

33 Silver to BNF Membership, December 14, 1992, Akanke Washington Collection, private collection. On the platforms that inspired BNF's, see Joshua Bloom and Waldo E. Martin, Jr., *Black against Empire: The History and Politics of the Black Panther Party* (Berkeley: University of California Press, 2013), 70–71.

34 "The Political Platform of Black Nia F.O.R.C.E," n.d., Akanke Washington Collection, private collection.

35 Ibid.

36 Jelani Makalani (Cobb) to BNF D.C. Chapter, May 23, 1992, Akanke Washington Collection, private collection.

37 Aarian Pope Punter, interview by the author, June 6, 2018; Aaron Lloyd, interview by the author, May 4, 2018; Flyer, "Black Nia F.O.R.C.E Presents the State of Black Youth Part 3: The Solutions," October 18, 1991, Akanke Washington Collection, private collection; and Karen Carrillo, "Black Nationalist Group Focuses on Feeding Homeless People," *New York Amsterdam News*, August 29, 1992.

38 Herb Boyd, "Black Groups in Newark Call for Their Own CCRB," *New York Amsterdam News*, October 31, 1992; Donald Rouse, "Youth Group Plans March in Newark for All Civilian Review Board," *New York Amsterdam News*, November 21, 1992, and "Youth Rally in Newark for an Elected All-Civilian Review Board," *New York Amsterdam News*, December 5, 1992; and Alecia McGregor, "Politics, Police Accountability, and Public Health: Civilian Review in Newark, New Jersey," *Journal of Urban Health* 93 (April 2016): 141–153.

39 See Angela Ards, "Organizing the Hip Hop Generation," in *That's the Joint! A Hip Hop Studies Reader*, ed. Murray Forman and Mark Anthony Neal (New York: Routledge, 2004), 311-324; Sekou Franklin, *After the Rebellion: Black Youth, Social Movement Activism, and the Post–Civil Rights Generation* (New York: New York University Press, 2014); and Bakari Kitwana, *The Hip Hop Generation: Young Blacks and the Crisis in African American Culture* (New York: Basic Civitas, 1992).

40 Kitwana, *The Hip Hop Generation*, 18. See also Andrea Mcardle and Tanya Erzen, *Zero Tolerance: Quality of Life and the New Police Brutality in New York City* (New York: New York University Press, 2001).

41 Shawn Houston, interview by the author, December 18, 2017; and Akanke Washington, interview by the author, December 18, 2017.

42 Aaron Lloyd, interview by the author, May 4, 2018.

43 Ards, "Organizing the Hip Hop Generation," 316.

44 "The Guidelines," 1; "Political Platform"; and "BNF Partial Summer Book List Assignments," April 24, 1989, all in the April Silver Collection, private collection; and "Black Nia F.O.R.C.E Summer Reading List: D.C. Chapter, 1992," n.d., Akanke Washington Collection, private collection.

45 Akanke Washington, interview by the author, January 24, 2017.

46 Killa Patterson, interview by the author, January 22, 2018.

47 Kitwana, *The Hip Hop Generation*, 156–157; Marcus Reeves, "Barakas: Father and Son Team Up to Unseat Newark Mayor James," *New York Amsterdam News*, March 26, 1994; and Jerry Gray, "Sharpe James Wins a Third Term as Newark Mayor," *New York Times*, May 11, 1994.

48 Lester Spence, *Stare in the Darkness: The Limits of Hip Hop and Black Politics* (Minneapolis: University of Minnesota Press, 2011), 95–129; Niamo Mui'd, "Live, from Newark: The National Hip-Hop Political Convention," *Socialism and Democracy* 18 (Fall–Winter 2004): 221–229.

49 See Andra Gillespie, *The New Black Politician: Cory Booker, Newark, and Post-racial America* (New York: New York University Press, 2012). Lester Spence has made the argument that hip hop–inspired figures often exhibit an acceptance of the neoliberal status quo represented by the likes of Booker. This notion of "hustle" has garnered necessary critique. See Spence, *Stare in the Darkness*, and his *Knocking the Hustle: Against the Neoliberal Turn in Black Politics* (Brooklyn, NY: Punctum, 2015).

50 Ted Sherman and Naomi Nix, "Ras Baraka Declares Victory in Newark Mayoral Election," *New Jersey Star-Ledger*, May 13, 2014, http://www.nj.com.

CODA

1 Kelly Miller, "The Howard Spirit," in *Howard Year Book: 1916* (Washington, DC: Howard University, 1916), 60, available via Digital Howard, http://dh.howard.edu.

2 See Jaimee Swift, "Meet the Women of HUResist: Leading the Charge against Trump at Howard University," *Huffington Post*, April 8, 2017, www.huffingtonpost.com. The quote from Sanchez that inspired HUResist was from April Silver's reflections on 1989, cited in the introduction, in this volume. On the idea of identity politics, see Mark Lilla, *The Once and Future Liberal: After Identity Politics* (New York: Harper, 2017). For a critique of Lilla and others, see Robin D. G. Kelley, "Births of a Nation," in "Forum I: Race Capitalism Justice," special issue, *Boston Review*, January 13, 2017), 117–135. Today's movements tend to center identities that are raced, gendered, classed, and premised on one's sexuality, reflecting an "intersectional approach." On the uses of intersectionality in activism, see Patricia Hill Collins, "Intersectionality's Definitional Dilemmas," *Annual Review of Sociology* 41 (2015): 1–20.

3 Here I am following Michael Blakey from his memorandum on Africana Studies and Afrocentricity. See Memorandum by Michael L. Blakey, "A Discussion of Afrocentrism for the Africana Studies Task Force," n.d., April Silver Collection, private collection.

4 Tatyana Hopkins, "HU Students Occupy Campus Building amid Financial Aid Scandal," *Washington Informer*, April 4, 2018, http://washingtoninformer.com; and Sarah Larimer, "Howard University Students Occupy Administration Building amid Financial Aid Scandal," *Washington Post*, March 29, 2018, www.washingtonpost.com.

5   Jazmin Goodwin and Autumn Dalton, "The Longest Student Sit-in in Howard's History Comes to an End," *The Hilltop*, April 6, 2018, http://thehilltoponline.com; Ahmari Anthony, "As an Organizer within HU Resist, Here's How We Recreated Activism on the Campus of Howard University," *Blavity*, n.d., https://blavity.com; Sarah Larimer, "Howard University Students End Occupation of Administration Building," *Washington Post*, April 6, 2018, www.washingtonpost.com.

6   The best statement on this remains Kwame Ture's pronouncement: "Howard presented me with every dialectic existing in the African community. At Howard, on any given day, one might meet every black thing . . . and its opposite. The place was a veritable tissue of contradiction, embodying the best and the absolute worst values of the African-American tradition." See Stokely Carmichael with Ekwueme Michael Thelwell, *Ready for Revolution: The Life and Struggles of Stokely Carmichael [Kwame Ture]* (New York: Scribner, 2003), 113.

7   Howard Newsroom Staff, "Howard University Board of Trustees Hosts Press Conference Marking End of Sit-in; Unveils Statement of Commitments to Campus community," Howard University, Office of University Communications, April 6, 2018, https://newsroom.howard.edu.

8   W. E. B. Du Bois, "Whither Now and Why?" in *The Education of Black People: Ten Critiques, 1906–1960* (New York: Monthly Review Press, 2001), 193–203.

9   See Roderick Ferguson, *We Demand: The University and Student Protests* (Berkeley: University of California Press, 2017).

10   Frantz Fanon, *The Wretched of the Earth* (New York: Grove Press, 2004), 145.

11   Cedric Robinson, *Black Marxism: The Making of the Black Radical Tradition* (Chapel Hill: University of North Carolina Press, 2000), 175–184.

12   Greg Carr, "Black Movements in America and Student Activism: Harmonies and Dissonances," *The Hilltop*, March 30, 2017, http://thehilltoponline.com.

13   Du Bois, "Whither Now and Why?" 193.

14   April Silver, interview by the author, January 29, 2017.

SELECTED SOURCES

MANUSCRIPT COLLECTIONS
Andrew Billingsley Papers, private.
Digital Howard, including Howard University Archives, Moorland-Spingarn Research
    Center, Howard University, Washington, DC, http://dh.howard.edu.
Haqq Islam Collection, private.
April Silver Collection, private.
Akanke Washington Collection, private.

INTERVIEWS
Makola M. Abdullah, June 8, 2018.
Ras J. Baraka, August 25, 2017.
Garfield Bright, April 4, 2018.
Nicole Brown, June 2, 2018.
Rich Byers, September 15, 2017.
Christopher Cathcart, January 31, 2018.
Imani Countess, March 24, 2017.
Anthony Dandridge, December 18, 2017.
Adwoa Dunn-Mouton, March 26, 2017.
Robert Edgar, March 14, 2017.
Kamal Harris, May 24, 2018.
Shawn Houston, December 18, 2017.
Haqq Islam, January 23, 2018, January 24, 2018, and January 27, 2018.
Stephen Jackson, February 19, 2018.
Fritz Jean, January 7, 2018.
Aaron Johnson, July 18, 2017.
Joseph Jordan, March 30, 2017.
Aaron Lloyd, July 22, 2017, and May 4, 2018.
Matt Middleton, January 2, 2018.
Killa Patterson, January 22, 2018.
Aarian Pope Punter, December 12, 2017, and June 6, 2018.
V. Jimale Ridgeway, March 26, 2018.
Carlisle Sealy, July 7, 2017.
Jam Shakwi, December 14, 2017.
Gail Sharps-Myers, October 2, 2017.
April Silver, January 29, 2017, September 1, 2017, May 6, 2018, and June 2, 2018.
Alvin Thornton, May 15, 2018.

274 | SELECTED SOURCES

Conrad Tillard, December 7, 2017.
Tunji Turner, December 18, 2017.
Sheri Warren, December 16, 2017.
Akanke Washington, January 24, 2017, and December 17–18, 2017.
Charles "Chuck" Webb, June 26, 2017.
Kevin Williams, July 9, 2017, and May 7, 2018.

Anderson, David C. *Crime and the Politics of Hysteria: How the Willie Horton Story Changed American Justice*. New York: Times Books, 1995.

Brady, John. *Bad Boy: The Life and Politics of Lee Atwater*. Reading, MA: Addison-Wesley, 1997.

Brown, Wendy. *Undoing the Demos: Neoliberalism's Stealth Revolution*. New York: Zone Books, 2015.

Byers, R. K. *The Real HU*. Kindle ebook. New York: Banned Books, 2012.

D'Souza, Dinesh. *Illiberal Education: The Politics of Race and Sex on Campus*. New York: Free Press, 1991.

Hampton, Henry, and Steve Fayer. *Voices of Freedom: An Oral History of the Civil Rights Movement from the 1950s through the 1980s*. With Sarah Flynn. New York: Bantam Books, 1990.

Holloway, Jonathan Scott. *Confronting the Veil: Abram Harris Jr., E. Franklin Frazier, and Ralph Bunche, 1919–1941*. Chapel Hill: University of North Carolina Press, 2002.

Jamieson, Kathleen Hall. *Dirty Politics: Deception, Distraction, and Democracy*. New York: Oxford University Press, 1992.

Kitwana, Bakari. *The Hip Hop Generation: Young Blacks and the Crisis in African-American Culture*. New York: Basic Books, 2002.

Matory, J. Lorand. *Stigma and Culture: Last-Place Anxiety in Black America*. Chicago: University of Chicago Press, 2015.

Mendelberg, Tali. *The Race Card: Campaign Strategy, Implicit Messages, and the Norm of Equality*. Princeton, NJ: Princeton University Press, 2001.

Perkins, William Eric, ed. *Droppin' Science: Critical Essays on Rap Music and Hip Hop Culture*. Philadelphia: Temple University Press, 1996.

Spence, Lester. *Stare in the Darkness: The Limits of Hip-Hop and Black Politics*. Minneapolis: University of Minnesota Press, 2011.

INDEX

Abernathy, Ralph David, visit to A-Building during protest, 149–50
Adams, Russell, 184
Adams v. Richardson, 198
affirmative action, 27, 32, 53, 226n14; and neoconservatism, 33, 145
AFL-CIO, 115
African diaspora, 165
African Liberation Support Committee, 32, 60
African Studies Research Center Outreach Program (Howard), 61
Africana/Black Studies, 1, 56, 196–97, 201; and Afrocentricity, 181, 251n38; and historiography, 4–5, 219n17; and Howard University, 21, 70, 76, 81, 107, 110–11, 154, 168, 183–88
Afro-American Studies. *See* Africana/Black Studies
Afro-American Studies Push Collective, 107
Afro-American Studies Resource Center (Howard), 61, 185
Afrocentricity, 110–11; and Africana/Black Studies, 181, 251n38; culture wars, 181, 262n61; Historically Black Colleges and Universities (HBCUs), 182; and hip hop, 181–82, 192; and Howard, 110, 180–88
Aid to Families with Dependent Children, 37
Ailes, Roger, 39
All-African People's Revolutionary Party (A-APRP), 77, 83; and Howard students, 79–80
Alexis, Carlton, 102, 169–70
Allen, Debbie, 116; and *A Different World*, 117
Allen, Harry, and Howard University hip hop conferences, 189–90
Alpha Phi Alpha (Howard), 97
Alpha Sweethearts (Howard), 97

Alston, Ona, 81
American Committee on Africa, 61
American Enterprise Institute, 39
American exceptionalism, 65
American universalism, 2, 116, 218n14
Anderson, Carl, 121
Andrew Mellon Foundation, 185
Andrews, Majorie, 158
Angelettie, Deric "D-Dot," 189, 191; and role in Howard protest of 1989, 136, 140; and Two Kings in a Cipher, 189–90
anti-apartheid movement, 3, 7; and divestment, 61–62; and Howard, 60–64, 70, 81, 239n45, 240n50; and student movements, 59–65
anticolonial movements, 77
anticommunism, 30
antiwar movement, 67, 192
Asante, Molefi Kete, 110–11, 181, 186, 265n92
Atkinson, Glenroy, 100–101, 105
Atwater, (Harvey LeRoy) Lee, 3, 7, 24; 1988 Horton campaign advertisement strategy, 42–45, 102–3, 145, 233n78; appointment to the Howard University Board of Trustees, 101, 110, 121, 124–25, 127, 146, 168; as Blues musician, 146; deathbed apology, 161; dialogue with Lee Atwater, 153; early life and career of, 40–41; lobbying work on Southern Africa, 102, 145; meeting with Howard University Student Association (HUSA), 144, 256n73; and Operation Outreach, 49, 153, 235n105; resignation from the board, 144; response to police siege on the A-Building, 144; as target of Howard student protest of 1989, 109–10, 113, 133–34, 151; "What I would Have Told the Howard Students" editorial, 145
Ayers, Gary, 20

ABOUT THE AUTHOR

Joshua M. Myers teaches Africana Studies in the Department of Afro-American Studies at Howard University. He serves on the editorial board of the *Compass* and is editor of *A Gathering Together: Literary Journal.*

Lightning Source UK Ltd.
Milton Keynes UK
UKHW041835230222
399138UK00001B/14